GEORGE ADE'S COMMON-SENSE ADVICE

GEORGE ADE'S COMMON-SENSE ADVICE

ON BUSINESS, INVESTMENT,
REAL ESTATE, LAW AND LIFE

Practical Wisdom from "America's Warm-hearted Satirist"
"Indiana's Aesop"

WILLIAM C. ADE

George Ade's Common-Sense Advice © copyright 2024 by William C. Ade. All rights reserved. No part of this book may be reproduced in any form whatsoever, by photography or xerography or by any other means, by broadcast or transmission, by translation into any kind of language, nor by recording electronically or otherwise, without permission in writing from the author, except by a reviewer, who may quote brief passages in critical articles or reviews.

Ade Royalties & Publishing
P.O. Box 313
Brook, IN 47922

Hardcover ISBN: 979-8-9856780-1-7
Ebook ISBN: 979-8-9856780-2-4

Library of Congress Control Number: 2024910053

Cover and interior book design by Mayfly book design

*To the Cordelias of my life: Mary, Sarah and Karen.
May they pass on these lessons to the next generation.*

Where ignorance is not bliss, get wise!

~ George Ade

Contents

Illustrations and Photographs; Sources and Credits xi
Preface xv
Introduction 1

On Business

The Heir and the Heiress 23
The Common Carrier 29
Life Insurance 32
The Fable of the Two Ways of Going Out After the Pay Envelope . . 38
The Fable of the Old Merchant, the Sleuth and the Tapioca 42
The Fable of the Divided Concern that Was Reunited Under a
    New Management 47
Vote For Landon 52
The Galley Slave Who Was Just About To but Never Did 54
On Glorifying the Grouch 61

On Investment and Real Estate

The Advantage of a Good Thing 69
The Fable of Prince Fortunatas Who Lived in Easy Street and
    Then Moved Away 72
House in Mercedes Street 86
The Fable of the Hard-Up Yeoman 92
Non-Essentials 107

On Law, Lawyers and Contracts

The Fable of the Bookworm and the Butterfly Who Went
    into the Law 111
The Maneuvers of Joel and the Disappointed Orphan Asylum 116
A Chapter of French Justice as Dealt Out In the Dreyfus Case 122
The Attenuated Attorney Who Rang in the Associate Counsel ... 129
George's Business Contracts and Correspondence 134
Tariffs 142

On Philanthropy and Estate Planning

Two Philanthropic Sons 151
The Fable of the Good Fairy with the Lorgnette, and Why
    She Got It Good 154
The Samaritan Who Got Paralysis of the Helping Hand 160
Vacations 165
The Fable of the Never-to-be Benefactor Who Took a
    Brand-New Tack 167
George's Legacy 172

On Life, Family and Success

The Set of Poe 179
The Galloping Pilgrim 185
Mr. Payson's Satirical Christmas 191
Away From Home (An Excerpt) 199
Effie Whittlesey 203
Chicago High Art Up to Date 213
Yellow! Yellow! The Poet of the New School Speaks 218
Whirligigs 222

The Married Couple That Went to Housekeeping and
  Began to Find Out Things 225
The Fable of The Last Day at School & The Tough Trustee's
  Farewell to the Young Voyagers 230
The New Fable of the Marathon in the Mud and the Laurel Wreath ... 236
The Fable of Almost Getting Back to Nature 245
George on America's "Spiritual Awakening" 248
The Fable of how Wisenstein did not Lose out to Buttinsky 250
The Fable of the Father Who Jumped In 256
Looking Back From Fifty 265
George's Mile Posts 268
Mr. Kakyak Decides to Be a Republican 270

Regrets

Lamentations on the Joys of Single Blessedness 279

Benediction

The Yankee's Prayer (1924) 289

Appendix

Theories X and Y 295
Ade Returns to City Room to Perform Labor of Love 297
  Wells Wills Nurse $50,000; Like Sum to Judge Landis 300
George's Last Will and Testament 302
Recommended Reading 327
Bibliography: Notable Writings Almost Included 329
Glossary 333
Acknowledgements 345
About the Author 347

Illustrations and Photographs; Sources and Credits

Cover: *George Ade*
Courtesy Purdue University Libraries, Archives and Special Collections

Spine: *George Ade*
Collection of William C. Ade

Photograph: *Rare photo of George Ade reading at Hazelden*
From *Revived Remarks on Mark Twain,* 1936

Sketch: *George and Spry*
John T. McCutcheon
From *The Letters of George Ade,* Terence Tobin, editor

George's inscription in his sister Ella's memory book
From *The Letters of George Ade,* Terence Tobin, editor

Photographs: *The Everleigh Club*
Wikipedia

Photograph: *Chapin & Gore Saloon*
Chicago History Museum

Photograph: *The Chicago Athletic Association Building*
Chicago History Museum

Photograph: *Chicago Athletic Association banquet*
Library of Congress

Photograph: *Chicago Athletic Association billiards*
Chicago History Museum

Photograph: *Chicago Athletic Association swimming pool*
Chicago History Museum

Photograph: *Hazelden, Brook, Indiana*
"Indiana Landmarks"; Town of Brook

Image: *1892 One Hundred Dollar Bill*
Antique Banknotes

Cartoon: *Found in a lonely Gulch near Death Valley*
John T. McCutcheon

Orson Collins Wells Obituary
New York Times, December 11, 1939

Cartoon: *Silas was a Putter-In and Claude was a Taker-Out*
John T. McCutcheon

Cartoon: *Within the Car sits Silas, one of the most hateful specimens of the Newly Arrived*
John T. McCutcheon

Cartoon: *The Grief that seemed crushing him to Earth*
John T. McCutcheon

Cartoon: *This, in a General Way, is Southern Europe*
John T. McCutcheon

Cartoon: *Over the Hills*
John T. McCutcheon

Cartoon: *Second Time on Earth*
John T. McCutcheon

Cartoon: *Learned Colleague*
John T. McCutcheon

Cartoon: *The Promoter*
John T. McCutcheon

Cartoon: *Sketching from a Model*
John T. McCutcheon

Cartoon: *Inhaling It*
John T. McCutcheon

Cartoon: *Thus it befell that a couple of Fortescues landed . . .*
John T. McCutcheon

Cartoon: *Wisenstein*
John T. McCutcheon

Cartoon: *Buttinsky*
John T. McCutcheon

Photograph: *Kankakee Sands Tallgrass Prairie Preserve*
Courtesy Ellen Jacquart

Chart: *Deficient—United States, federal budget, % of GDP*
The Economist

George Ade's Last Will and Testament
Courtesy Purdue University Libraries, Archives and Special Collections

Preface

> *The philosophy of Ade is a reassuring one, since everywhere there is a deep compassion of a man who has been there and seen it.*
>
> ~ Jean Shepherd, Introduction to *The America of George Ade*

Isaac Newton once wrote, "If I have seen further [than others] it is by standing on the shoulders of giants."[1] My great-great uncle, turn-of-the-20th century author and playwright George Ade, was one of the giants upon whose shoulders I've stood. It was by a familiarity with his life and works that I was prepared to leave the small Indiana farm where I grew up to explore the world for minerals on a royalty basis. The royalties I've earned through that endeavor are essentially the same as a writer's royalties for plays, books and articles.

I inherited no money or land. However, due to my success in my profession as a geologist and investing in stocks and real estate, I became one of the storied 1% in America[2]. I was a member for over ten years at TIGER 21, an exclusive group of ultra-high-net-worth entrepreneurs, investors and executives; and then a founding partner at R360, a member-owned, member-led community where wealth creators and their families navigate the unique challenges of leading significant family enterprises.

I doubt that I could have achieved these things without Uncle

---

1. Letter to Robert Hooke, February 5, 1676
2. Today the 1% in America begins at $13 million, according to DQYDJ.

George as my example and inspiration. **Jack Backstreet's brief biography of George states, "Unlike his literary idol Mark Twain, Ade was particularly financially savvy. He became a millionaire in his 40s and an enthusiastic philanthropist, bestowing numerous Indiana-based educational, medical and fraternal endowments."**[3] He truly was a titan—not only of the arts, but also of business and fiscal dexterity.

George's first mentors on business and investing were memorialized in his story "The Prairie Kings of Yesterday" in which his admiration for the previous generation of great empire builders was set out in some detail.[4] However, George was operating in the gay 90s, a time much different from that in which the pioneer Prairie Kings prevailed. At first George floundered in this environment and wound up, as he put it, "back home again and broke." He later met the legendary stockbroker Ort Wells[5] and other mentors who brought him into the 20th century and helped him learn to successfully manage his business affairs and money. Under Ort's mentorship, George constructed what today is called a "barbell portfolio."[6] In building back his finances after going broke, George bought farms 50% leveraged with his brother Will acting as his agent. Once one farm was paid off, Will would mortgage it to buy another, and then another and another until George had over 2,000 acres paid off. This was the low-risk side of the barbell, hereafter never to be leveraged again. The risk side of George's barbell portfolio was his royalties and stocks. Ort acted as his broker and financial advisor in matters relating to the royalties from his plays.

---

3. https://www.imdb.com/name/nm0011748/bio/, accessed November 14, 2023.
4. See Chapter 18 of *A Pioneer in the Fullest Sense: The Wit and Wisdom of George Ade's Father*, 90-111.
5. See the Appendix for George's tribute to his friend Ort Wells: *Ade Returns to City Room to Perform Labor of Love*.
6. I first heard the term "barbell portfolio" from David Russell at TIGER 21 meetings in Miami. It is a sophisticated way to manage very risky investments by pairing them with low risk investments in one's portfolio.

In 1996, journalist Bill Granger memorialized George in a *Chicago Tribune* story that succinctly and beautifully describes George's genius and his rise to fame and fortune:

George Ade's Common Touch

Bill Granger, Chicago Tribune, March 24, 1996

George Ade heard the talk and walked the walk through a fabulous decade of work in Chicago as columnist on the Chicago Record, the morning newspaper of the afternoon Chicago Daily News, both owned by the same publisher, Victor Lawson (who helped start the Associated Press.)

Ade was the quiet reporter, a man who was willing to work with the ordinary clay of human life he found in all the forgotten corners of the city and mold stories of his life and times—bereft of the usual columnist's ego.

"My ambition was to report people as they really were, as I saw them in their everyday life, and as I knew them to be. Consequently, I avoided exaggeration, burlesque and crude caricature; and I did not try to fictionize or to embroider fancy situations, as was common in the fiction of the day. In the stories, there was not much emphasis upon plot, but instead carefully sketched, detailed incidents in the delineation of real characters in real life, depicting various episodes in their lives as related through the medium of their own talk . . . There is nothing more native than speech."

Before he was done, Henry L. Mencken praised his work, calling it "as thoroughly American, in cut and color, in tang and savor, in structure and point of view, as the works of [William Dean] Howells, E. W. Howe or Mark Twain."

Speaking of Twain, Samuel Clemens sent a note to William Dean Howells, critic, novelist and father of the American school of realism in fiction, about Ade after reading one of his many collections of Chicago stories. "My admiration of the book has overflowed all limits, all frontiers," Clemens wrote. "I have personally known each of the characters in the book and can testify that they are all true to the facts and as exact as if they had been drawn to scale."

That lofty praise was for a farm kid born Feb. 9, 1866, in tiny Kentland, Ind. He was a child with big eyes and a sense of wonder that never left him, surviving even his move from Chicago newspapering into playwrighting and a string of Broadway successes that made him rich.

One of his earliest memories was of the Chicago Fire, which destroyed the city in 1871, when Ade was 5: "That one night in October, just as far back as I can reach into the past, we sat on the fence and looked at a blur of illumination in the northern sky and learned that the city which we had not seen was burning up in a highly successful manner."

That line contained the soul of his genius as a writer and reporter and ironic observer. He carried such lines off with quiet dignity both for himself and the subject, even when he was one of the first whites to write touching stories of black city life in his columns, later collected in his "Pink Marsh" stories (1897). Marsh was a black man who shined shoes in a barber shop, and humanity passed before his eyes. Ade polished Marsh's observations into prose.

Ade attended Purdue University, where he met a student who would become his lifelong friend, John T. McCutcheon, artist and cartoonist who preceded him to a job on the Record (then called The Morning News) up in the big city.

After college, Ade drifted into writing around Lafayette, Ind. He worked on the papers there, getting paid partly in meal tickets at a cheap restaurant that was a big advertiser. He also wrote testimonials advertising a tobacco-habit cure. When he was ready to leave Indiana for the big city, McCutcheon got him a job on the Record. Ade began reporting on the weather at $12 a week. In no time, he wrote the weather news right onto Page 1. He covered the city as a reporter but made an early impression on the editors with his skills as a writer and with his sense of humor.

He started in 1890, and by the time of the World's Columbian Exposition of 1893, he was assigned by managing editor Charles H. Dennis to join a small cadre of reporters who covered the great fair every day and pulled stories out of it.

"Ade was the star writer of that small galaxy," Dennis recalled later. "His stories were all honored without a byline—in fact, through the thousands of days that passed while he recorded his later stories, he never got a byline from the Record. After the fair closed . . ., Ade went back on the city desk staff and saw his copy routinely butchered by the copy editors."

"Ade's articles suffered grievous mutilation," Dennis wrote 50 years later. "Knowing that whatever he wrote was amply good enough to appear in print exactly as it came from his hand, I shared his exasperation over the terrible hash made of his articles. So I told Ade soon that he and McCutcheon might have the two columns on the editorial page lately vacated by the World's Fair feature and that they might use it every day, subject to my supervision, in any way they liked. I chose for the new feature the title which it bore from first to last."

The title was as boring as any editor could conceive: "Stories of the Streets and of the Town." But the prose written by Ade—and McCutcheon's touching illustrations—were not.

The two men were close and shared lodgings in the south Loop. They were pals and delighted in working together and rooming together—even if they were not delighted with their domicile. McCutcheon later wrote of the room: "You had to take accurate aim to walk between the bed and the sofa. One window opened to the west, admitting a flood of sunlight in the afternoon when we were at the office."

McCutcheon later went on to draw for The Tribune, including the famous "Injun Summer" cartoon that once graced the front page every autumn.

Ade was prolific, a quality that counted on newspapers at the time. He was also good. His columns were published in various small books, and he achieved best-seller lists in 1897 with a compilation of a weekly syndicated feature, "Fables in Slang."

The fables came out of the same Chicago school of gentle cynicism that fathered Finley Peter Dunne's "Mr. Dooley" and included morals like this: "Early to bed and early to rise, and you'll meet very few prominent people."

He turned to writing for the stage at the turn of the century and left behind his body of work. His first light opera, "The Sultan of Sulu," achieved a long run on Broadway. He then wrote a series of successful comedies, including "The County Chairman" and "The College Widow," that made him the toast of New York. At one point, he had three successful plays running simultaneously.

Unlike most newspapermen, he made a lot of money, and he used some of it to buy 2,000 acres of farmland back at his roots, near the small town of Brook, Ind. He lived on the farm there for the rest of his long life and never stopped writing, even publishing a funny bit of nostalgia called "The Old Time Saloon" in 1931 at the height of the hysteria called Prohibition. He died at Brook on May 16, 1944.

He is difficult to categorize as a writer, despite the praise of his contemporaries, because his sort of essay in realism has gone out of style in journalism. He lived quietly, at the edge, observing and recording.

A final word from Mencken: "Ade himself, for all his storyteller's pretense of remoteness, is as absolutely American as any of his prairie-town traders and pushers, Shylocks and Dogberries, beaux and belles. He is as American as buckwheat cakes." So he was.

My purpose in putting together this volume is to cull from George's great opus his best common-sense advice on business, investment, real estate, law, philanthropy and life so that others might have the same advantage I had as a young man. You'll find no stern finger-wagging or condescension in George's counsel. He was always kind in his moralizing and advice. He never talked down to anyone. Thus he was known as "Indiana's Aesop" and "America's warm-hearted satirist." This is what makes him such an ideal mentor and encourager.

Let's begin with this uplifting piece:

Don't Believe Those Who Say You Can't Do the Job Tackled

It happens that I have just finished writing a picture play in which I tried to prove, by a story, that there are no lazy people in the world. The so-called lazy man or woman is simply one who has been put at the wrong job and gets up every morning with no interest or enthusiasm in the daily task ahead.

The first recipe for doing good work is to pick out the kind of work for which you have a real liking. Go at your undertaking with a degree of confidence. Don't believe the people who keep telling you that you can't get away with the job you have tackled. No one can estimate how much harm is being done every day by the discouragers. A lot of people who do not mean to handicap and hold back young people are forever warning them and filling them full of doubts and fears. The youngster who is very cocky and self-assertive may be a kind of nuisance at times, but he has more chance of getting ahead than the one who absolutely believes before he goes at any work that he is going to fall down and flatten out and be a positive failure.

After you have loaded yourself with courage and determination, the next part of the recipe is to learn to be a very severe critic of your own work. Study your output in cold blood and make sure that you are doing the very best you can. When you are on a job try to discover the faults in your work, and you will be better off in the long run than if you try to delude yourself into believing that everything you do is necessarily perfect just because you do it. Give a little more than is expected of you.[7] *When you are rendering a first-class service don't always be worrying for fear that you are giving someone else more than he pays for. Be satisfied with the knowledge that you are becoming more efficient and valuable every day and, therefore, sooner or later will command a better price in the open market.*[8]

This is perhaps the best advice that young people today need to receive. Even the great Warren Buffett approves this message. "You've gotta keep control of your time, and you can't unless you say no," he said. "You can't let people set your agenda in life. Never give up searching for the job that you're passionate about."[9]

George had it right all along!

In the pages ahead I will present to you what are, in my mind, the Best of the Best of George Ade's wisest insights told in the form of his fables, articles, letters, play excerpts and essays. George liked to give his readers a good jolly as well as good advice, so be aware when reading the original "morals" of his fables and stories that he often uses satire (says the opposite) or makes them a joke.

After presenting each of George's pieces I've tried to use my own life experiences to illustrate the relevancy of his wisdom to modern times. My success is evidence that his lessons still resonate, for they are timeless. As it turns out, character, integrity, forethought, work ethic and a sense of humor are as vital to one's success in the modern era as they were in George's day.

To facilitate your understanding, I have footnoted and prepared a glossary of the many obscure names and words George

---

7. As a consulting geologist I always submitted an extra map, cross section or analysis beyond what was required by the contract.
8. See "Theories X and Y" in the Appendix for more on this topic.
9. *Warren Buffett's Key to Success: "Say No to Almost Everything"*, https://finance.yahoo.com/news/warren-buffett-key-success-no-161048764.html#:~:text=%E2%80%9CThe%20difference%20between%20successful%20people,almost%20everything%2C%E2%80%9D%20Buffett%20said.

used in his writing—particularly slang words from the turn of the 20th century. Serving as the book's Introduction is George's *Fable of the Old Fox and the Young Fox*. I believe it to be the perfect kick-off for everything that follows. And for the Benediction to close the book, I offer an insightful piece that George wrote circa 1924 entitled *The Yankee's Prayer*. As I write this 100 years later, *The Yankee's Prayer* remains as fresh as a spring breeze across the Indiana prairie.

I sincerely hope you enjoy this volume. I pray that George Ade's wisdom amuses, inspires and guides you and yours toward greater prosperity and contentment just as it has my family for generations.

William C. Ade
Brook, Indiana
Spring, 2024

Rare photograph of George Ade reading in Hazelden
From *Revived Remarks on Mark Twain*, 1936

"This previously-unpublished sketch of Ade and his dog Spry was found in one of Mildred Gilman's scrapbooks." ~ Terence Tobin, *Letters of George Ade*

Be true to yourself is the wish of Your brother Geo. Ade

Sixteen-year-old George's inscription in his sister Ella's memory book on April 1, 1881. From *The Letters of George Ade*, Terence Tobin [editor], Purdue University Press, 1973

Introduction

One of George Ade's most enduring one liners is this timeless classic:

Early to Bed and Early to Rise is a Bad Rule for any one who wishes to become acquainted with our most Prominent and Influential People.[10]

And where does one meet our most prominent and influential people? Why, on the Streets and in the Town, of course! As a reporter-at-large for the *Chicago Record* writing under his own byline, George was expected to find his own material. He became quite good at it—so good that the paper started publishing his essays in a series called *Stories of the Streets and of the Town*. By the time George was in his mid-twenties he was very well acquainted with the citizens and streets of Chicago where he lived, worked and played from roughly 1890 to 1904. In order to create his news stories, fables, books, plays and screenplays, George spent his time in the Windy City watching, listening and chronicling what he saw and heard. His writing made him more than just rich and famous. It also made him worldly and wise.

---

10. Lester Cohen included this quote of George's in his 1926 book *Sweepings* and also in the subsequent screenplay of the same name (movie directed by David O. Selznick, future director of *Gone with the Wind*). The quote was so popular by then, Cohen did not even reference George as the creator. *Sweepings* is a great movie for anyone wanting to get a feel for the Chicago of George's day.

In other words, Young George got around.

According to author Karen Abbott, George sometimes pursued his stories at the infamous Everleigh Club on South Dearborn Street in Chicago. The Everleigh Club was a posh brothel that was in operation from 1900 to around 1911 and was run by two sisters of the surname Everleigh. I have spoken with Ms. Abbott by phone because she mentioned George in connection with the Everleigh Club in her book *Sin in the Second City: Madams, Ministers, Playboys, and the Battle for America's Soul*.[11] The sisters kept a registry of the prominent men who visited their club and according to Ms. Abbott, George's name came up.

Located in Chicago's red-light district, the Everleigh Club wasn't much to look at from the street. Once inside, however, the gentlemen callers were treated to the height of style and luxury. There were elaborately-decorated parlors, ballrooms, bar rooms, dining rooms, music rooms, bathing rooms and yes, bedrooms.

The Club employed up to two dozen cooks and maids (among others . . .) who catered to the Everleigh's exclusive clientele.

---

11. https://a.co/d/0UP2OfU, accessed November 24, 2023.

Everleigh Club Exterior

Oriental Music Room

Entry Hall

"Throne Room"

The Everleigh Club wasn't George's preferred source for stories, though. His and his friends' main hangout was Chapin & Gore's Saloon on West Monroe Street in Chicago. This was by far the best saloon in town and arguably one of the best in the country... maybe even the world. In his book *The Old-Time Saloon*, George, who had wet his whistle in saloons all around the globe, claimed that the bars in Chicago ranked right up there with any he'd ever encountered anywhere:

> [I] had to and [I] did snoop the wicked city from one end to the other. The Chicago of the nineties had nothing to learn from Port Said, Singapore, the lake front at Buffalo, the sea front at Bombay, or the crib section of New Orleans—the aforesaid spots having a world-wide reputation for wild wickedness. Chicago was just as tough as it knew how to be, and that's as much as you can ask of any town. Saloons everywhere and many of them open all night and all day Sunday.

When George wasn't looking for a scoop at the Everleigh Club or a saloon, he could be found at the Chicago Athletic Association

Chapin & Gore Saloon circa 1904

(CAA), his home for many years. Located on Michigan Avenue, the magnificent CAA building was modeled after the Doge's Palace in Venice. The association itself was established in 1890 as "a not-for-profit organization that provide(s) a setting for athletic, business, and social activities."[12] The founders were a group of elite and powerful Chicago men that included Marshall Field, Cyrus McCormick and A. J. Spalding (a baseball player and the founder of the eponymous athletic gear company). The CAA was the most exclusive private men's club in the country, and it had everything: the finest athletic accoutrements, dining, billiards, poker rooms, and of course, bars. It also had living quarters for the city's upper crust bachelors (of which George was one, as was his financial mentor Ort Wells who also lived there). The CAA was at the very top of Chicago society and George knew something about how to get into society. I don't believe he had to wait outside too long before being invited in.

The CAA was filled with self-made millionaires and up-and-comers. It must have been a fabulous and exciting place for George to live. However, it did not afford much peace and quiet for him to do his work. Thus, he built a "cottage" on his farm outside

---

12. https://www.loc.gov/item/il0935/, accessed November 29, 2023.

Chicago Athletic Association Building
circa 1910

CAA Banquet, 1906

Introduction

Billiards, 1905

Swimming pool

Hazelden, Brook, Indiana

of Brook, Indiana as a writing retreat. He christened this lovely Tudor Revival-style home "Hazelden."

George moved from the CAA into Hazelden in 1904. He was 38 years old. He had risen in prominence and wealth in the gay 90s only to lose it all and then build it back up again. He must have felt like he'd learned a great many lessons going from rural Indiana to Purdue University to the *Chicago Record* newspaper as its most poorly paid employee, and then rich, and then broke, and now even richer ... and not yet 40 years old. Perhaps George looked back on those experiences and sat down with his No. 2 pencil and yellow note pad and wrote out the following story, *The Fable of the Old Fox and the Young Fox*, for his extended family? In any case it was one of the last things he would have written before moving from Chicago into Hazelden.

George would return to the themes of this piece as a source for many of his future fables and short stories. I have annotated the fable as the Introduction here because several of its one-liners turned into the fables, stories and screenplays included in this collection. I believe it's a wonderful way to set the stage for all that's to come.

The Fable of the Old Fox and the Young Fox

From *True Bills*, 1904

After he had lived in Town for many Years and had come to know the Animals and their Ways, even to the occasional Running Amuck of the Bulls and Bears[13], the Old Fox had gathered to himself a few Hard Lessons which he set down for the Instruction and Betterment of Fox, Jr. One Day he took his Young One into the Private Office for a Session of Fatherly Advice.

---

13. Wall Street booms and crashes.

"I have a few Nuggets of Truth," said the Old Fox, showing some loose Scraps of Paper on which he had written. "I hesitate to offer them, for, if I remember correctly, the Member of our Family who was best Posted on Business Epigrams went under as far back as 1873[14]. Still, some of these may help you. The Work of turning them out has been a pleasurable Respite from my ordinary Routine. Proverbs are easily Manufactured, my Son. They are Self-Evident Truths, blooming in the Garden of Inexperience. Those which happen to be the right Length to fit into Copy-Books are most likely to Endure.

Forty Years Ago I was competent to turn out Dozens of Maxims and Proverbs, each glistering with Truth. You are in the Fluff of Youth, while I am marked with Gray, yet doubtless you could give me Cards and Spades in the Making of Precepts for the Guidance of the Immature. The dear little Girls in the Grammar-Schools write Essays in which Mighty Conclusions are linked together end to end, Emerson Fashion. With one Reading of Poor Richard and some timely Inspiration from Rochefoucauld and Hazlitt, any Upstart may set down our Common Weaknesses and catalogue a full Set of Danger Signals. The Letter of Advice has been the easiest Form of Composition from the time of Chesterfield. However, in preparing you to go out and be of the City Tribe, and come Home each Night with your Brush unbedraggled and your cool, smooth Nose unmarked by Scratches, I flatter myself that I have omitted the usual Rigamarole of Weighty Instructions, my Experience having convinced me that the machine-made is seldom brought out except to be Misapplied."

"Thank you, Father," said the Young Fox. "I am glad that you have saved yourself the Trouble of formulating the Generalities for which the Rising Generation is always prepared. I have fixed up for my own Use a Set of Rules which, doubtless, is more

---

14. Also known as the Long Depression. See https://en.wikipedia.org/wiki/Panic_of_1873

Comprehensive and Beautiful than anything you could put together at your Time of Life."

Saying which, the Young Fox showed a pretty Morocco-Leather Booklet, made to fit the Waistcoat Pocket, in which he had written many meaty Paragraphs, the Substance of the same having been deduced from what he had read of the Struggle for Existence.

"Read a few Selections," said the Old Fox, with a Tolerant Smile. "I love to hear the resounding Conclusions of an Oracle."

"But I am not an Oracle," said the Young Fox, modestly. "I am not even an Authority. I am only a bright Juvenile who has sorted out the Essentials for Success and set them down neatly with my Fountain-Pen."

"Do not flatter yourself that I credit you with the Authorship of any of the Matter contained in your little Book," said the Old Fox. "We do not intend to Plagiarize, but all of us absorb our pet Proverbs from the Text-Books, the learned Monthlies, and the Editorial Page. We paraphrase Benjamin Franklin, and put Two and Two together to make Four, and change a Preposition, and presto! the Old Saw seems to be a new Truth evolved without Help or Suggestion. No doubt you have written in your little Guide to Life that a Youthful Frugality insures Comfort throughout the Declining Years, and a Good Name is better than Riches, and to be sure you are Right before you go Ahead."

"Not in those Words, I assure you," said the Young Fox, somewhat testily. "It is true, however, that I have composed certain General Directions in favor of Honesty, Temperance, Economy, Punctuality, Candor, Politeness, and Business Caution."

"All Men declare for these Admirable Traits in their Pocket Note-Books," said the Old Fox. "And no sooner is the Ink dry than they are led astray by the Caprice of Small Happenings. The Trouble with a world-wide Maxim or a great bulky Truth is that it does not dovetail nicely into the Exigencies of a Petty Case. Here at the beginning of the Twentieth Century, my Son, when all Endeavor is being subdivided and specialized, a Technical Instruction under a Sub-Head has more Practical Value than a huge Proverb that has come bumping down the Ages. The Health Officer who tells you in a terse Bulletin to boil your Drinking-Water does you an Actual Service and the Results are immediate, as the Bacilli can testify. But you might have to hunt around all Day without finding an Opportunity to make use of Mr. Emerson's tremendous Suggestion, 'Hitch your Wagon to a Star.' I am not poking Fun at the Large Rules for Conduct, but I beg to remark that very often you will find that they are Shelf Ornaments instead of Working-Tools kept bright by Use. Like the other Classics of our Literature, they are profoundly respected and seldom Utilized.

"What you need now, my Son," continued the Old Fox, "is a Set of Proverbs, Precepts, and Maxims brought up to Date and peculiarly adapted to an Era of Horseless Carriages, Limited Trains, Colonial Extension, Corners in Grain, the Booming of New Authors, Combinations of Capital, the Mushroom Growth of an Aristocracy of Wealth, and the Reign of Tailor-Made Clothes. A Majority of the Points to which I shall call your Attention may seem to be Frivolous and hardly worth while, but, as I have already intimated, it is the small Rule, made to fit the Individual Instance, that proves most valuable in the Long Run. Years ago I made a silly little Rule, as follows: 'Never extend Credit to any one who wears a Blue Necktie.' Childish, say you? Perhaps, but it has saved me Thousands of Dollars. If you will give sincere Heed to what I have inscribed here, you may be able to duplicate my magnificent Career."

Fox, Jr., took the Slips of Paper and read as follows:

1. Get acquainted with the Heads of Departments and permit the Subordinates to become acquainted with you.

2. Always be easily Familiar with those who are termed Great in the Public Prints. They are so accustomed to Deference and Humility, it is a positive Relief to meet a jaunty Equal.[15]

3. As soon as you get an Office of your own, put in a Private Exit, marked, "Escape in Case of a Dear Friend with an Invitation to Dinner."

4. The first Sign of Extravagance is to buy Trousers that one does not need. Every Young Man on a Salary should beware of the Trousers Habit.[16]

5. If you were Cut Out to be a homely American, with a preference for Turnips and Tea Biscuits, do not attempt to Live It Down. The most pathetic Object this year is the Man who wants to be a Degenerate and can't quite make it.[17]

6. A Bird in the Hand may be worth Two in the Bush, but remember also that a Bird in the Hand is a positive Embarrassment to one not in the Poultry Business.[18]

7. Do not give Alms promiscuously. Select the Unworthy Poor and make them Happy. To give to the Deserving is a Duty, but to help the Improvident, Drinking Class is clear Generosity, so that the Donor has a Right to be warmed by a Selfish Pride and count on a most flattering Obituary.[19]

---

15. See *Don't Believe Those Who Say You Can't Do the Job Tackled*, p xxi
16. See *The Fable of Almost Getting Back to Nature*, p 245
17. See *George's handwritten note to his sister, Ella*, p xxvi, and his views on *Chicago High Art*, p 213
18. See *The Samaritan Who Got Paralysis of the Helping Hand*, p 160
19. See *Little Buck the Trapper, Wildcat Road Vol I*, p 50-55; also *Two Philanthropic Sons*, p 151

8. There is Everything in a Name. A Rose by any other Name would Smell as Sweet, but would not cost half as much during the Winter Months. This means that you should get a Trade-Mark and keep it displayed on the Bulletin Boards.[20]

9. Never try to get into Society, so-called. Those who Try seldom get in, and if they do edge through the Portals they always feel Clammy and Unworthy when under the Scrutiny of the Elect. Sit outside and appear Indifferent, and after a while they may Send for you. If not, it will be Money in your Pocket.[21]

10. All the Apostles of Repose and the Mental Scientists tell the Business Slave to avoid Worry, but an old Trader's Advice is to Worry until you have had enough of it and then do something Desperate.[22]

11. Never write when you can Telegraph, and in Wiring always use more than Ten Words. This is the Short-Cut to being regarded as a Napoleon. The Extra Words cost only a few Cents, but they make a Profound Impression upon the Recipient and give the Sender a Standing which could not be obtained by an Expenditure of Four Dollars for a Birthday Gift. A Man never feels more

---

20. Today this is what we call "branding." See *The Attenuated Attorney Who Rang in the Associate Counsel*, p 129; and *The Fable of the Bookworm and the Butterfly Who Went into the Law*, p 111

21. See *The Fable of the Old Merchant, the Sleuth, and the Tapioca*, p 42

22. I believe what George had in mind is what he wrote in his *Vacations* essay, p 165 . . . take a vacation. For someone who grew up in an era where vacations were rare to unknown, taking one was an act of desperation. See *The Fable of the Divided Concern that Was Reunited Under a New Management*, p 47; and *Father and the Boys, Plays Worth Remembering, Vol I*, p 355

Important than when he receives a Telegram containing more than Ten Words.²³

12. Remember that the latest Outline for a Business Career is to Rush and Bustle and Strain to accumulate enough Money to pay your Expenses to Carlsbad or Southern California after you have dropped from Overwork. The only Failure is the one who Breaks Down without having got together his Recuperation Fund.²⁴

13. An Ounce of Prevention is worth a Pound of Cure and costs more. Don't attempt to prevent Trouble or you will lose your Eyesight watching so many Corners at the same time. Wait until Trouble comes and then consult a Specialist.²⁵

14. When a Man is in a New Town his Prospects are determined (1) by the class of Hotel at which he is registered, (2) by his Wardrobe, (3) by the Style of his Business Card, and (4) by the Manner of his Address.²⁶

15. A Rolling Stone gathers no Moss and therefore will not be derided as a Moss-Back. Roll as much as possible.²⁷

16. If you must Economize, dispense with some of the Necessities. You can bear up under the Realization that the Gas Company knows of your keeping the Jets turned low, but if you go out of a Café followed by the Reproachful Gaze of a Waiter who regards you as Stingy,

---

23. George's friend Will Rogers did George one better. When Rogers was not able to attend George's birthday party one year, he sent a life-size photograph of himself to stand in his place. That photograph holds a spot of honor in George's office at Hazelden to this day.
24. See *The Galley Slave Who Was Just About To but Never Did*, p 54
25. See *The Maneuvers of Joel and the Disappointed Orphan Asylum*, p 116
26. See *The Fable of the Two Ways of Going Out After the Pay Envelope*, p 38
27. See *Vacations*, p 165; and *Away From Home (An Excerpt)*, p 199

you will feel Small and Unhappy for Hours afterward and your Work will suffer.[28]

17. It has been accepted as a Law that there can be no absolute Waste of Energy, but you will be putting the Law to a Severe Test if you permit yourself to be drawn into a political Controversy on a Sleeping-Car with a Stranger who wears a wide Slouch-Hat.[29]

18. The Shorter the Hours, the Larger the Income. Don't get into the Habit of putting in Long Hours or you may be set down into a permanent Subordinate Position.[30]

19. When you believe that you love a Young Woman so earnestly that you will have to Marry her, take a Long Ride on the Cars to find out if the Affection endures while you are Travelling. The Beauty of this Test is that if you really Love her, you never will start on the Trip by yourself.[31]

20. If you expect to be a popular After-Dinner Speaker, don't attempt to work at anything else. That is a sufficiently large Contract for one brief Existence.[32]

21. If you take care to Pronounce correctly the Words usually Mispronounced, you may have the Self-Love of the Purist, but you will not sell any Goods.

---

28. The British concepts of "keeping a stiff upper lip" and "keeping up an exterior" are more important than "letting your hair down." This comes from the stoic school of literature which included Rudyard Kipling and Theodore Roosevelt.
29. The slouch hat was preferred by Civil War veterans, especially from the old confederacy. And one can imagine George, who idolized Lincoln, being trapped in a sleeping car with the likes of Marse Covington! See *Tariffs, p 142*, plus the play *Marse Covington* in *Plays Worth Remembering, Vol I, p 39*
30. See *The Attenuated Attorney Who Rang in the Associate Counsel*, p 129; and *The Fable of Prince Fortunatas Who Lived in Easy Street and Then Moved Away*, p 72
31. See *The Fable of the Father Who Jumped In*, p 256
32. See *The Fable of the Never-to-be Benefactor Who Took a Brand New Tack*, p 167

22. Never accuse a Man of being Lazy. There is no such thing as Laziness. If a Man does not go about his work with Enthusiasm, it means that he has not yet found the Work that he likes. Every Mortal is a Busy Bee when he comes to the Task that Destiny has set aside for him.[33]

23. Early to Bed and Early to Rise is a Bad Rule for any one who wishes to become acquainted with our most Prominent and Influential People.[34]

24. Always interline a Contract before signing it, merely to impress the Party of the First Part. The one who puts his Signature to Articles of Agreement drawn up by the Other Fellow is establishing a Dangerous Precedent.[35]

25. Never pretend to have Money except when you are in Straits. The Poor Man who pretends to have a Bank Account betters his Credit and takes no Risk. But the Prosperous Individual who counts his Money in the Street, forthwith will be invited to attend a Charity Bazar.[36]

"Is that all?" asked the Young Fox, when he had concluded the reading.

"I thought that would be enough for one Dose," replied the Old Fox.

"But you have not put in anything about depositing a certain Sum in the Bank every Week," said Fox, Jr. "I had always supposed that was the inevitable No. 1 of Parental Suggestions."

"I omitted that time-honored Instruction because I hope you

---

33. For an interesting take on this subject, see "Theories X and Y" in the Appendix. See the Preface of this volume beginning on p xv.
34. See the book *Sweepings* by Lester Cohen, or the movie *Sweepings* by David O. Selznick
35. See *The Maneuvers of Joel and the Disappointed Orphan Asylum*, p 116
36. See Screenplay Sketch from *A Pioneer in the Fullest Sense: The Wit and Wisdom of George Ade's Father*, p 295-297

Introduction

will keep your Money out of the Bank," said the Old Fox. "It is so easy to sign Checks. If you find a Surplus accumulating, go in for Life Insurance, and then you may reasonably hope for the allotted Threescore and Ten Years."

And the Young Fox took the Truth Tablets out to have them Framed.

MORAL: *Even the Elders can give a number of Helpful Hints.*

The Lesson:

All in all, my career was greatly enhanced by the common-sense advice of George Ade. His lessons are timeless because they are lessons about people and how they interact.

For example, the Old Fox's advice to the Young Fox to "permit the Subordinates to become acquainted with you" helped me immeasurably in my career. Once a secretary I knew worked at a company I was consulting for. She sent me a copy of a secret contract between four companies that owed me a royalty. It was specifically designed to cut me out of my royalty by fraud. I gave it to my lawyer, Phil Sotel. At the arbitration proceeding in Houston it was presented in a true "Perry Mason" moment. The nineteen opposing lawyers for the corporations had no defense and meekly whined, "Where did you get that contract?" They paid the royalties, litigation expenses and a penalty but never ever figured out how the cat got out of the bag. By all means, permit subordinates to become acquainted with you!

And how about George's advice on saving, when he had the Old Fox instructing the Young Fox to buy a life insurance policy? Granted, a life insurance policy may have been the best vehicle for "forced savings" in George's day but today we have much better tools—namely IRAs (especially Roth IRAs) and any employer matched savings program. These should all be used to the maximum today. The S&P 500 index fund, Real Estate Investment Trusts (REITs) or Berkshire Hathaway are all excellent things to put in these accounts. Had they been available when George was investing, I am certain he would have utilized them.

The bottom line: investment tools such as life insurance and technologies like the telegraph may have slipped into the past, but as George knew, how people feel—either when they get something a little bit extra and unexpected or when they don't—has not changed, as you will see time and again in the pages ahead.

On Business

The Heir and the Heiress

From *Knocking the Neighbors*, 1912

Once upon a Time there was a Work-Horse who used to lie awake Nights framing up Schemes to Corral more Collateral to leave to the Olive Branches.

They may have looked like Jimpson Weeds to the rest of the World but to Pa and Ma they were A-1 Olive Branches.

Pa was a self-made Proposition—Sole-Leather, Hand-Stitched and Four-Ply, with Rivets around the Edge.

His Business Career had been one long Rassle with Adverse Circumstances. Nothing was ever handed to him on a Sheffield Tray with Parsley around it. The World owed him a Living, but in order to collect it he had to conduct his Arguments with a piece of Lead-Pipe.

He was out for the Kale, if you know what that means. He was collecting Hebrew Diplomas and he had a special Liking for the light-colored Variety with a large C in the Corner.

He was going to provide for his Family, regardless of what happened to other Families.

He had a little Office back of the Bank and made a Specialty of helping those overtaken by Trouble. Any one in Financial Straits who went into the Back Office to arrange for a Loan was expected to open Negotiations by removing the Right Eye and laying it on the Table.

1892 One Hundred Dollar Bill

Pa had Mormon Whiskers and a Mackerel Eye and wore a Shawl instead of an Overcoat and kept a little Bag of Peppermint Drops in his Tail-Pocket and walked Pussy-Foot and took more Stock in Isaiah than he did in the Sermon on the Mount. The Above is merely a Rough Outline, but it will help you to understand why his Wife preceded him to the Other Shore.

She was a Good Woman who never formed the Matinee Habit and up to the Day of her Death she could put her Hand on her Heart and truly say that she had not wasted any Money on Jewelry or Cut Flowers.

But she could have written a large Book on how it feels to get up in the Morning and stir a little Oatmeal.

Pa and Ma saved and skimped and held out and trimmed and maneuvered for Years.

They had been brought up in the School of Hard Knocks, but they wanted Bertrand and Isabel to go through Life on Ball Bearings.

Pa finally went to his Reward, according to the Local Paper, and then it came out that Bertrand and Isabel had $400,000 each, which was more than Pa had ever turned in to the Assessor.

These two Children had been sheltered from the Great World, although never stinted in the matter of Sassafras Tea or the Privilege of reading Books written by Josephus and others.

As soon as he came into his Inheritance, Bertrand looked about in a startled Manner and then bought himself a Plush Hat and began to cultivate Pimples.

A few Days later he might have been seen riding in a Demonstrating Car with a Salesman who wore Goggles and who told him that all the Swell Guys were putting in Orders for the $6,200 Type with the jeweled Mud-Guards. And next Morning the Sexton observed that Father, by turning over in the Grave, had somewhat loosened the fresh Earth.

Bertrand had Modern Plumbing put into the Old House and built a Porte Cochere[37] on the Side and moved a lot of Red Velvet Furniture into the Parlor. Some said that the Moaning Sound heard at Night was only the Wind in the Evergreens, but others allowed that it was the returned Spirit of the Loan Agent checking over the Expenses.

Isabel stopped wearing Things that scratched her and began ordering from a Catalogue, because the Local Dealers didn't carry anything but Common Stuff. Also she began to Entertain, and the first time she served Hot-House Asparagus in January, the House rocked on its Foundations.

Bertrand soon knew the Difference between a Rickey and a Sour and was trying to pretend to let on to be fond of the Smoky Taste in that Imported Article which has done so much to mitigate the Horrors of Golf.

In the meantime, Isabel had got so far along that she could tell by the Feel whether the Goods were real or only Mercerized, and each Setting Sun saw a new Crimp in the Bank Account.

All Statisticians agree that a couple of Heirs can spend Much Money and yet besides if they do not work at anything else. Especially when every Pearl in the Rope represents a Chattel Mortgage

---

37. A porch where vehicles stop to discharge passengers.

and a fancy Weskit[38] is a stand-off for One Month's Rent of a good piece of Town Property.

Bertrand married a tall Blonde who knew that Columbus discovered America and which kind of Massage Cream to buy, and let it go at that.

They went abroad and began to Ritz themselves. Every time Madam walked into one of those places marked "English Spoken while you Wait"—Zing! The Letter of Credit resembled a piece of Apple Pie just after the willing Farm Hand has taken a Hack at it.

Isabel hastened to make an Alliance with one of the oldest and toniest Families west of Bucyrus and north of Evansville. She succeeded in capturing an awful Swell Boy who wore an Outside Pocket on his Dress Coat and made a grand Salad Dressing (merely rubbing the Bowl with a Sprig of Garlic) and was otherwise qualified to maintain Social Leadership all the way from the Round House up to the Hub and Spoke Factory on the Hill.

Isabel's Husband built a House near the Country Club so as to get the Automobile Trade, coming and going. Some of the Best People would drop in and show the Ice-Box how to take a Joke.

Late at Night, when a Hush fell upon the $28,000 Bungalow, the Deep Quiet signified that some had Passed Away and others had locked Horns at Bridge—10 Cents a Point.

Even Lake Superior would go Dry if tapped at two different Points by Drain Pipes of Sufficient Diameter.

After Bertrand returned from Europe with his Paintings and a Table d'Hote Vocabulary, he and Brother-in-Law began to compare Mortgages. By consulting the Road-Map they discovered that the Primrose Path would lead them over a high Precipice into a Stone Quarry, so they decided to take a Short Cut at Right Angles and head for the Millionaire Colony.

---

38. An informal word for waistcoat.

The Day they started for New York City with a Coil of Strong Rope, their purpose being to tie Kuhn, Loeb Co.[39], Hand and Foot, it is said that a long vertical Crack appeared in one of the most expensive Monuments in Springvale Cemetery, as if some one underneath had been trying to break out and Head Off something.

In preserving the form of a Narrative it becomes necessary to add that Bertrand is now the obliging Night Clerk at a Hotel in Louisville, with a Maximum Rate of $1.50 Single and a Shower Bath.

Brother-in-Law is Assistant Treasurer at a Temple of Amusement which guarantees all the latest and best Films.

What became of the Bundle?

Listen.

When Pa locked up his Desk and started for the Pearly Gates, he left behind in the office an humble Man Friday, who took care of the Books and did the Collecting.

This Understrapper was a Model Citizen of 35 who wore a plain String Tie, drank Malted Milk and was slightly troubled with Bronchitis.

When the Children began throwing it at the Birds, he bought himself a Net and got Busy.

Any time Anybody wanted to plaster a Mortgage on a Desirable Corner he was there with a Fountain Pen and a Notary.

It nearly broke his Back to carry all the Property, but he kept buying it in and then hung over his Desk until all Hours of the Night figuring how he could meet the Payments.

He wore the same Overcoat for nine years and his Wife never saw one of those Hats with Bagoozulum and Bazoosh flounced all over it unless she went down town and looked through a Window.

One Day a friend remonstrated with the Slave.

"Why are you wearing yourself to a Shadow and getting Old before your Time?" he asked. "What shall it avail a Man if he is

---

39. An investment bank in New York City.

Principal Depositor at a Bank when it comes to riding behind Horses that wear Plumes?"

"I will tell you," replied the Slave. "I have a Boy named Bertrand and a little Girl named Isabel and my Wife and I have decided that it is our Duty to leave them Well-Fixed."

> MORAL: *Somebody must rake up the Leaves before the Young People can have a successful Bon-Fire.*

The Lesson:

As a former longtime member of TIGER 21 and a founding partner of R360,[40] I have witnessed many examples of first-generation wealth creators who put away lots of wealth for the next generation only to see it ignited into a bonfire soon after the wealth was transferred. It's just as common today as when George wrote this story.

One of the goals of R360 is to address this problem. There are six forms of capital: intellectual, social, human, emotional, spiritual and financial. Research by one of our managing partners, Michael Cole, has shown that these financial capital bonfires do not usually occur for lack of training in finance.[41]

Money is only a tool. More important than financial capital are the other five forms of capital. These are the forms of capital that provide purpose. When someone has no purpose in life, they will make a bonfire out of the tools—the financial capital.

---

40. https://www.r360global.com/
41. Michael Cole, *More Than Money: A Guide to Sustaining Wealth and Preserving the Family.* (Bloomberg Press, 2017), Chapter 1.

The Common Carrier

From *Knocking the Neighbors*, 1912

Once there was a little E-Flat Town that needed a Direct Communication with a Trunk Line.[42]

A Promoter wearing Sunday Clothes and smoking 40-cent Cigars came out from the City to see about it.

The Daily Paper put him on the Front Page. Five Dollars was the Set-Back for each Plate at the Banquet tendered him by the Mercantile Association. A Bonus was offered, together with a Site for the Repair Shops and the Round House.

When the College Graduates in Khaki Suits began to drag Chains across Lots, a wave of Joy engulfed Main Street from the Grain Elevator clear out to the Creamery.

Then came 10,000 Carusos[43], temporarily residing in Box Cars, to disarrange the Face of Nature and put a Culvert over the Crick. Real Estate Dealers emerged from their Holes and local Rip Van Winkles began to sit up and rub their Eyes.

One morning a Train zipped through the Cut and pulled up at the New Station.

---

42. The main line of a railroad.
43. Young workers, possibly Italian immigrants.

The Road was an Assured Fact. The Rails were spiked down; the Rolling Stock was in Commission; Trains were running according to Schedule.

There was no longer any Reason for Waiting, so the Citizens hiked over to the Court House and began to file Damage Suits. The Town Council started in to pass Ordinances and the Board of Equalization whooped the Taxes.

Horny-handed Jurors hung around the Circuit Court Room waiting for a Chance to take a Wallop at the soulless Corporation.

When the Promoter came along on a Tour of Inspection, the only Person down to meet him was the Sheriff.

Children in the Public School practised the new Oval Penmanship by filling their Copy-Books with the following popular Catch-Line: "When you have a Chance to Soak the Railroad, go to it."

And the Trains never ran to suit Everybody.

MORAL: *Go easy with Capital until you get it Roped and Tied.*

The Lesson:

This story has a good lesson, for today it is very possible to chase all the so-called evil corporations away. When I was living in Singapore I met then-Prime Minister Lee Kuan Yew. I spoke with, listened to and read everything that I could about him and I highly recommend to everyone that they read his books. During his administration, Lee declared that his city state would be "the nest for the goose that lays the golden egg." The goose that lays the golden egg of which he spoke was First World multinational corporations that would bring employment and development for the inhabitants of his then Third World land. Thus, Lee's policy was to court large multinational corporations by making Singaporean taxes and regulations as modest as possible. It was a good strategy. Today the GNP per capita in Singapore is over $100k per person (by contrast, per capita GNP is perhaps $70k in the United States). In his book *Third World to First*, Lee explained in detail how anti-corporate thinking in the West would lead to its decline and Asia's rise.

As I am writing this, the United Auto Workers are striking and requesting a starting salary of over $100k for union members with no college and perhaps not even a high school diploma. That's just a start. Union rules are based on seniority, not merit.

My daughter who is a lawyer tells me that after a four-year undergraduate degree and a three-year Doctor of Jurisprudence, a new lawyer can expect to start out at $70k.

Social justice?

I do not understand how people can shout about social justice when they're extorting from big corporations salaries for high school dropouts that exceed the salaries of those who have spent years improving their minds and talents. To me, that is the exact opposite of any literal meaning of social justice.

Pray, let us stop killing the goose that lays the golden eggs!

Life Insurance

From *In Babel: Stories of Chicago*, 1906

The moment you see him coming toward you, you are sensible of the fact that his personality towers above your own. He stoops a little, figuratively and literally, when he comes to address you.

"Mr. Mark, I wrote to you some time ago in regard to a business matter in which I supposed you might be interested," he says.

You do not remember having received any communication from him and you are moderately certain that you never saw the man before, but memory is fickle and you tactfully say "Yes," nodding your head.

"I had intended to come around and see you before this," he says. "A friend of yours, Mr. A. J. Booster, in the Behemoth building, was very anxious that I should call in to see you, and I promised him that I would."

You remember Mr. Booster, dimly, as a restaurant acquaintance, who makes puns. You wonder why he has put on such a solicitude.

You look at the plain card in front of you, "Mr. Percival Conway," and wonder if he has come to buy those lots in Prairie Glen, which you have been holding at $800, without an offer in four years.

"Now, I don't want to interrupt you if you are busy or take up any of your time needlessly," says Mr. Conway, as he glances at a heavily engraved gold watch. "It is now 10.30. If you will have more time at 11.30 or at 2 this afternoon, or at any other hour, I can break my engagements and come here to see you. What I have to say will probably take ten minutes. It's a simple and straightforward business proposition, and I think it will appeal to you as a business man. (This flatters you, in spite of the fact that you haven't an ounce of business sense and never made a success of a trade.) As I said before, I won't take up more than ten minutes, but I don't care to bring the matter to your attention until you feel that you have the time at your disposal."

To tell the truth, you are very busy. Your day's work lies before you on the desk and beckons you to activity. But who can resist a man who is so considerate? Besides, it will be over in ten minutes, so why not have it out of the way? You ask him to be seated and put yourself into a serious attitude for listening.

"Mr. Mark, I believe that I can put you in the way of making a little money for yourself, or at least of saving some money year after year, and, at the same time, protecting your family or relations," he begins.

This has a suspicious phrasing.

"Let's see, you're about twenty-nine years old, aren't you?" he asks.

"More than that—thirty-four."

"Indeed! I wouldn't have believed it. Now let me see (taking a small book from his inside coat-pocket), you say thirty-four—thirty-four—well, that isn't so much more. There isn't so much difference in the expectation. Now, Mr. Mark, how much money could you spare every year—money to be put aside simply as a sure investment, with the privilege of drawing it out at any time if you saw fit to do so?"

You begin to catch the trend of his remarks.

Life Insurance

"Is this another life-insurance scheme?" you ask as you feel the wrath slowly spreading toward your extremities.

"Not exactly, although we guarantee you the incidental insurance the same as the old-line companies. Our proposition, however, differs from all others in this important respect: We allow the interest accumulating on the tontine policy[44] to become a reserve fund, and at the end of twenty years you can either draw this principal or you can apply it on a paid-up policy at four per cent. interest. Now, for instance, you are thirty-four years old and you take out one of our non-reversible twenty-year policies with the reserve-fund clause. You would pay the first year $186.13, and of that sum $22.49 would go into the contingent department and be applied on the policy direct, while $76.87, as you can see by a glance at this chart, will be put aside, and out of that we allow you the discount, so that the second year you can either pay the $186.13 or you can allow the $14.92 set down here as premium, to apply on the payment, or you can withdraw and take a nine-months' paid-up policy for $1,800, but if you do this you lose the four per cent. interest which I mentioned a few minutes ago, so that, if you care to accept my advice in the matter you will take the same kind of a policy that I wrote for your friend, Mr. Booster—that is, the reactionable endowment policy, with the clause permitting the accumulation of both premium and interest, so that, after the termination of eleven years, you being only forty-five years old at that time, you can withdraw all that you have paid in up to that time, less the $22.49 indicated in the left-hand column, or, as I said a while ago, you can accept a paid-up policy at the uniform rate, which in your case would be equivalent to $3,400. Now, I suppose the question presents itself to your mind: 'In what respect does this

---

44. An early system for raising capital where individuals pay into a common pool of money. In the U.S., tontines were popular in the 1700s and 1800s, then faded in the early 1900s. Tontine investors paid lump sums upon joining and received annual dividend-like payments until death. ~ Investopedia

proposition vary from one that might be offered by an old-line insurance company'?"

It is possible that such a question has presented itself, but the probability is that you are wondering what it is all about.

Your mind gropes through the murk of technical verbiage as Mr. Conway proceeds to elucidate the difference between his proposition and one that might be made by an old-line company.

"In the first place, we apply the premium direct and compute the insurance at the rate of $2.06 a year per $1,000, so that the entire residue goes into the sinking fund[45] and there it draws compound interest for you at the rate of four per cent. per annum. This is made possible under our new system of reducing operating expenses to a minimum and putting the executive department into the hands of men who do not seek pecuniary reward, but are actuated by unselfish and philanthropic motives. Now in this twenty-year automatic policy, which you will probably prefer to any of the others when you have given the matter thorough study, you pay in $2,247.67 and you get at the end of twenty years your $5,000, to say nothing of the incidental protection during that period. Now, in one of the old-line companies you would pay in $4,862.54, so that we save you $2,600 right there, as well as guaranteeing to you the privilege of withdrawal and the computation of interest, or the acceptance of a paid-up policy. Doesn't that strike you as a generous proposition?"

There can be but one answer to this question. You must say "Yes."

Suppose you say "No." He will ask you, "Well, to what particular feature of the policy would you object?"

Then you would be helpless.

If you were to say that you didn't know what he was talking about and that all his arguments were as Greek or Sanscrit, that

---

45. A fund established by setting aside revenue over a period of time to fund a future capital expense, or repayment of a long-term debt.

would be evidence of a feeble understanding, because he gave you to understand at the beginning that he was going to be simple and direct.

There is but one way in which to cover your confusion of mind, and that is to nod gravely and say "Yes."

However, this is a dangerous thing to do. The moment that you say "Yes," that becomes a practical admission on your part that you are partly under conviction.

Immediately he does the magician's trick. He pulls a huge book from under his coat (you wonder how he managed to conceal it) and begins to fill out an application for a policy.

Here you must enter a protest or you are lost. It must be an emphatic protest. You must give some specific reason for not desiring a policy. Whatever that reason may be, he is ready to bombard and demolish it with unanswerable arguments, business proverbs, and figures of speech. Hundreds of men have given him that same reason at various times, and he has studied out his reply, rehearsed it carefully, and fortified himself at every point.

So when you start in to dispute ground with Mr. Conway you are in the position of a bewildered novice who is going against the champion of the world.

If you say that you have all the insurance you can carry, he will demonstrate to you that you have not. If you mention that you are investing all of your money, he will prove to you that his company offers the only safe and profitable field for investment. If you raise the point that you are unmarried and have no one dependent upon you and therefore feel no disposition to carry insurance, he will produce a green book and read the figures to prove that of every 1,000 men who, at the age of thirty-four, announce that they never will marry, no less than 860 afterward weaken and go to the altar, and this, too, at a time of life when the insurance rates are becoming very high.

So you see, there is no chance for you. The only thing to do is to take out a policy for any amount that he may suggest.

The Lesson:

I have encountered just such an insurance salesman, perhaps even the same salesman! More frequently, it is telemarketers who all seem to have my phone number . . .

Just say "No thanks," hang up and block the phone number. They will soon call back from a new number, and the cycle goes on and on forever. . .

But the lesson is to just say "No thanks" and stick with it!

The Fable of the Two Ways of Going Out After the Pay Envelope

From *True Bills*, 1904

A man who had been given the Fresh Air by a Soulless Corporation was out rustling for another Job. He went around to see all the General Managers. Usually he had to sit outside and permit a beautiful Stenographer to look Holes in him. When he was finally admitted to the Sacred Presence of the head Gazooks, he would approach the Roll-Top on tiptoe and stand there with his Hat in his Hand and beg for Work. He wanted a Job, and Salary was no Object. Thereupon the Main Torch would slip him the Old One about putting his Application on File and notifying him in case anything turned up. The Morgues are full of People who have Applications on File.

After he had been Drilling from one Office to another for about a Month, he had about 350 of these vague, indefinite Promises, but there was nothing doing in the Salary Line.

So he decided to try a new Tack.

"This Humble Pie doesn't seem to agree with me," he said. "I shall cut out the Apologetic and try being Nifty."

Accordingly, he went to a Friend and braced him for a Century[46] as if asking for a Match. Then he engaged a Suite at the Principal Hostelry and sent engraved Notifications to all the General Managers that he could be seen any Day between 11:45 and 12:15 on presentation of Visiting-Cards.

They knew that he was a Big Gun or he wouldn't be paying ten per for his Rooms. So several hurried over and began to Bid for him.

MORAL: *Those who have tried Meekness know the Importance of being Important.*

The Lesson:

In 1986 I found myself unemployed in Jakarta needing to support a wife and three small children who were still in diapers. I went around to all of the companies asking for a job, and because it was the great oil recession there were none. I had no source of income whatsoever.

At this point, I remembered "The Fable of the Two Ways of Going Out After the Pay Envelope."

I took the repatriation airline tickets for our family of five and cashed them in. This was all of the cash I had. Actually, I was insolvent, owing more money than I had in assets due to having bought the family farm to keep it from entering bankruptcy. With these few thousand dollars I moved my family from Jakarta to Singapore and rented a small two bedroom walk up in the less fashionable district of Jurong with the goal of turning it into a home office.

I printed up deluxe stationery and business cards with my telephone number, a fax number, and the telegraph cable number (yes, telegraphs still existed at that time). I registered a new business and got legal papers, a work permit and a green card. I also bought

---

46. A $100 bill.

tailor-made tropical-weight suits and ties. I was representing a consulting company, after all.

I went to all of the companies that were likely to hire a geologist and told them that I wasn't looking for a job; rather, I was the manager of a consulting business and I understood that they couldn't hire anyone because of the mandatory 30% staff layoffs. I also understood that after layoffs they had more work than they had people to perform it. My consulting business could take on any work whatsoever on a turnkey basis. One single price for a job. Any job. To be completed for a fixed price in a fixed timeframe.

The managers all shouted, "Eureka! We're guaranteed to be on time and under budget, we're not adding to the headcount, which is forbidden, and we don't have to go to all of the trouble of having an employee or getting them work permits, or a place to live," etc. etc.

Meanwhile, everyone else who was laid off was wandering around looking for a job; an expatriate job with a work permit, income taxes paid, incentive compensation and bonuses, company-provided housing, company medical, paid vacation time, a company car, company-paid private school for their kids and of course American Club membership for their families. The overseas benefits could exceed the base salary of an expatriate geologist. The "salarymen" didn't have a chance competing with me, not a prayer. On any job I was much less than half the cost with none of the Human Resources hassle.

Within a few months I not only had half a dozen bidding for my services but I also did George one better. I took all of the jobs and called my competitors, who by then were back in their home country, usually Houston, Texas, still looking for a job. I'd ask if they'd be willing to do a short-term interpretation for a fixed price with a deadline of a month or two. They always said an emphatic YES! Then I'd quote the corporation twice the price and double the time so in case the Texan dropped the ball, I would have the time to do it myself. In each and every case the corporation immediately said YES! Then we would sign the contract and I'd get 50% up front. Worst case scenario, I'd make a good consulting wage. Best case, I'd make a fortune.

The result: many of the geologists who had followed the conventional path were not able to find jobs and consequently lost not only income but, in some sad cases, their homes and families. I, on the other hand, earned more money on my own than I had ever made as a salaried oil exploration company employee. I had the field all to myself until OMS came to town . . . to be continued in another story.

The Fable of the Old Merchant, the Sleuth and the Tapioca

From *Forty Modern Fables*, 1901

A High-Priced Detective was sitting in his Lair, trying to look Mysterious, when there came to him a gray-muzzled old Business Man. The Latter was noted for his Probity, his Keenness and the Fact that he never Thawed. In the Commercial Agencies he was Rated AA Plus A1, which meant that he had it in Bales.

"I wish to enlist your Services," said the Great Merchant. "A Young Man who lately has come into a World of Money desires to be admitted to Partnership in our Large Business. We are an Old and Reputable Concern, and before associating ourselves with this Stripling we wish to know all about his Character and Habits. We want you to Camp on his Trail and give us a straight Line on his Daily Life."

So the Main Detective called in a couple of Ferrets, who drew Twelve a Week, and they began to Shadow the Young Man at $8 a Day. They put on Gum Shoes and covered their Faces with black Muffs, such as are worn by the Train Robbers in a Davis and Keogh Melodrama. They peeked over Transoms and shinned up Fire Escapes and hid behind Bill-Boards, and every time the Young Man made a Move they were Next. At the end of a Week the Celebrated Detective made a Report to the Pious Patriarch who had employed him.

"I regret to tell you that the Young Man who seeks a Connection with your Well-Known House is a Night Hawk and a Spender," said the Superintendent. "He is trying to dim the Record of Coal-Oil Johnny. He opens Cold Magnums for the Merry-Merry almost every Midnight, and he is having Diamonds set into the Teeth of Nine of the Peroxide Sisters. By the time that he lands into his Happy Clothes of an Evening he is fairly well Corned, and he sees the Dawn of Morning through a Purple Haze. In the Afternoon, when he arises, he has a Hang-Over which is made the Foundation of something very Tidy in the way of a Skate. He begins to Push the Button and absorb the tall Pick-Me-Ups. For a six o'clock Breakfast he has a few Cigarettes and some of the cold Zippy-Zip. Thus he contrives to be the Custodian of a continuous Bun and stave off the Katzenjammer, his Life resolving itself into one long Honolulu Sunset. His Associates are a fine Bunch of Rowdy-Dows, who lean over when they Walk, and wear Lilac Gloves in the Summer Time. Their one Joy is to purchase little Hot Birds and big Johannesburg Twinklers for the Ladies depicted on the Lithos."

"My! My!" said the staid old Merchant, as he shook his silvered Head. "He must be a Lah-Lah if he can hold to that Gait. I suppose he plays the Drunken Sailor with his Money."

"I regret to say that he does," replied the Eminent Sleuth. "All the Tin-Horn Sports and Shoe-String Gamblers speak of him as their Meal Ticket. He is put against a new Brace Game every Week. He is so Soft that sometimes even the hardened Sheet-Writers feel that it is a Shame to take it away from him. But they need the Vulgar Mazume, so they lighten him."

"Is it not Sad to see a pin-headed Rake dissipating a Large Fortune built up by some one who Walked to save Car Fare?" asked the Old Gentleman. "You are sure that he has no Business Gumption?"

"No more than a Rabbit," was the Reply of the Detective. "He is a Come-On for any Bunco Game in the List. He is a Ninny. Should you give him an Interest in your Business he would show up at his Desk about once a Month, and if you handed him an Assessment he would think it was a Dividend."

"I thank you for your Report," said the Pillar of Trade. "We will admit the Young Man to a Full Partnership and urge him to put in all the Coin at his Command."

"I am surprised," said the Sleuth. "He is a horrible Light Weight."

"That is why he will be a Mark for a cool-headed Johnny Wise who lives on Cereal Food and gets into his Pajams at 9.30 every Evening," said the Prominent Merchant with a slight Grin. "Why should all this lovely Money go to Cabmen and straw-colored Sou-brettes[47] when it might as well be Garnered by an Honored Citizen who would know how to Invest it? From what you tell me of the Rapid Youth I conclude that he would be Meat for a crafty Side Partner."

Next Day the Chorus Girls' Friend was Taken In, and eighteen Months later the steady old Partner with the Snowy Locks had him euchred[48] down to the Clothes on his Back.

His Fortune was permanently Invested in an Old and Reliable Establishment, and he was on his Uppers for fair.

MORAL: *Any one who has the Qualifications can get in with a First-Class Firm.*

---

47. A flirtatious young woman.
48. (Pronounced You-Kur) As a noun, Euchre is a card game. Used as a verb, to euchre means to gain advantage over someone.

The Lesson:

Soon after setting up my consulting firm in Singapore following the oil price collapse in 1986, I secured some good paying clients including the Belgian company Petrofina, Marathon Oil out of the United States, the Malaysian-Singaporean conglomerate ProMet, etc. I was working out of my modest two-bedroom home and making more money than I had ever made before.

However, I was not the only one setting up consulting companies in Singapore, for there had been a huge layoff of geologists around the world. One of my competitors was the firm known as OMS. This firm had the backing of an Australian venture capitalist. They set up their office on Orchard Road, the "Fifth Avenue" or "Boardwalk and Park Place" of Singapore in a high-rise office with beautiful views. There they had two managing directors, secretaries, office boys, drivers, and so on. And one single very cheap client, Petrocorp of New Zealand.

The two managing directors of OMS called me to their office in the clouds and invited me to be part of their firm. They showed me the lovely office and the desk that I would have, as well as a secretary. They asked that I disclose the value of all my consulting contracts, which I did. Then I asked them to disclose the value of all their consulting contract—singular. I was bringing in approximately ten times as much money per month as they were. This came as quite a surprise to both of us.

Over a long and sumptuous executive lunch, they went into great detail about all of the wonders of their vision and their mission to serve the exploration companies throughout the greater Asia-Australia region, and how they had a couple hundred thousand dollars of seed capital from the Australian venture capital company and that it would be useless—futile, even—for me to try to make it on my own.

I told them I would think it over. On the bus ride home that evening I recalled George's *Fable of the Old Merchant, the Sleuth, and the Tapioca*, and I smiled. I was not going to serve myself up as a tapioca dessert for OMS. I politely declined their offer to become a partner.

Within six months OMS had burned through all their seed capital, closed up shop and laid off every one of their employees.

The Fable of the Divided Concern that Was Reunited Under a New Management

From *True Bills*, 1904

Once upon a Time there was a Firm doing Business under the Name of Hailfellow and Grouch.

They had a large Retail Establishment, upon entering which the Customer was greeted by the mingled Odors of Kerosene, Roasted Coffee, Leather, Herkimer County Cheese, Navy Plug, Dried Apples, and petrified Codfish. In the good old Summer-Time it was not necessary to go into the Store in order to get the complicated Aroma. Farmers driving by could come very near guessing what Hailfellow and Grouch carried in Stock.

The Firm did a Nice Business and used to split quite a Piece of Money every January 1st. But neither one was satisfied. Each felt that he was entitled to at least two-thirds of the Net Profits.

Mr. Hailfellow was the Hand-Shaker for the Outfit. His Long Suit was to know everybody and call him by his front Name.

On every pleasant Day he stood in front of the fragrant Emporium, in his Shirt Sleeves, holding a public Levee.

He was a quiet Josher and knew a lot of good Jokes that he had once heard in a Minstrel Show at Columbus, Ohio, and that made him very strong with the Country Trade.

Furthermore, he was a good Mixer. He belonged to the K. P.'s and the Odd Fellows and a few others, so that about four Nights out of the week he would fill his Pockets with mild Smokers, usually neglecting to make out a Ticket, and then he would pike for the Lodge-Room and let his Partner and the Boy with the Pink Shirt attend to the Store.

If there was an Auction Sale or a Baseball Game or a Circus anywhere within a Radius of twenty Miles, then Mr. Hailfellow would put on his Dark Suit and stand-up Collar and drive over, just to get his Mind off of his Business. In one Way and another he managed to keep his Mind off of Business about seven-eighths of the Time.

Sometimes, when he was around the Store, and there was a Saturday Rush, he would have to wait on a few Customers, but he was a shine Salesman because he never could make out what the Cost-Mark meant.

Mr. Grouch, the Partner, possessed a Good Head for Business, but he had the Social Disposition of a Coffin-Trimmer. While Hailfellow would be up and down the Street, kidding the local Population and making himself well liked, Grouch would be in the back end of the Store straightening out the Books and figuring Discounts.

Grouch was at the Store by 7 o'clock every Morning, keeping Tab, for fear that some one who was No Good would get his Name on the Books.

Hailfellow would land in about 9.30 and open the Day by reading the Morning Paper through from the Weather Bulletin in front to the Testimonials on the last Page. After which he was ready to go out and plant himself on a Salt-Barrel and discuss the Issues of the Day.

Grouch had only one Day off in Four Years, and then he had to attend the Funeral of a Relative. So that when he did get a Vacation there was not much Enjoyment in it.

There was no denying his Industry, but no one liked him. He seemed to have some kind of an inward Grudge against every one who came in to buy a Bill of Goods. If a Customer remarked that it was a Nice Day, he didn't seem to believe it. The Trade would not have stuck at all, had it not been for Hailfellow, who had a way of giving Stick Candy to the Kids and beautiful Colored Pictures, advertising Breakfast Foods, to the Women Folks.

Each Partner naturally believed that he was getting the Short End of the Arrangement. They would go home and tell their Troubles to the Wives. Mrs. Hailfellow went around to Sewing Societies and Missionary Meetings telling how Mr. Hailfellow had to put up with a lot and was really the one who brought all the Trade to the Store.

Mrs. Grouch loved to let all her Friends know that her Husband slaved like a Dog while the Partner soldiered, but, just the same, always came in on the cut-up of the Profits.

When the Wives begin to take part in a Business Row, the Dissolution Notice is about Due.

Hailfellow and Grouch agreed to disagree. Hailfellow took his Share and opened a New Place across the Street, with a Gilt Sign and nickel-plated Show-Cases.

Almost immediately it was the most popular Joint in Town. At Times there were as many as ten Men sitting around the Stove swapping Fish Stories. Hailfellow employed a couple of Clerks who knew more about a Cash Register than the Man that invented it.

He issued Pass-Books[49] to all those who cared for his Jokes. The Drummers[50] would jump several Towns in order to get to him in a Hurry, because, if Hailfellow liked a Drummer, he would order a

---
49. A booklet provided by a bank to keep track of deposits and withdrawals.
50. Slang for a salesman. As in, "He's out drumming up sales."

thousand gross of Lamp Chimneys rather than appear cold and unsociable. In a short time he had a Magnificent Stock, but he could not remember exactly how much it cost him. So he sold Goods at whatever seemed to be Reasonable and the Farmers drove long distances so as to give him their Trade.

In the meantime Grouch was reaping the sure Reward of one who is not kind to his Fellow-Man. People did not care to patronize one whose Conversation consisted very largely of Grunts, and why should they do so when they could go right across the Street and buy Stuff below Cost, and a Joke given away with every Purchase?

Grouch began to lose Money and the Rent ate up his Invested Capital. At last the Jobbers closed in on him and asked the Sheriff to step in, and the Sheriff said he would do so as soon as he got through closing up the Hailfellow Matter.

Mr. Hailfellow had done a rushing Business. He owed nearly every Wholesale House west of New York, and in addition to laying up the most remarkable mess of Junk ever seen under one Roof, he had collected the Autograph Signatures of all the Paupers in the County. Four Experts worked for a Month trying to find out where he stood, and at last they figured out Fourteen Cents on the Dollar.

It is always pleasant to record a Reconciliation. After all their Differences and Misunderstandings, Hailfellow and Grouch came together and resumed Friendly Relations.

Both are employed by a New Concern which bought up the Bankrupt Stocks.

Grouch is keeping the Books at not very much per Month, and Hailfellow receives exactly the same Salary for standing around the front Doorway and glad-handing the Yaps.[51]

Which proves that it is impossible for a Business Man to side-step his Destiny.

---

51. A mouth that talks continuously and/or a hillbilly-type person.

MORAL: *Pick out the Other Kind for a Partner.*

The Lesson:

My late partner Bogue Hunt was a superb regional geologist and perhaps the best collector of geological data since Everette Lee DeGolyer. Bogue had amassed a collection of geological and geophysical data that was larger than that held by any of the governments in Asia at the time.

Bogue reached out to me to be his partner not because of my regional geologic knowledge or my ability to collect and organize a database, but because he knew I would turn his database into a portfolio of prospects. He and I complemented each other in innumerable ways, each of us often correcting the other. Bogue had a profound grip on exploration history and the regional geology of Asia, while my knowledge of geophysics, sequence stratigraphy and more modern prospect generation was unfamiliar to him.

In the long run, perhaps the greatest thing I added to the partnership was the simple observation that we needed outside legal advice on overriding royalty contracts, etc. Eventually we brought in attorney Phil Sotel as a sometimes partner and all-of-the-time friend. Although the three of us were very different individuals, we accomplished more together than any of us would have been able to do alone.

Vote For Landon

From *The Trumpeter* Magazine, September 25, 1936

I am very strongly for Landon and Knox because I have a lingering prejudice in favor of the old-fashioned virtues of economy, frugality and careful management. It seems to me that any individual or business organization or government which gleefully and recklessly goes head over heels into debt just because it has a chance to extend its credit is headed for trouble. It is never a safe plan to live away beyond one's income unless one is prepared later on to meet all the obligations assumed and pay all debts.

The present administration at Washington has shown a reckless disregard for all of the time-honored rules of conducting a safe business. It has padded the payrolls and multiplied the number of bureaus and departments and built up a vast political machine at the expense of the taxpayers. While doing this it has seemed to suggest, in all of the proclamations and propaganda, that the citizen who, by economy, frugality, private enterprise and careful management, has built up a successful enterprise of any kind and acquired a surplus, is an enemy to the general good and needs to be penalized and punished. I cannot believe that the American plan under which we have grown and developed is entirely bad or that a citizen is unworthy just because he has invested money and is an employer of labor.

I think we have tackled too many wild experiments and have wasted great sums of money on projects which were carelessly conceived and foolishly executed. I am for a return to safe and sane methods.

The Lesson:

Pure and simple common sense on business, investments and government—that's what this piece represents.

The Galley Slave Who Was Just About To but Never Did

From *Breaking Into Society*, 1904

Once there was a Youth who tackled the Mercantile Career at a very light Stipend.

His chief Ambition in Life was to get so far ahead of the Game that he could afford a nice Cutaway Suit, a swell Derby for Sunday, and a 14-karat De Beers[52] set in a massive Gold Band.

He learned to embrace the Country Trade and talk 175 Words per Minute, so that in a little while he had an Offer from an Opposition Concern. Whereupon he said he hated to leave, but—and the House stood for an Increase.

He came into the Cutaway and the Ring, and then he found that he needed a Spike-Tail and a Folding-Hat and a Cape-Coat. His Glad Raiment carried him right into Sussiety[53], and he began to meet Gazelles[54] that suited him, so he figured on the Probable Expense of Keeping House.

He thought that if he could annex a good-looking Tottie with

---

52. De Beers was (and is) a diamond consortium founded in the late 1800s, so George was referring to a diamond.
53. George's take on the phonetic spelling of "society."
54. An attractive, aloof girl.

large, soulful Eyes, and take an Apartment and keep a Girl, then he would be fixed for sure.

So he went out for more Salary and carried the Bunk-Book next to his Heart. At last the Proud Day arrived when he had his own Flat, with a rented Piano in the Front Room and Tidies[55] on the Chairs. Before the Lease expired Pet discovered that the Dining-Room was too small, and began to dream Dreams of a House of their Own in which they could Entertain. So he tucked back his Cuffs and took a fresh Grip on the World of Trade, and honed like a Turk, making Payments on the House. He was beginning to look round-shouldered, but he drank plenty of Coffee and smoked fat Cigars and buckled down.

He had it all planned to take a good Rest as soon as he had lifted the Mortgage. He went so far as to send out for Time-Tables[56] and look at the Pictures of People sitting around in Steamer Chairs enjoying the Sea Air.

He would have taken a nice, long Vacation, only he saw a Chance to break into the Firm. Accordingly he went in Debt up to his Eyes. He would lie awake at Night casting up his Liabilities and computing Interest. He talked to himself on the Street, and acted just the least bit Dippy. But he was determined to swing the Deal, and then, as soon as he was out of the Woods, he could take a Trip and hang around Picture-Galleries and ride in Gondolas and have the Time of his Life, with nothing to worry him.

For Years he had said that it was a Crime for any one Man to pile up more than $100,000. As soon as he went above that Figure it was a Case of sitting up Nights to count it. As soon as he had that Hundred Thousand raked up and tied in Bundles, then for a Quiet Spot near a Body of Water and a Naphtha Launch[57] and the free, open Life of the Golf Links.

---

55. A tidy is a small cloth draped over furniture to protect it. Today we might call it a doily.
56. A printed schedule of train departure and arrival times.
57. A small boat powered by an external combustion engine (Naphtha engine).

To the 50-cent Table-d'Hote Fellow, 100,000 Samoleons[58] in one Lump looks bigger than the Union Station, but the Man who is being gnawed by the Mazuma[59] Bacillus thinks he is a Pauper unless he can count up Seven Figures. He is always sizing up alongside of Rockefeller and Morgan, and he feels like a Piker sitting in a stiff Poker Game with one White Seed.

Just about the time the Business Man counted up $100,000 to the Good he discovered that he needed seven Servants around the House. And the Missus could float downtown on a sunny Afternoon and make $1000 look like a Pinch of Small Change.

He set his Mark at One Million. Then, when he had that, out to the Sylvan Dell. He was going to be a Gentleman Farmer.

Every Office Building on Earth is congested with hollow-eyed Prisoners who are planning to be Gentleman Farmers. About next Year or Year after—away from the Hurly Burly and nothing to do except raise Chickens.

All of them have those Chicken Dreams. This Business Man whom we are describing even went so far as to pick out the kind of Chickens he was going to raise—Plymouth Rocks. He figured how many Eggs he could get per Hen, and sometimes, when the Pencil was working well, he estimated that he could make the Place self-supporting.

In the mean time he was humping himself and eating Pepsin Tablets[60] and taking a little something every Night to make him Sleep.

The Business had developed so that he had kept two Stenographers busy, and was jumping from the Long-Distance Phone to the Private Office most of the Time, and chewing up 30-cent Cigars, and in other Ways giving a correct Imitation of a Man who has a large and ambitious Family on Hand.

---

58. Slang for dollars.
59. Slang for money.
60. A digestive aid.

He began to look Wild out of the Eyes and had a severe Case of the Jumps, but he had to postpone that Rest for a little While, because no one else understood all the details of the Business.

When the Doctor hinted about Nervous Prostration he said that he was trying to get the whole Organization down to a System, so that some one else could step in and run it, after which he expected to take a Place in the Country and raise Chickens. He told the Chicken Story so often he began to believe it himself.

In order to systematize the Large Business so that he could turn it over to some one else and then have his Vacation, he began to put in 16 hours a Day, and landed in the large Corner Room, with a Trained Nurse putting Ice on his Head and telling him he would be all right in a Day or so.

He had a Ticker put in at one side of the Bed, and kept a Stenographer on hand up to the Afternoon that he departed this life.

It is said that when he went to his Reward he was met by a Celestial Attendant, who proved to be the Recording Angel.

"If you're the Recording Angel, get out your Book," said the Business Man. "I want you to take a few Letters for me."

MORAL: *The Chicken Ranch is always in the Future Tense.*

The Lesson:

I often hear friends and associates who founded their own businesses say, "I'm trying to get the whole organization down to a system, and then I'm going to retire." Every time I hear this, I recall George's story of *The Galley Slave Who Was Just About To but Never Did*. It's so very easy to become completely and totally immersed, fascinated, and occupied by a successful business—especially if it's *your* business.

I have witnessed men who literally worked themselves into an early grave exactly this way. Men who were advised to ease up by fellow TIGER 21 or R360 members. It is as true today as it was in George's day: "The Chicken Ranch is always in the Future Tense" for some people. Alas, one day the chickens *did* come home to roost, but the businessmen weren't there to enjoy it.

Poker

George mentions poker in this story, which is no surprise because he had a lifelong fascination with the game. He even wrote the Foreword to Webster's book on poker[61]:

> *You remember ping-pong. You may remember even the 13-14-15 blocks of wood. Two good indoor pastimes which died before they could be weaned. If you are not too young and have felt the urge to get all that life offers, maybe you have croakinaled yourself, wrestled with the double Canfield, tried your hand at "authors" (nadir of diversions), and even taken a gay hand at "pitch" or "sniff." As the missing word contest sinks for the third time, the cross-word puzzle bounds into our midst and acquires an immoderate popularity which is the surest omen of an early demise.*
>
> *No person of normal bringing-up could play charades, write limericks or try to answer those animal, vegetable and mineral questions for seven nights in succession without becoming sleazy under the bonnet. They are giggling games and giggling is a trade at which no one can work all of the time without becoming the human equivalent of poison ivy.*
>
> *Do you want to know of a game which is practically devoid of giggling? Some profanity all of the time and now and then a dash of manslaughter, but hardly any laughter except an occasional cackle*

---

61. https://a.co/d/99tKfd9

from the dirty dog who runs a whiz in a jack-pot? Referring, of course, to poker.

Poker—essence of the adventuring traits of the ambitious Yankee. The world's champion recipe for getting something for nothing in a hurry. The only game in which courage so often triumphs over intelligence, guided by caution. Popular, because so many of our best people are bold without being either intelligent or cautions.

No matter how often you have played it, something new turns up every game. And no other pastime permits you to discover so many criminal traits in your life-long friends. An utter vacuity of expression is given credit as a display of magnificent self-control. Social standing, pedigree, intellectual superiority and personal pulchritude cease to be assets when the cut-throats move up to the round table and begin to level their stacks.

Euchre and seven-up[62] *have gone over the hill, but poker is still doing as much business in the winter as baseball does in the summer. Some one will say, "Ah, the survival of the fittest." Possibly a more accurate explanation would be that poker is the survival of the fightin'est.*

But George wasn't the only one who saw poker as significant. The great mathematician John Von Neumann used it as a basis for the mathematical formulation of game theory (business strategy) which I studied as part of my MBA. Here's how *Forbes* explained it[63]:

Von Neumann was only interested in poker because he saw it as a path toward developing a mathematics of life itself. He wanted a general theory–he called it "game theory"–that could be applied to diplomacy, war, love, evolution or business strategy. But he thought that

---

62. A Dutch card game originally called All Fours. It was first written about in England in the 1600s. In the 1800s it became popular in America and was called Seven-Up.
63. https://www.forbes.com/2006/12/10/business-game-theory-tech-cx_th_games06_1212harford.html?sh=21b8fa9d5e94, accessed December 7, 2023.

there could be no better starting point than poker: "Real life consists of bluffing, of little tactics of deception, of asking yourself what is the other man going to think I mean to do. And that is what games are about in my theory."

In 1944, Von Neumann teamed up with the economist Oskar Morgenstern to publish the bible of game theory, A Theory of Games and Economic Behavior. The essence of the theory was the mathematical modeling of a strategic interaction between rational adversaries, where each side's actions would depend on what the other side was likely to do.

So yes, a knowledge of poker was not only useful in taking my MBA, but also was a source of income that provided me with meals every Friday night when the dorm cafeteria was closed.

On Glorifying the Grouch

From *The Rotarian*, September 1937

It isn't always advisable to be satisfied with things as they are. It is all right to advocate optimism and smiling faces and serene confidence for the future, but sometimes it's a good idea to be a grouch and register an occasional kick. In other words, don't accept halfway results and compromises as an easy way to solve problems. Be the devil's advocate and try to find out what is wrong with your surrounding conditions instead of taking it for granted that everything is "O. K."

How much better off we would be if every board of directors handling a bank or a factory or a mercantile concern, in the years just prior to 1929, had contained a larger percentage of fault-finders and grouches! We had too many Sunny Jims and not enough Prophets of Gloom. The "crab" who didn't believe in reckless extension of credits and a frenzied whooping of quotations on the stock exchange was a pretty deserving citizen, even if he was unpopular while the boom lasted.

In our part of the country, the bankers couldn't hear anything except the birds singing in the trees. They welcomed no prognostication except one of enduring prosperity and blue skies and everlasting sunshine. They said that land was worth $200 an acre and made their loans to relatives and friends and casual applicants on that basis of valuation. They hooted at the fogies who advocated conservative methods and safety reserves of cash. When the notes they held began to shrivel and the panic came sweeping along every Main Street, they exploded like so many firecrackers. The scraps of wreckage are still being picked up and distributed skimpily among the unhappy depositors. Only the tight-fisted grouches survived the calamity.

The good bench-working and thoroughly useful "grouch" is not merely an ill-mannered person who works overtime at being disagreeable. He is the fellow who discovers the cloud before he sees the silver lining. He is the rugged individualist who doesn't like to take orders unless he has great confidence in the head man who gives the orders and figures out, for himself, the full significance of the orders handed him.

He is the original man from Missouri. He wants to be shown. He doesn't believe everything he reads in the papers. Like our old friend, "Al" Smith,[64] he wants to "look at the record" before he commits himself. His very make-up prevents him from being a serviceable "yes man" because he has a private hatchery in which he grows his own opinions and he glories in being a member of a belligerent minority. He is a thorn in the side of complacency. Very often his grouchiness is a divine discontent with the present layout of affairs in general. The man who is not entirely pleased with the landscape in general is usually the man who is going to improve the scenery.

In diplomatic and legal circles, one hears much about the *status quo*. An advocate of the *status quo* is in favor of things "as is." A true grouch always speaks up for things as they ought to be. He doesn't hesitate to throw a monkey wrench into the machinery, if convinced that the machinery is all wrong. Consequently he is often feared and even hated, but usually he is respected as a disturbing

---

64. Alfred Emmanuel Smith (1873-1944) was a four-term Governor of New York and the Democratic presidential nominee who lost to Herbert Hoover in 1928.

element to be placated and conciliated. Even a smooth-working Rotary Club is usually a more lively and progressive organization if it contains a few vigilant grouches who are always investigating things and clamoring for greater efficiency and more tangible results.

The grouch is usually a close trader and a "tough bird" with whom to close a deal because he "wants what he wants when he wants it" and does not choose to be worked upon or hornswaggled. In many years of travel I have discovered that the man gets more for his money who lets out a yelp unless he receives all the service and attention for which he is paying. His wishes are respected because he is a hard man to please. When the fowl is being served, the grouch gets the second joint and the "easy mark" gets the neck.

It was by travelling with a determined grouch[65] that I learned a few valuable rules about dealing with hotels. Suppose you are motoring and have been entrusted with the job of handling the sordid business arrangements for your little group of four or five persons. You drive up to a hotel which you have selected as a possible stop for the night. It is a large and reputable establishment with many rooms, not all of which are occupied unless the rush season is on or there happens to be a convention in town. Your guidebook and many billboards along the route have informed you that the rate at the hotel is so much a day "and up." Well, the minimum rate, multiplied by the number of people in your party, will represent a reasonable sum to be paid this hotel for the privilege of finding rest and shelter for a few hours. In other words, when you pay this sum, you need not feel that you are cheating anyone. The job for you, as grouchy spokesperson for your party, is to keep within your budget.

In describing the formula to be observed, I am following the directions laid down by my "tight" and grouchy friend. I am, it must be admitted, merely a synthetic grouch. By inclination I am

---

65. My guess is that George is referring here to his friend and financial mentor Ort Wells, a frequent traveling companion and, by all appearances, a proud grouch.

a weakling and, if I followed my own timid promptings, I would go into the hotel, followed by all the luggage and passengers, ask for "good rooms" and accept the ones offered, without inquiring as to the tariff, and then, next morning, discover that all our rooms had been among the "and ups" and that the bill was away in excess of my reasonable budget.

That is not the routine of the certified grouch. His Rule No. 1 is to remove no luggage from the car until he has engaged the rooms and come to a definite understanding with the man at the desk. If the clerk's chart shows plenty of vacant rooms, it is his plain duty to make sure that no prospective guest shall be turned away. He may quote fancy prices at first, but he will talk sense later on if he discovers that he is up against a stubborn grouch who has his own idea of how much he is going to spend. Remember that the prospect has not committed himself by unloading his luggage—and both parties know that there is another hotel farther along the road.

Perhaps you say that this bargaining and bluffing are undignified, but the negotiations need not involve the loss of temper or the use of hard language. The spokesman for his party simply states the facts in the case and quotes the advertised rates and indicates the proposed limit of his expenditure. The average hotel clerk is a model of patience and politeness and he does not resent the attitude of the buyer. In fact, he probably recognizes his trading ability and he immediately begins checking up on rooms.

It is a fact that for overnight visitors, travelling in a handbag, the minimum-priced room is just as desirable as a suite, and perhaps more so. The suite will be on the main corner overlooking the noisy street and the cheaper apartment is tucked away somewhere in the rear where there is a larger supply of quietude. But a room is a room if it has a bath, a bed, two pillows, and a reading lamp. Those are the essentials and the two pillows and reading lamp are usually to be found in every room. If the inquiring grouch is skeptical, he will make a final impression at the desk if he asks for the privilege of inspecting the rooms before he signs the register. He can then just make sure about the two pillows and the reading lamp and the amount of ventilation through the windows. When he finally approves and the rates have been adjusted, he can unload his car and move into his new home and be just as welcome as if he were paying twice as much.

Not even the grouchiest grouch will haggle over prices at a retail shop or try to get his gasoline at a cut rate, but it seems to me that he is simply doing his duty by his own pocketbook when he takes advantage of a sliding scale of prices and avoids extravagance. And, as already suggested, a good hotel man does not object to the customer who is a careful buyer. Any way you figure it, he will get, from a party of four or five, a very fair rental for his rooms.

It will be discovered at clubs, restaurants, and boarding houses that the man who is a little hard to please gets prompter service and a little more careful attention to his orders than the meek and humble patron who hasn't the nerve to complain. The rule seems to be, "Take good care of Mr. Grump or you will hear from him." He isn't afraid to turn down a food order that comes on cold or is improperly prepared. Because he is impatient with stupidity and bungling methods and second-class goods, he becomes an influence for efficiency and speed and a full return for money expended.

We glorify the grouch not because he is the perfect roommate but because he speaks up and says the things which need to be said and which we would say if we were not so all-fired polite and considerate.

The Lesson:

At TIGER 21 one of the sayings was, "TIGER is not about *getting* rich, it's about *staying* rich." Every member was required to have an annual "portfolio defense" where we had to defend all of our investments to the group. One of the questions we had to answer was: *What would you do if your portfolio lost 50% of its value and you simultaneously lost 50% of your income?* After the financial crisis of 2008, the question was revised thusly: *What would you do if your portfolio lost **60%** of your assets and simultaneously **60%** of your income?* Such was the reality of the Great Recession. It's basic risk management.

In George's day it was the Great Depression which saw a 90% drop in the stock market, the suspension of most dividend payments and farm income so low that it couldn't even pay the property taxes.

TIGER estimates that a 60/60 event will occur at least once in everyone's lifetime.

During my lifetime, the oil industry suffered a drop in oil prices from over $40 per barrel to less than $10 in 1986. Many of my friends and associates went bankrupt. The president of Jackson Exploration USA, the domestic branch of the company I worked for, committed suicide. However, one company, Parker Drilling, famously survived and thrived. Just before the crash they had a board meeting. The younger Parker was CEO and "Old Man Parker" was still on the board but usually slept through the meetings. When his son proposed leveraging up the company to build a fleet of ultra deepwater drilling rigs, the Old Man stood up.

"Son, you ain't never seen hard times," he said. "When times are hard you can't eat an oil rig."

The board voted against the motion to lever up. Within months the oil price collapsed.

I witnessed many TIGER members who had to resign due to their net worth falling below the minimum. The cause was usually leverage.

Companies with boards of optimists don't survive the hard times.

On Investment and Real Estate

The Advantage of a Good Thing

From *Knocking the Neighbors*, 1912

Once there was a prosperous Manufacturer who had made his Stake by handling an every-day Commodity at a small Margin of Profit.

One Morning the Representative of a large Concern dealing in guaranteed Securities came in to sell him some gilt-edged Municipal Bonds that would net a shade under 5 per cent.

"I'll have to look into the Proposition very carefully," said the Investor, as he tilted himself back in his jointed Chair. "I must have the History of all previous Bond Issues under the same Auspices. Also the Report of an Expert as to possible Shrinkage of Assets. Any Investment should be preceded by a systematic and thorough Investigation."

Having delivered himself of this Signed Editorial he dismissed the Bond Salesman and went back to his Morning Mail.

The next Caller wore a broad Sombrero, leather Leggings, and a Bill Cody Goatee—also the Hair down over the Collar. He looked as if he had just escaped from a Medicine Show. After lowering the Curtains he produced from a Leather Pouch a glistening Nugget which he had found in a lonely Gulch near Death Valley.

Found in a lonely Gulch near Death Valley

The careful Business Guy began to quiver like an Aspen and bought 10,000 shares at $2 a Share on a Personal Guarantee that it would go to Par before Sept. 1st.

MORAL: *It all depends on the Bait.*

The Lesson:

This piece was written long after George had been "back home again and broke" after the "sharpies" had gotten to him early in his career. George had lost all of his money to speculative investments and learned his lesson the hard way.

After that George became friends with his financial mentor Ort Wells at the Chicago Athletic Association where they both lived until Hazelden was built. Ort was a very rich and famous stockbroker in Chicago and he taught George all the ins and outs of investing in the market and the difference between an investment and a speculation.

You can almost see the hand of Ort Wells in this extremely short short story.[66]

Personally, I've always enjoyed the story for another reason. My very first job working for Phillips Petroleum prospecting for geothermal energy sent me to what is now Death Valley National Park! We found no commercial prospects of geothermal energy in Death Valley.

ORSON COLLINS WELLS

Retired Broker, Once a Partner of Charles G. Gates, Dies at 80

Special to THE NEW YORK TIMES.

CHICAGO, Dec. 10—Orson Collins Wells, retired Chicago broker, clubman and world traveler, died today at his home in Clearwater, Fla. He was 80 years old.

Mr. Wells, once a partner of the famous speculator Charles G. (Bet a Million) Gates, was born at Neenah, Wis., and accompanied his parents in his youth to Lafayette, Ind. At the age of 14 he went to work as a railroad telegrapher in Wisconsin. Later he entered the employ of the Western Union Telegraph Company, remaining until 1884, when he became associated with George C. Eldridge & Co., Chicago brokers.

He was in the service of a number of the larger Chicago brokerage houses until 1904, when he became a member of the firm of Charles G. Gates & Co., brokers in stocks, grains and other commodities. When the firm was dissolved in 1907 Mr. Wells retired.

He never married, and for more than forty years resided at the Chicago Athletic Association.

The New York Times
Published: December 11, 1939
Copyright © The New York Times

---

66. See Appendix for George's tribute to his financial mentor.

The Fable of Prince Fortunatas Who Lived in Easy Street and Then Moved Away

From *Handmade Fables*, 1920

Once there was a Boy named Claude, born with a Plated-Ware Spoon in his Mouth. When he was 21 he came into a very salubrious Chunk of Property.

Before the Family Plunder was pushed over to him, by order of Court, he lived on Expectations.

While the less-favoured Lads of the Village were learning Trades or clerking at the Bee Hive, Claude was reading the Ads and picking out what he would get for himself when he was of Age.

Why arise at chilly Dawn and hot-foot to a Slave Pen when it is so pleasant under the Covers?

Why strain the Ligaments for a wretched Dole of Ten Bucks Per, when both Tens and Twenties are waiting in the Bank to be wadded up and thrown at the Robins?

It is said that Parents who have Gone Before sometimes rest from their Harp Exercises and walk to the edge of the Golden Parapet to look down and Keep Cases on the Loved Ones still detained on Earth.

If the Ex-Plumber and Gas Fitter was acting as Look-Out for Claude, he did not have much News to report.

About all he got was a Bird's-Eye View of a pale Gillie[67] engaged in rolling these little Fire-Cracker Cigarettes and watching the Fellows play Kelly[68].

Just about the Happy Day when Claude was getting all set to Snip the twine on his Bundle there came to Town a plain product of the Suburbs answering to the name of Silas.

Silas had failed to discover that Life held any large Percentage of Lavender for the Son of a Teamster.

Silas was simply a Rear Private in the large Army that beat it down-town every Morning, with the Wolf trotting along behind.

When his Laundry failed to get back on time he was in a Bad Way.

He wasn't a Good-Looker or a Swell Dresser or quick with the Organs of Articulation.

He was a Flumpie, which is a Cross between a Gugg[69] and a Yap.

On the day which brought him the right to Vote against the Party in Power, his only Assets were the contents of a frail Steamer Trunk, an eager Willingness to serve his Chief, and a permeating Wish to be a Depositor and carry his own Pass-Book with an Elastic around it.

Just two Blocks away, Claude was counting the Leaves in his new Check-Book and trying to grapple with and encompass the Stupendous Fact that he had One Hundred Thousand[70] gleaming Simoleons.

This Sum is either Large or Small, according to its Habitat.

In New York City at the present Writing, it represents what a good Head Waiter is expected to spend on a Christmas Present for his Wife.

---

67. A man or boy who attends his male employer or guest.
68. A type of pool game played with sixteen balls.
69. A dimwitted or silly person.
70. $100,000 in 1920 = $1,594,762 in today's buying power, according to the Consumer Price Index calculator.

In some of the interior Counties of Arkansaw, it would look like the National Debt.

Thirty years ago, many an Inland Town looked up to the local Croesus[71] who had corralled One Hundred Thousand. He was supposed to be Fixed.

To Claude the Amount seemed Sufficient, and to Silas it was simply Himalayan.

Such was the Get-Away for the Long-Distance Championship—Silas without a Bean, and Claude smothered with Greenbacks.

It was to be a hard and wearing Race toward the setting Sun.

Only a real Dopester[72] would have given the Tip that Claude carried all the Weight and that Silas was an Odds-On Favourite.

Silas believed that he had been cruelly handicapped, and Claude was so busy being measured for Silk Underwear that he never suspected that there was going to be any Contest.

He thought Life was a Parade.

They were of the same Age. Each had enjoyed the Disadvantages of High School Training, wore a Number Seven Hat, and carried a very Moderate Voltage above the Neck-Band.

The main Difference seemed to be that Silas was a Putter-In and Claude was a Taker-Out.[73]

Each Nightfall the humble Climber was slightly Plus, while the merry Tobogganer was more or less Minus, thereby supplying us with the whole Plot of the Drama.

It does not signify one Iota or Scintilla where you may be pegged on the Chart at 4 o'clock of a certain Afternoon. But the

---

71. The king of Lydia (present day Turkey) in the 500s BC known for his wealth.
72. A person who collects and supplies information, especially on sporting events and elections. As in, "He's got the dope on that."
73. George wrote that Silas was a "putter- in" and Claude was a "taker-out". This story anticipated the wonderful book "The Millionaire Next-Door", where authors compare the behavior of those they call "UAWs" (Under Accumulators of Wealth) and those who are "PAWs" (Prodigious Accumulators of Wealth).

Direction in which you are headed makes it a moral Pipe to bet on your Terminus.

It is not of Record that any one ever coasted to the top of Pike's Peak.

One day, while Silas was still working on Page 1 of the Red Book given to him by the Bank, he passed the mid-Victorian Morgue in which Claude was signing most of his Checks.

The shabby Servitor stood at a Safe Distance and watched the high-flown Aristocrat climb into an English Vehicle and gather up the Ribbons.

At that date, the pampered Worldling did not ride in something shaped like a U 27 Submarine while seated on his Floating Ribs and peering out through a Wheel.

He was perched some 14 feet above Terra Firma and favoured the Brown Derby and Pearl Buttons.

Silas gazed at the Proud Pup and became coagulated with Bitterness.

For about 15 Seconds he was a Bomb-Thrower.

"It is no Fair Shake," he told himself. "Why should he spend more for Florida Water[74] every week than I pull down in Stipend?"

As for Claude, he experienced no emotional Disturbance whatever as he glanced at the Person in Hand-me-Downs.

To him, the mere Wage-Earner was an unconsidered Item, the same as a Tree or a Policeman.

So the One Hundred Thousand Dollars went spinning up the Boulevard and the Pauper proceeded homeward, grimly determined to get some of the Coin in which so many undeserving Folk seemed to be wallowing.

Claude could have lived within his Income if he had worked at anything other than Ordering Things sent up to the House.

---

74. An American version of Eau de Cologne.

Silas was a Putter-In and Claude was a Taker-Out

A yearly Windfall of Five Thousand[75] would be Nuts for one too busy to go Shopping. It is not such a much for one of those wrap-it-up Kids.

Especially if the jolly little Spender gets led to the Altar by a Damsel who wants all of her Dreams to come true.

The Boy who makes two Check-Books grow where one flourished before is certainly Santa Claus for the Tradespeople.

Each year the Rentals and Coupons went up in graceful Curls of Smoke and the Young People, not wishing to Starve or be deprived of their Stick-Pins and Brooches, began to hack large irregular Blobs out of the Principal.

Every January 1st they had less Money working for them. With the Income dwindling and the Spending Habit asserting itself in new and startling Ramifications, there was no let-up to the Melting process.

---

75. $5,000 in 1920 = $79,738 in today's buying power according to the Consumer Price Index calculator.

When Claude and Silas were 30 years of Age, the Latter was only $5,000 to the Good but he had spikes in his Shoes and Rosen all over his Dukes and knew the Ropes.

Claude still had Seventy-five Thousand[76] and had learned that when one needs immediate Rhino[77], all one has to do is open the Tin Box and sell Some-thing. Even so.

Silas was an Oatmeal Fan and Claude was getting so that he could tell one Vintage from another with his Eyes Shut.

And now, grabbing the License afforded every writer for the Movies, flash Sub-Title "Five Years Later" and dissolve into Close-Up of Claude seated in a Booth at the Safety Deposit Vault anxiously shuffling his Securities. Let the Picture reveal the Fact that he is alarmed over the High Cost of Living High.

He has Fifty Thousand[78] of the Original Stake. His Income has been sliced in two, the same as a Cantaloupe. His Expenditures have doubled. He is thinking that probably he had better do a quick Sashay into Wall Street, fill a couple of Suit Cases with soft Jack[79] and then get out again, just like that.

It was a very pretty Inspiration, of the kind that enables the Stock Broker to play Golf every Summer for a Box of Balls a Hole.

Just as Claude started out to place an Order for a Thousand Shares of anything that was sure to go up, he met Silas coming in to plant the Deed for a Desirable Corner.

Claude did not speak to Silas. He could not be expected to know a Grubber of the Middle Class, who controlled only about Twenty Thousand and never had Dined Out.

Silas did not pause to envy the Social Leader. He was too busy

---

76. In 1920, $75,000 = $1,196,071 in today's buying power according to the Consumer Price Index calculator.
77. British slang for money.
78. In 1920, $50,000 = $797,381 in today's buying power according to the Consumer Price Index calculator.
79. An American slang word for money.

with his Mental Arithmetic, figuring what his Real Estate would fetch ten years hence, after everything had moved farther Up Town.

Without going into all the Details of eating the Tape as it came out of the Ticker, the occasional call for Bromo Seltzer, and inside Tips from prominent Head Waiters, it may be announced without fear of Contradiction that Claude's Operations on the Exchange did not lead up to any extensive Slaughter.

It was not generally known at the corner of Broad and Wall that he had been sitting in.

Claude knew it, however, because he had so much more Room in his Tin Box.

When Silas was 38 years old, he met Claude at a Dinner given by Prominent Citizens to a Statesman from Washington who had hopes.

They were brought together because each was a trembling Conservative.

Claude had Twenty Five Thousand[80] Bucks of the evaporating variety, which he wished to retain as long as possible.

Silas had Forty Thousand[81] Iron Men, trained to work 24 Hours every Day, which he proposed to pyramid into a Million if Congress did not get fidgety and spill the Beans.

Silas no longer hated Claude. He did not so much as recall the Day when he gnashed his Teeth at the Young Swell in the Driving Togs.

At this Stage of the Game, Silas reserved his Envy for someone who could show more than Forty Thousand.

It was Claude's turn to be set back into the Two-Hole.

He found himself deferring to the Money-Maker; it being fairly well understood between them that one was a Comer and the other was a Goer.

---

80. In 1920, $25,000 = $398,690 in today's buying power according to the Consumer Price Index calculator.
81. In 1920, $40,000 = $637,905 in today's buying power according to the Consumer Price Index calculator.

In fact, they closed a little Deal involving two encumbered Lots right there at the Table.

The Reader will be given Three Guesses as to which of the Traders had an Ace in Reserve.

The Shift from Crackers and Milk to Guinea Hen can be managed nicely, as we learn by glancing into any First-Class Hotel.

But a Jump from Guinea Hen to Dairy Products by one never having gone against the Lacteal Stuff is what Sherman said about People shooting at One Another.

Shortly after Claude went limping past the 40th Mile Stone, he had to blow the Whistle on Friend Wife, who was getting ready to send Daughter to Europe and put Son in Yale.

The Family threw three individual Fits when the Producer showed them his Stack and warned them to get braced for a rattling good Bump.

He had a few scattering Assets but he could not remember the names of all the Mortgage Holders or when the Paper fell due.

All he knew for Sure was that the proposed Income Tax would not gouge him very deep.

The Loved Ones felt that they had been double-crossed and flimmed.

For 20 years they had been permitted to nurse a Delusion that Papa had Nothing But.

His Private Fortune had seemed to them a pleasant and permanent Source of Supply, something like the Croton Reservoir.

Mother sat there with her Fingers spread apart by the Rings and wanted to know what he had done with it. She seemed to wonder if he had been slathering it on Another Woman.

It was agreed that Claude had to get busy and Do Something.

The Idea of chopping Expenses just when the Children were making Headway in the Younger Set was almost too painful for Discussion.

So Claude decided to put his Pride in his Pocket and accept

The Fable of Prince Fortunatas

a Position as Head of some Respectable and Hefty Corporation, starting in at Ten Thousand[82] a year and working up.

He had a Proud Chance.

All of those Show-Me Sharks who pull the Strings probably toss about on their Pillows every Night, wondering where they can find a high-salaried Gazimbo who looks well in Evening Clothes and knows how to carve a Duck.

Silas had elbowed his way into a gigantic Merger Proposition and was just getting his Full Stride when Claude blew.

So it was to Silas that Claude hied[83] himself and said he was willing to accept a Position as one of the Executive Heads of the blossoming Combine.

He knew how to walk into an Office and sit at a Mahogany Desk, because he had been managing the Estate.

In fact, he had managed it so much that he had worn it out, and now he wanted to start in on Something Fresh.

Silas should have pulled something like the Following:

"Well, Claude Dexter, the Tables have been turned. Yuhs ago, when I was a struggling Stripling, your Eyesight did not carry 10 Feet in my Direction. Now that I am Rich—Aye, and Powerful withal, you come to Cringe and Fawn. Take That and That!"

On the Contrary, he merely Stalled.

He felt sorry for the poor Fluffie and respected him moderately because of the superior Cut of his Clothes.

He had the Application put on File and promised to speak to the other Directors.

In fact, he showed that he was willing to do almost anything for Claude except hire him.

---

82. In 1920, $10,000 = $159,476 in today's buying power, according to the Consumer Price Index calculator.
83. Went quickly.

Claude had a fretful Time trying to discover a good Business Opening for one whose Training had consisted of telling the Waiter to keep the Change.

Sometimes he felt that he should have clapped on the Brakes before smashing into the large Boulder at the Foot of the Grade.

While he was thus Brooding, the Creditors divided up the Residue.

In the period of Blue Gloom following any Domestic Catastrophe, it is usually the Wife who takes off her Long Gloves and proceeds to save the Pieces. When it came to reorganizing, Claude was just as useful as a One-Legged Man at a Fire.

He sat back with his Head in a Sling and watched the Society Matron get ready to conduct a Boarding House for Refined People of Moderate Means.

Claude is now 50 years of Age and a great help to his Wife, because he does nearly all of the Marketing.

He would play a fairly good game of Cards if he could remember what is Out.

At that, he has the Manner of one who has enjoyed Advantages. Otherwise he is Nix.

Sometimes, when he is on his way to the Corner to order the Lamb Chops and Celery and a few boxes of snappy Crackers, he hears a low purring Sound, which continues to crescendo until a huge Motor Car of next year's Design goes zipping by. Within the Car sits Silas, one of the most hateful specimens of the Newly Arrived.

Silas knows that about next September he will be taken up by the Old Families who have been prominent since the Panic of '73.

All of the Phenomena herewith related have been observed time and again in every town on the Map.

The only surprising Climax to the Tale is provided by Silas, who now has four Children.

Within the Car sits Silas, one of the most hateful specimens of the Newly Arrived.

He is planning to make them happy and useful Citizens by leaving each one of them about a Hundred Thousand.

MORAL: *The only safe Income is Self-Hatched.*

The Lesson:

George had a profound understanding of real estate investing, and his views are as pertinent now as they were 100 years ago. Consider the passage:

> Silas had Forty Thousand Iron Men, trained to work 24 Hours every Day, which he proposed to pyramid into a Million if Congress did not get fidgety and spill the Beans.

In real estate, pyramiding means using equity from existing properties as down payments for new ones, thereby resulting in little out-of-pocket expense.[84] Employing this strategy, one can increase one's real estate portfolio without having to dip into savings or take on traditional mortgages. It can be risky because it relies on property appreciation and the investor's capacity to refinance, but done intelligently and prudently, it can result in major gains over time. George certainly used pyramiding in building up his Hazelden Farms estate!

The story of Prince Fortunatas was published in 1920 after the United States had a major round of inflation following World War I. Real estate investors were able to get fixed interest rate loans ($40,000 Iron Men) of long duration that allowed them to pyramid (leverage) their wealth and get a free ride on the inflation caused by excessive government spending. So long as "Congress did not get fidgety and spill the Beans" of course refers to the tax code that allows interest expense to be tax deductible even when government-caused inflation is greater than the interest rate.[85] Making interest expense tax deductible has resulted in ongoing deliberations on Capitol Hill. As Wikipedia puts it:

> *The deduction is the focus of policy debate in the United States. The standard justification for the deduction is that it incentivizes home ownership, but most economists believe the deduction is bad policy and is counterproductive. They note that it increases inequality, is an unnecessary market distortion, and contributes to housing unaffordability.*[86]

---

84. https://www.economictheories.org/real-estate-license/pyramiding-not-just-for-the-pharaohs.html, accessed January 12, 2024.
85. https://www.ft.com/content/426c1465-9561-4300-8d3e-2430e4124c93, accessed January 11, 2024.
86. https://en.wikipedia.org/wiki/Home_mortgage_interest_deduction#:~:text=The%20deduction%20is%20the%20focus,bad%20policy%20and%20is%20counterproductive, accessed January 12, 2024.

This is virtually identical to the run up in real estate values we are experiencing today after Congress blew out the budget under both Trump and Biden. Those who invested in leveraged real estate at this time, just as at the close of World War I, were able to pyramid (leverage) their wealth due to inflation so long as "Congress does not get fidgety and spill the beans."

Did Congress ever "spill the beans"? When the Great Depression came they raised taxes everywhere and on everyone. They not only spilled the beans, they tipped over the whole Apple Cart![87]

The larger lesson that George is teaching is based on the Chinese proverb, "Give a man a fish and you feed him for a day. Teach a man to fish and you feed him for a lifetime." It does little good to leave the next generation financial capital without first teaching them how to make their own financial capital themselves.

My cousin Donald Kleinkort is an active real estate investor who prefers to buy his houses at sheriff sales far below the market value. It is as if George had a premonition of his great-great nephew Donald as the model for Silas in this story. Donald recently sent me this message about his real estate holdings and philosophy:

> *Both my lake house and my Lafayette house were purchased far under the market and all three [of my] homes are 100% financed at 3% fixed rate for 30 years. The cost of ownership including repairs, taxes, interest on loans is zero. The appreciation of the properties equals all the expenses not including utilities.*
>
> *Florida home purchased in 2018 for $425,000. Value today $1 million.*
>
> *Lake house purchased 1990 for $175,000 (including addition in 2001). Value today $475,000.*

---

87. https://www.taxpolicycenter.org/briefing-book/how-do-federal-income-tax-rates-work, accessed January 11, 2024.

> KleinKreek bought in 2018 for $510,000 which includes renovations. Value today $1 million plus.
>
> All 100% financed sub 3%.
>
> Long term cost of ownership = zero
>
> Personally owned and used homes aren't money makers, but if bought and financed correctly they don't cost much either, and give tremendous lifestyle enhancements!!!

Of course Don does exactly the same thing with the houses he buys as rental properties, resulting in a very high rate of return.

House in Mercedes Street

From *In Babel: Stories of Chicago*, 1906

I am one of a large family. We stand in a row along Mercedes Street. When first I had any knowledge of myself I was a mere skeleton frame-work of scantling. There were six of us, just alike, and we were knee-deep in bright yellow lumber. All day long the workmen crawled over our ribs. I felt the rap-a-tap-tap as I became decently clad in weather-boarding and shingles. They shouldered the clean, sweet-smelling pine through every gaping door and window.

At last I was a completed house with the brass knobs glittering and the raw wood hidden under two glossy colours of paint.

The shavings and litter were carried away. Tufts of green grass began to show in the trampled front yard. To be sure I had a sort of damp feeling in my joints and was still untidy with the siftings of saw dust and the splatterings of paint and plastering, but I had the pride of knowing that I was as handsome as any other house in Mercedes Street.

Since then I have learned by eaves-dropping that Mercedes Street is supposed to be a shabby and uncounted thoroughfare and that our sextette is not in the fashion. One day a very gay little house, with scalloped decorations fastened to it, came along Mercedes Street on rollers and I remember it was very reluctant to take up with our society and had to be dragged a few feet at a time. Sometimes, by lifting myself and peeping, I can see the bulky shapes of large buildings far away. They are behind the clouds of smoke and I do not envy them their largeness. In fact I envy no other house, for contentment has come to me.

For a time I was inwardly troubled. The first blow to my pride came soon after the painters had given me the last finishing caress.

A man and a woman stopped in front of me and stared critically. The woman said, "Dear me!" in a tone of such disappointment that I felt a tremor in every rafter. They unlocked the front door and walked through the rooms, their foot-falls starting the hollow echoes, and the woman found fault with me. The man said they would have to take me, with all my imperfections.

The two were childless and out of luck, and they seemed to regard me as a place of exile, so how was I to cheer them when they always wore a frown for me? I had hoped to be loved, but I was merely tolerated. Still, I was rather glad they came. I will admit that it felt good to get the carpets and rugs and shiny furniture and looped curtains, for a house, after being well furnished, has the same satisfaction that a man has after he has dined properly.

The inner warmth drove away the lingering chill and damp, and it was certainly pleasanter to glow with lamps than to stand lonesomely in the darkness.

Yet I was constantly saddened by the thought that those whom I held and sheltered and gathered under my warm plastering, even as a hen gathers her brood, did not think well of me.

The woman used to have an occasional caller, to whom she would apologise for my poor dimensions (think of it!), and she would say that the neighbourhood was unattractive. I will confess that I was indignant. Leaving my own merits out of the question, there is certainly no excuse for saying evil things of Mercedes Street. The men work for their money and the women love their children. And such children! I have seen the street white with them on a Sunday evening, for every little girl had a white dress and every boy a white waist. The men sat in the open air and smoked. The women called gayly from door-step to door-step, and the children fluttered everywhere like sparrows. It has seemed to me on such a night, that I would rather be here in Mercedes Street than anywhere else.

When the unhappy couple moved out one day in early spring I did not care so much, although that night I had to stand in conspicuous gloom and feel the sweep of cold draughts. The woman said she hoped she would never see me again, but the man, as I believe, did not feel so unkindly toward me. The waggons disappeared down the street, but wherever they stopped, I don't believe that house will be a home for the man.

After my first family went away there followed a cheerless month. Company is company, even though it offend you. I had the feeling of being neglected when I saw the smoke curl from other chimneys and heard the children shouting at the houses across the way.

But one day—and I must always call it the best of days—a pudgy, red-faced little man stopped squarely in front of me and said, "Oho!"

I think all of my front panes must have crinkled back a smile at him, for I liked this little man.

Then there came into view a plump woman with two red spots on her cheeks and a little boy who had his mother's cheeks and his father's wrinkly eyes, and two very small girls with braided hair, who hopped and skipped like springy little frogs.

"Is it the place, Henry?" asked the woman.

"Yessee," he replied, pointing to my number.

"Isn't it fine? All this nice grass in front."

"But behind!" exclaimed Henry. "Ah, behind—for a garden—big—plenty of room!"

"Is this where we're going to live?" shouted the boy, dancing on the front stoop.

"Maybe—yes," replied the father, laughing. Then the boy laughed and the mother laughed and the two little girls laughed, and for the first time I wanted to laugh too, although it was utterly preposterous for a house to expect to laugh.

That day, within the hour, my self-respect came back and I fear I was almost as vain as I was on the day when the painters got through with me.

The laughing family said my rooms were the prettiest in the world, my closets the snuggest and my kitchen the tidiest. So I knew they were coming back, and they did come, with some of the queerest bales and chests and bundles that I had ever seen on a waggon in Mercedes Street. The furniture was new, but the bales and chests and bundles had come from the old country, and, being unpacked, they brought forth strange dishes, cutlery, pictures, clothing, bedding and the like, all cumbersome and showing service, but mightily home-like.

Once more I felt my rafters warmed, and once more the light from my windows fell across the sidewalk where the young women and their sweethearts promenaded slowly each pleasant evening and held hands secretively.

The new family loved me! So, of course, I had to love the new family, because a real home always tries to multiply the affection brought into it.

Summer was coming. Now the open windows were filled with plants, and the grass spread over the front-yard, covering the bare spots. The whole family went gardening in the back-yard, and there was such shouting and laughing at work that all the work was like play.

I came to know the family secrets. In the old country the little man had been poor and the family lived in two rooms, and did not have meat oftener than once a week. They would tell of the old country sometimes, and when they sat down to eat the wife would say: "Oh, Henry, in the old country this would be a holiday feast."

What a stroke of fortune to be found by these people, who could delight in having a house of their own, with a garden at the back and the vines beginning to climb in front!

No wonder I was proud. They said the best things about me, and wrote about me to their friends in the old country, and they even had me photographed. That day I squared up and looked my best, for I could not remember that any other house in Mercedes Street had been photographed.

Through fall and winter they kept me warmed with their simple goodness, and I was so grateful that on windy nights I would soothe the children to sleep. When the wind whistled at my eaves I would change the whistle to a crooning sound, which none but the children could understand, and which is never heard except where there are children to listen.

The three would lie in their beds and listen to the droning lullaby, and soon all three would go to sleep smiling. They thought it was the wind singing to them, but I did my part, for I am sure the song did not sound the same at any other house in Mercedes Street.

Spring and summer came again. The vines hung in showers of green around the front windows and the children sang in the street.

One morning I drowsed in greater happiness than usual, for now there were four children instead of three.

Such bantering as they had! He said it was his and she said it was hers, and I longed to speak up and say it was mine also.

It is winter now. The fourth one sits strapped at the window and laughs at the children outside.

I believe I am the proudest house in Mercedes Street.

The Lesson:

Perhaps the world's greatest investor is Warren Buffett, who is also famous for living in the same relatively modest house[88] that he bought in the 1950s, even though he could afford mansions larger than king's palaces.

I have lived in many houses in the United States and overseas, from a very old farmhouse in Newton County, Indiana to an extremely modest walk-up apartment in Singapore to true mansions in the Philippines and Bandar Seri Begawan.

It's not the house . . .

---

88. It's interesting to note that TIGER 21 doesn't let members count home equity in their net worth. Also interesting: Warren Buffett says he would have made more money renting rather than living in his famously humble home, which he bought in the 1950s. https://finance.yahoo.com/news/warren-buffetts-31-500-house-181400983.html

The Fable of the Hard-Up Yeoman

From *Handmade Fables*, 1920

One Day a serious-minded Disturber of the Soil named Ebenezer, living out where the Prairie Loam is very Brunette and the Cattle are broad across the Hips, got up in the Morning so borne down by Business Anxiety that all he could take on for Breakfast was a few Eggs and a couple of Patty Cakes of a rare kind of Sausage containing Pork and several Strata of Flapjacks and a Tureen of Coffee.

The Grief that seemed crushing him to Earth had been engendered by a steady Increase in Land Values.

Like every other nifty Agriculturist, he had a Chronic Hankering to own all the good Property adjoining.

There was one Eighty in Particular that he coveted until he couldn't bear the Thought of some Neighbour beating him to it.

For several Years he had been doing a little gumshoe Dickering to get hold of that dandy little Patch of Corn Land.

Every time he inquired the Price, the Owner boosted the Figure a mite, and then told our Good Friend that he could either take it or leave it or do a Run and Jump into the Crick, it didn't make no difference which.

The Grief that seemed crushing him to Earth had been engendered by a steady Increase in Land Values

---

One of the bitter Ironies encountered during the Vaudeville Tour known as Mortal Existence is that when the Articles we sell go up like a Rocket and Life begins to look like a Feather Bed, then the Commodities we wish to Purchase likewise get into a Bull Market and go sailing, and Joy evaporates.

No matter how much of the Crisp a Fellow handles, he feels like a Lazarus if he cannot acquire all of the desirable Items that he seems to think he wants.

That is why Ebenezer was feeling awful Blue when he wound up his little hank and started for Town to pick out some new Records for the Talking Machine.

He alighted in front of the Bank, and there he plumped right into a mess of Calamity. Although he tried to duck into the Drug Store, the Trouble-Maker nailed him.

All the Overture Stuff about the Spring Planting and the Health

The Fable of the Hard-Up Yeoman

of the Family did not camouf[89] Ebenezer. He could feel a Touch coming.

The Person accosting him was of a Species which had multiplied without increasing in Popularity.

In other Words, this Party was around sticking up People in the name of a large Undertaking for the General Good.

He was there with a line of glib Cackle about every Citizen having a real proprietary Interest in his own Country.

He went at Ebenezer hammer and tongs and told him to Come Across with a Handful.

"I can't do it, Bill," said Ebenezer, with a quaver in his Voice. "I think all this Work ought to be done by the Govamint, but, even at that, I'd dig if I wasn't so Poor just now. You don't see me romancin' along Main Street in any Twin Six[90] that costs Four Thousand. I have to put up with a little Coffee Grinder. Never in all my born Days did I ride in a Private Car, the same as them Railway Presidents. They're the Fellows to go after. Did I ever own a Plug Hat[91]? Does my Woman sport any Diamonds? Here I am, strugglin' along an' just makin' both Ends meet, an' you come and try to slip me some more Tribulation. Sometimes I wonder what they do with all the Taxes I pay in. Now I've got to stand in front of a Table an' answer a lot of fool Questions about my Income. It always seemed to me that, when a real Producer gets hold of some Cash, it's His'n, an' nobody's got any Right to go feelin' into his Pockets for it. Besides I've had more than seven quarts of Trouble. Many's the Wallop that's been handed to me in the last Year. Last Season, after I sold my Corn for a Dollar Ten, it went to a Dollar Fifty on the Board of Trade. You can figure that on 5,000 Bushels I certainly lost a pile of Money. I've felt pinched ever since. I understand, of course, that it's all right for them that have it stacked

---

89. Slang for deceive, as in camouflage.
90. Packard's roadster with a 12-cylinder engine, the first of its kind.
91. A round hat with a narrow brim. Also known as a derby hat or bowler hat.

up to be reckless an' throw in big Donations an' get their Names in the Paper, but it does strike me they ought to lay off of us Grangers that are hard pushed. Why, I need more Land right now, but I can't get it without bein' Gouged, and I'm Fussed. You must know that my Grocery Bills are bigger than they used to be. Honest, Bill, I don't see how you can look me in the Eye an' tell me it's my Duty to let go at a Time like this. I think you Aristocrats that loll around in the Towns and live off of us ought to put up all the Spondulix[92] needed just at this time."

The Solicitor was slowed up. He began to feel ashamed of himself for trying to take the Hot Biscuit and the Spareribs right out of the Mouths of Ebenezer's Offspring.

He went back to the Local Committee and reported that inasmuch as Eb had been compelled to order Gasoline at the advanced Rate and Casings at the new Price for Rubber, and had been stood up so hard by the Chicago Tailoring Firm which specializes on Garments for College Students, and had been put to extra Expense because the McCormack[93] Records cost quite a bit of Money, and was trying to lay in such a large advance supply of Nut Coal for the Base-Burner, probably it wasn't fair to expect him to get wrought up over Public Weal.

He reported that a good many rapacious Combinations had swooped down on Ebenezer and rassled his Feelings and stripped him of his Assets.

It looked as if Eb would have to be marked up as a Dead Pigeon.

The Committee considered the Case carefully, because there were several Ebenezers right in this same Township.

The Members of the cruel Hold-Up Gang knew that Ebenezer was sincere in his tearful Declarations.

What with the High Cost of Necessary Luxuries and the Contemptible Methods lately adopted by Tax Ferrets and the

---

92. 19th century slang for money or cash.
93. John McCormack was a famous Irish tenor.

Prohibitive Price on all Land adjoining him, it was evident that this particular specimen of Farmer felt that he was being persecuted beyond Endurance.

They had to admit that he was right about the Private Car and not having as much Jewellery as those mentioned in the Sunday Papers. Also, he never frittered away any time at Golf.

One Member of the Committee, having no Pity in his Heart, then suggested that Poverty was a Relative Term.

He said that Ebenezer was a well-meaning Citizen and there was just one Prescription needed to make Eb a useful Patriot of comprehensive Vision, and that was an Inspection Tour.

He called attention to certain biographical Data.

Ebenezer had started out in Life as a Farm Hand.

His only Assets at the beginning were a set of willing Muscles, the habit of Industry, and about as much technical Knowledge of Agriculture as he could absorb from his Neighbours. He believed him-self to be self-made.

It never struck him that the Institutions of a Free Country, and the Privileges sprouting under a Western Sky, and the virgin richness of a new Soil, and the kindly help of an intelligent Community had cooperated to make him a Present of 240 Acres worth $300 an Acre.[94]

Someone suggested that it would be a Grand Thought if Ebenezer could visit some of the other Geographical Divisions on this limited Globe and study the Daily Life and Domestic Affairs of other Men who had started with Nothing much and worked hard, and practised Economy and persevered in their Efforts to set aside a few Rubles for a Rainy Day.

So the Committee pulled off a very bright Stunt.

It learned that a smart Yank had perfected an Airplane of incredible Speed.

---

94. Today circa $1,500/ac.

It could do a Mile in practically Nothing, flat.

Motor-Cars had minimized all Mileage, but the new flying Contraption simply eliminated Distance.

The Committee sent for a Machine that had a separate Perch for a Passenger and invited Ebenezer to take a free Ride.

The Lad at the Wheel was instructed to show Ebenezer the Sights that would do him the most good.

"Our respected Neighbour has got it into his Bean that a Raw Deal has been framed and that he is the Fall Guy," explained the Committee to the Aviator. "Load him on your Rubberneck and let him get wise to the Happy Lot of those who are not subject to the Oppressive Conditions which have caused him to holler."

They sailed away, and a strange assortment of changing Landscapes began to unroll beneath them.

By the time they had gone a paltry Thousand Miles in a southerly direction, it was revealed to the pop-eyed Traveller that even the Home of the Brave was made up largely of Mountain Ranges and Scrub Forest. The Bottom Lands were subject to overflow and the Slopes consisted of Mineral Deposits.

Presently they hovered over a sun-baked Expanse studded with prickly Vegetation.

"I invite your Attention to the Peon of Mexico," said the polite Guide. "He puts in the usual number of Hours per Day. Once in a great while he is permitted to look at a small piece of depreciated Tin Money. He lives in the Mud Hut that you see nestling among the Cacti. His food consists of Injun Meal and Black Beans touched up with Pepper Sauce. If he lives to be 60 Years of Age, he still lacks about $18 of having enough to pay the Funeral Expenses."

They shot eastward above blue Waters and paused to admire an Island of tropical Aspect.

"This is somewhere in the West Indies," said the Guide. "It doesn't matter where, because the Farmer is just as well off one place as another. You will notice the Gentleman wearing the

20-cent suit of Pajamas and chopping down Sugar Cane. He is quite beyond the reach of the Coal Trust, being surrounded by a genial Temperature of 100 degrees Fahrenheit. He resides in yonder Store Box mounted on Stilts. When he shows up after a Hard Day in the Fields, he finds a stewed Banana waiting for him. If he is frugal, some day he will own both a Guitar and a Mule."

Still eastward they clove their way, and up from the Sea rose a whole Continent of Spired Cities and tiny Gardens and first-class Scenery.

"This, in a General Way, is Southern Europe," explained the Conductor of the Tour. "I am bearing to the south because the Agricultural Districts somewhat to the North have been cultivated to a depth of 4 feet and planted with explosive Shells. It is my purpose to show you the more favoured Regions. Look at the huge Hotels and the dandy Palaces. They are not frequented by members of the Farmers' Protective Association, but the humblest Toiler can look at them every time he straightens up. The Tower you see yonder is not a Silo. It is part of a Chateau. Do you make out all the Truck Patches? Well, those are not Truck Patches at all. They're Farms. You will note that all the Women and Children are permitted to take Exercise in the Open. Each of them will dally with a hunk of Black Bread and a large Radish later in the day. We are now looking at what is known as the Home of Laughter and Song. This is a grand Spot in which to settle down if you don't object to rooming with the Live Stock and can subsist on the aforesaid Laughter and Song."

On they went, with tumbling Waters and white Deserts beneath them. They came to a mere ribbon of Green bordering a River which wound through a Desolation of burning Sand.

"I thought you would enjoy a close-up of Egypt," said the Guide. "This is where Agriculture was invented a good many Centuries before the Year One. Countless Millions have been working at it ever since, and the most that any Tenant ever got ahead was

This, in a General Way, is Southern Europe

the Privilege of facing eastward twice a Day and giving Thanks to Mohammed. The Exhibit to which I call particular Attention is the Fellah with the Breech-Clout[95] driving the Oxen and guiding the Plow made from a crooked Limb. He is still pulling the Ptolemy Stuff because he is not taxed for Free Schools and Experiment Stations. Please get next to the Bunch lifting the Water out of the Nile in buckets and pouring it into Irrigation Ditches. How's that for the little old 20th Century? Each member of the Bucket Brigade earns almost enough every Day to buy a good 5-cent Segar. The Grain is trampled out according to the most approved Old-Testament methods. I forget the name of the Staple Food in this Vicinity, but it is a kind of Ragweed en Casserole. Please take notice that these dark-skinned Persons are Hustlers. You don't catch one of them loafing on his Job. He scratches just as hard as any Township

---

95. A type of loincloth made of tanned leather, fabric or fur, tucked between the legs and held up by a strap or strings. Typically American Indian.

Trustee in the Mississippi Valley. Does he get anywhere? After a long and sweaty Day, he sleeps on the bare Ground under a Canopy of Twigs plastered with Mud. He looks at an unchanging Horizon. After a while he dies. Don't pity him. He never heard that somewhere in the World the weary Plowman goes to the Circus and eats Ice-Cream Cones. We will now proceed to India, one of the favourite Haunts of those who go forth to Sow and Reap."

During the next Jump through Space, Ebenezer confirmed what he had learned in the Geography Class; viz., that most of the Earth's Surface is covered with Water.

He picked up the further Information that most of the so-called Land looked like a Gravel Pit that had been spread out to dry.

India, he had read somewhere, was the Land of Mystery.

The Mystery turned out to be that Swarms and Myriads of skinny Individuals with large, mournful Eyes and fluttering Cotton Nighties somehow managed to wrench a Sustenance from the blistering Plains.

Each Human Work-Animal was escorted to his daily Task by the Spooks born of Superstition, while behind him stalked the dim Specter of Famine.

"Sometimes a Crop does not come up to Expectations," explained the Guide. "When that happens, about as many People as you will find in the State of Pennsylvania curl up and die of Starvation. Land is owned by the Rajahs and Princes. The hereditary Privilege of the Son of Toil, here as in almost every nook and corner of our happy Planet, is to remain alive for a Period of Years. I need hardly tell you that the hungry Vegetarians you see grubbing in the Fields as far as the Eye can reach never heard of Mince Pie, never attended a Band Concert, never took a Joy Ride, and never sat in a Rocking Chair to read the Home Paper. They expect to get their Reward in the Hereafter. It's a great Scheme for a Landowner to meet his Pay-Roll with Checks payable in Paradise."

They moved on. Below them spread the vast Beehives of the Old World—Burma and Java and Siam.

"These Natives over here are Nice Folks," explained the Guide. "They can't Read or Write and they don't Vote but, on the Other Hand, they don't have to conceal anything from the Assessor, because they have nothing to conceal."

China proved to be well worth seeing.

All the checkered Fields were green and gold with heavy Crops.

The wide Expanses of farming Country were unmarked by Public Highways and the Residents were far removed from the excessive Freight Charges demanded by Railways.

Each Producer carried his Crop to Market in a Basket.

"Here we find the truly independent Farmer," said the Lecturer, indicating the ornery little Villages which huddled in the Valleys. "The greedy Manufacturers and the Trust Combines have not been able to get to him and load him up with Self-Binders and Grand Rapids Furniture and Cream Separators and Fancy Groceries and all the other Items for which you and your unfortunate Neighbours are overcharged at Home. By reason of his living far from the operations of the Octopi, he is enabled to get along on an average Wage of 2 cents per Day. Is he unhappy? Not at all. Once a Week he sits down to a Banquet consisting of a Bowl of Rice with a piece of dried Fish in it."

By this time, Ebenezer was ready to admit that almost every fool corner of the Earth that had even a skim of Soil on it was being cultivated, but he was surprised to discover that the Foreigners had failed to equip their Farms with Front Porches and Garages and other Essentials.

Either he knew something about Farming that they didn't know or else there was some other Reason.

On the homeward Tack the Airplane took in Japan, so that Ebenezer could observe Conditions in a progressive Nation where the Harvest Hand pulls down 14 Cents a Day and can afford to put dried Fish into the Rice two or three times a Week.

The Fable of the Hard-Up Yeoman

During the hasty skip across the Pacific, the Guide addressed Ebenezer as follows:

"Well, my jolly Home-Seeker, if you decide later on to flee from the predatory Inflictions which have caused you so much sorrow in the U. S. A., to which part of this Terrestrial Sphere will you emigrate? Of all the drudging Farmers on the outside Map, is there one with whom you would trade Places? Can you see any one of them running a Shoe-String up to 240 Acres?"

They began to make out the white Houses and the big Red Barns and the Fat Stock and the ribbons of Macadam[96] and the flivs[97] moving hither and thither, while in between and all around were the unhampered and generous Fields.

"How do they look to you?" asked the Conductor.

"Oh, Boy!" was all that Eb could exclaim.

MORAL: *Where Ignorance is not Bliss, get Wise!*

The Lesson:

When this was written 100 years ago, George noticed that Japan was leaving behind much of the rest of the poor countries in terms of its agricultural productivity. American productivity was such at that time that the yeoman farmer who traveled the world would see nothing to compare it with the productivity of Indiana farms; the rest of the world was mostly consumed by poverty, and stagnant poverty at that.

But the Industrial Revolution was coming to farms everywhere. What began on the farms in America is catching on across the globe. The world hasn't caught up with us, but we should know that we are in an agricultural productivity race.

---

96. The small pieces of gravel compacted in layers to surface roads.
97. Slang for cars, usually of poorer quality.

When I lived in Singapore in 1982, I heard Lee Kuan Yew give this speech[98]:

Speech by Prime Minister Lee Kuan Yew at the Launching of Productivity Month in Singapore Conference Hall on 1 Nov 82

Productivity: Who Benefits?

In August 1982, The Times Organization had a survey on productivity awareness. The survey shows that practically all Singaporeans have heard about productivity. But they still have deep misunderstandings of the concept. Eighty-one per cent of Singaporeans considered teamwork to be a very important factor for higher productivity, which is correct. However, the survey also showed that 70% felt that the company would benefit most from productivity improvement. In other words, 70% did not understand that higher productivity is in the interests of the workers as much as management because it will enhance their job security through making their goods and services competitive internationally.

So long as workers believe that productivity is for the benefit of managements to make bigger profits through workers working harder and smarter, we shall not succeed. It is only when our workers understand that productivity means that the company they work for becomes more competitive and will stay viable even under the most severe of economic conditions, that the productivity movement will be on the move. And with the world economic outlook bleak for the next few years of economic and banking uncertainties, the increased productivity of our workers will help multi-nationals to

---

98. https://www.nas.gov.sg/archivesonline/data/pdfdoc/lky19821101.pdf, accessed November 10, 2023.

expand in Singapore even when they retrench elsewhere. For higher productivity is the way managements are able to give their workers job security in bad times, and more benefits and higher wages in good times. A keen sense of productivity must become part of the ethos of our people as it is with the Japanese. This is the long road we must travel if Singapore is to become a developed society by the 1990s.

The benefits of productivity must be shared and enjoyed by all management and workers. Then workers will develop that sense of a common destiny in the survival and prosperity of the company. Workers will give of their best only if their well-being is closely related to the performance of their companies. Hence we must gradually move away from broad and uniform NWC recommendations towards a system of wage increases based on increased productivity and profitability of specific companies and industries.

If we are to succeed, managers must learn to manage effectively. They must make productivity a major function of corporate operations. Every member in an enterprise must be motivated to increase productivity. A management which does not place priority on the productivity-consciousness of the workforce must fail in competition against those who do.

Productivity is a complex issue involving many factors. All Singaporeans must gradually grasp this concept and its full significance. Then their attitudes will undergo a profound change. This will take time. The quickest start is to convince the central or core group of managers, supervisors and union leaders, people who are able to make changes in the work environment and influence other workers, to change their attitudes and increase their comprehension of productivity. That is the first phase target of this Productivity Month.

Our political stability and sound policies have made for good economic progress in the past two decades. Foreign businessmen have invested in Singapore and have enabled our industrious workers to produce goods and services that are competitive in international markets.

As we climb up the technological ladder, the going will get tougher. Diligent workers, excelling individually, will not be good enough. Managers and workers must work together as a team. Those countries where management and workers are locked in adversarial combat, like Britain, are losing out to those like Japan where management and workers cooperate to achieve ever higher productivity.

The old "them and us" attitude between labour and management Singapore inherited from the British, and which the communists accentuated and exploited, must be expunged. Our new cooperative approach, which has contributed to our success, is now to be enshrined by amending the Trade Unions Act, which is based on British practices, to redefine the role of trade unions from one of confrontation with management to one of cooperation, to increase productivity to the benefit of both management and workers like in Japan and in Korea.

The present definition of a trade union is negative and out of date. A union's principal object is to represent its member in trade disputes; or to promote, organise or finance industrial action; or to impose restrictive conditions on the conduct or any trade or business. Our new definition has been adapted from Japanese and Korean legislation. It defines a trade union as any association or combination of workmen or employers to (1) promote good industrial relations, (2) improve the working conditions of workmen or enhance their economic and social status, and (3) achieve the raising of productivity for the benefit of workmen, employers and the economy of Singapore. In these two different definitions lie two different attitudes to work and cooperation. It is this difference in attitudes which account, in large measure, for Japan's success, and Korea's rapid growth.

All successful managements have in common a man-centred philosophy. Healthy labour-management relations and good work attitudes amongst all workers depend on good management philosophy in which care and concern for the workers are high in management priorities. It is more important for management to have sincere concern for their workers than to provide increasing employee benefits. Next, there must be good communication between management and workers and between workers themselves. Effective teamwork requires good leaders and good communication, thus ensuring a proper sharing of work, with every member performing the work he knows best.

In nearly all work situations, small consultative groups can help get the workers involved and motivated, and also tap their intimate knowledge of the work. Hence QC circles is one of the best tools to increase productivity. Workers' involvement and contribution will also create in them a sense of pride in their work and an identity with the enterprise they work in. The public sector has made a good start with WITS or Work Improvement Teams.

It may take 15 to 20 years to get Singaporeans as productivity conscious as the average Japanese or Korean. A change in outlook cannot be achieved in a productivity month. It is only the beginning.

Like George, Prime Minister Lee Kuan Yew understood that the key is productivity. We should not forget how important productivity is to our well-being. Singapore and much of East Asia today understand this, perhaps better than we do.

Non-Essentials

From *Single Blessedness*, 1922

hich traveller collects the hardships—the one with the toothbrush or the one with three indestructible trunks?

Happy is he who can put within reach the things he needs and avoid becoming a haggard caretaker.

If our friends acquired only those items which are indispensable to reasonable contentment, what would they do with all the cedar chests and extra closets and attics and storerooms and safety deposit boxes?

The founders of the family name arrived with an axe, a rifle, a skillet, and a spinning wheel. While building an empire, they frequently gave thanks for all the bountiful goodnesses vouchsafed to them.

And now, granddaughter thinks that the Fates are treating her rough if she doesn't get her facial massage once a week.

Civilization means the banking up of material accessories which we do not need.

The fun of spending money is to garner things for which we hanker, without being compelled to explain why.

But the shopping pastime can be worked up into a dreadful mania for collecting non-essentials.

The problem is to find a happy compromise between living in a tree and endeavouring to carry a ton of personal property under each arm.

Do you ever play the new game of solitaire called "Looking Backward"? You get all the cancelled checks of last year and finger them over and ask yourself, "Why?" If you can find the answer, you win.

The article we covet begins to shrink the moment the price-tag is removed.

Every poor man in America would like to own an orange grove and a yacht. Did you ever see an orange grove or a yacht that wasn't for sale?

What becomes of the beautiful specimens of neckwear seen in shop-windows? Men rush in and buy them and then hide them.

We of the U.S.A. are the greatest little tribe of buyers in the world, specializing on gorgeous tomfooleries.

Maybe after a while you will learn to project yourself into the wiser realms of the future. Before signing a check or committing yourself to a venture, you will find it possible to see the transaction as it will appear two years away, on the road behind. When you acquire this gift, you will lose much of your fretful desire for freak golf clubs, mining stock, striped shirts, platinum cigarette cases, hair tonics, toy dogs, and midnight suppers.

The Lesson:

Being a consumer is a very poor substitute for having a purpose in life. The pioneers made sacrifices and endured great privations because they had one objective: making a better life for their children. It is purpose, not possessions, that lead to happiness. And the best investment you can make is in the next generation's education. After that—helping the next generation get a good start in life. Our pioneer ancestors understood this.

On Law, Lawyers and Contracts

The Fable of the Bookworm and the Butterfly Who Went into the Law

From *Forty Modern Fables*, 1901

Two Brothers started away to College at the same Time. Just before they boarded the Train, Pa led them aside and handed them some splendid Advice. He told them that they were now ready to mold their Futures. He said he wanted them to stay in of Evenings and Bone hard, and he hoped they would mind the Faculty and keep away from the Cigarette Fiends who play the Banjo and talk about Actresses. He wanted them to stand high in their Classes and devote their Spare Moments to Reading rather than to the Whimsies and Mimical Fooleries of a University Town.

William listened solemnly and promised to Behave. Cholley fidgeted in his Chair and said it was nearly Train-Time.

So they rode away on the Varnished Cars, William reading about the Goths and Vandals and Cholley playing Seven-Up with a Shoe Drummer from Lowell.

At the University William remembered what Pa had said, so he cooped himself up in his Room and became a Dig and soon enough was greatly despised as a Pet of the Professors. Cholley wore a striped Jersey and joined the Track Team and worked in to the Glee Club. He went to his Room when all the other Places had closed up. Every Time a Show struck Town he was in the Front Row to guy the Performers and pick up some new Gags. He went calling on all the Town Girls who would stand for his Fresh Ways, and he was known as the best Dancer in the Ki Ki Chapter of the Gamma Oopsilon Greek Letter Fraternity. The Reports Sent Home indicated that William was corralling the Honors in Scholarship and Cholley was getting through each Exam by the Skin of his Teeth, but he had been elected a Yell Captain and could do his 100 Yards in Ten Seconds Flat. Pa would write to Cholley now and then and tell him to Brace Up and give him a Hunch that Life was full of Sober Responsibilities and therefore he had better store his Mind with Useful Knowledge and Chop on all the Frivols and Fopperies, whereupon Cholley would write back that he needed Fifty by Return Mail to pay for Chemicals used in the Laboratory.

By the Time that both were Seniors, William had grown a fuzzy Climber in front of each Ear and was troubled with Weak Eyes. He always had a Volume of Kant under his Arm and seemed to be in a Brown Study[99] as he walked across the Campus. Cholley kept himself Neat and Nobby[100] and seemed always Cheerful, even though he had two or three Conditions to his Discredit and had only an Outside Chance of taking his Degree. He was Manager of the Football Team, and he had earned the affectionate Nickname of "Rocks." He was a great Hand to get acquainted with any Girl who dared to show herself near the Halls of Learning and by constant Practice he had developed into a Star Chinner[101], so that he could Talk Low to almost any one of them and make her believe

---

99. Daydreaming or deeply contemplative.
100. Fashionable, elegant, stylish, chic; as per Nob Hill, the poshest part of San Francisco.
101. A talkative, bombastic person.

that of all the Flowers that ever bloomed she was the one and only $30,000 Carnation.

William kept away from Hops and Promenades because he remembered what Pa had said about the Distracting Influence of Fripperies[102] and the Twittle-Tattle of Artificial Society. The only Girl he knew was a Professor's Sister, aged 51, with whom he was wont to discuss the Theory of Unconscious Cerebration. Then he would drink a Cup of Young Hyson Tea and go Home at 8.45 P. M. Cholley at about that Time would be starting out in his Primrose and Dockstader Suit to write his Name on Dance Cards and get acquainted with the Real Folks.

On Commencement Day William received the Cyrus J. Blinker Prize of a Set of Books for getting the Highest General Average of any one in the Class. Cholley just managed to Squeeze Through. The Faculty gave him a Degree for fear that if it didn't he might come back and stay another Year.

After they had graduated, Pa gave them another Talk. He said he was proud of William, but Cholley had been a Trial to him. Still he hoped it was not too late to set the Boy on the Right Track. He was going to put both of them into a Law Office and he wanted them to Read Law for all they were worth and not be lured away from their Work by the Glittering Temptations of Life in a Big City. William said he was prepared to Read Law until he was Black in the Face. Cholley said he wouldn't mind pacing a few Heats with Blackstone and Cooley[103] now and then, if he found that he could spare the Time. The Father groaned inwardly and did not see much Hope for Cholley.

When the two Sons became Fixtures in the Office of an established Law Firm, William kept his Nose between the Leaves of a Supreme Court Report and Cholley was out in the other Room

---

102. Things that are not necessary, not serious, not important.
103. Issued in 1870, Sir William Blackstone's *Commentaries on the Laws of England* was a book of English common law edited by Thomas Cooley.

warming up to the Influential Clients and making Dates for Luncheons and Golf Foursomes.

Within three Months after they started at the Office, William had read all the Books in the Place and Cholley was out spending three weeks at the Summer Home of the President of a Construction Company, who was stuck on Cholley's Dialect Stories and liked to have him around because he was such a good Dresser and made it lively for the Women.

Out at this Country Place it happened that Cholley met a Girl who didn't know how much she was worth, so Cholley thought it would be an Act of Kindness to help her find out. When he sat out with her in the Cool of the Evening and gave her the Burning Gaze and the low entrancing Love Purr that he had practised for Four Years at the University, she stopped him before he was half finished, and told him that he need not work Overtime, because he was the Boy for Nellie. She said she had him Picked Out from the Moment that she noticed how well his Coat set in the Back.

In one of the large Office Buildings of the City there is a Suite finished in Dark Wood. At a massive roll-top Desk sits Cholley, the handsome Lawyer, who is acquainted with all the Club Fellows, Society Bucks and Golf Demons. When a Client comes in with a Knotty Question, Cholley calls in a Blonde Stenographer to jot down all the Points in the Case. Then the Client departs. Cholley rings a Bell and Brother William comes out of a Side Room with his Coat bunched in the Back and his Trousers bagged at the Knees. His Cravat[104] is tied on one Side only and he needs a Shave, but he is full of the Law. Cholley turns all the Papers over to him and tells him to wrestle with the Authorities for a few Days and Nights. Then William slips back into his Hole and Humps himself over the calf-bound Volumes while Cholley puts on his slate-colored Gloves and Top Coat and goes out to where Simpson is holding a Carriage

---

104. A neckband, the precursor to a modern necktie or bow tie.

Door open for him. He and Nellie take the air in the $2,200 Victoria[105] that he bought with her Money and later in the Day they dine with the Stockson-Bonds and finish at the Theater.

Cholley often reflects that it was a great Piece of Foresight on Pa's part to counsel Studious Habits and Rigid Mental Discipline, for if William had not been a Grind at College probably he would not have proved to be such a Help around the Office, and although William gets the Loser's End of the Fees and is never Called on to make a Witty Speech at a Banquet given by the Bar Association, he has the Satisfaction of knowing that he is the Silent Partner of the best-dressed Attorney in Town and one who is welcome wherever he goes.

MORAL: *There are at least two Kinds of Education.*

The Lesson:

There is a word for lawyers like Cholley who are great at schmoozing and attracting new clients to the firm, and that word is "rainmaker." Rainmakers are like hunters who go out into the field, look for likely targets, kill them and bring them back to the village for the feast. They can't write a contract or litigate in court, but they're great on the back nine.

Then there are the lawyers like Will who actually know what they're doing. What they lack in charisma they more than make up for in expertise and legal prowess. They are the ones who deliver the goods to the clients the rainmaker brings in.

So the next time you need the services of an attorney, remember: if you hire the schmoozer, you're going to end up paying for two lawyers!

---

105. A doorless French carriage with a forward-facing seat for two covered with a folding top, or calash, and a removable, elevated coachman's seat above the front axle.

The Maneuvers of Joel and the Disappointed Orphan Asylum

From *People You Know*, 1903

An old Residenter, who owned a Section of Improved Land, and some Town Property besides, was getting too Feeble to go out and roast the Hired Hands, so he turned the Job over to his Son. This Son was named Joel. He was foolish, the same as a Fox. Any one who got ahead of Joel had to leave a 4:30 Call and start on a Lope. When it came to Skin Games[106] he was the original High-Binder[107].

Joel took the Old Gentleman aside one Day and said to him: "Father, you are not long for this World, and to save Lawyer Fees and avoid a tie-up in the Probate Court, I think you ought to cut up your Estate your own self, and then you will know it is done Right."

"How had I better divide it?" asked the Old Gentleman.

"You can put the whole Shooting-Match in my Name," sug-

---

106. A rigged gambling game or swindle. Or, a dishonest business or scheme.
107. Unscrupulous person, originally a New York gangster.

gested Joel. "That will save a lot of Writing. Then if any other Relatives need anything, they can come to me and try to Borrow it."

Joel sent for a cut-rate Shyster[108], who brought a bundle of Papers tied with Green Braid, and assured the Old Gentleman that the Proceeding was a Mere Formality. When a Legal Wolf wants to work the Do-Do on a Soft Thing, he always springs that Gag about a Mere Formality.

Joel and the Shell-Worker moved the Old Gentleman up to a Table in the Front Room and put a Cushion under him and slipped a Pen into his Hand and showed him where to Sign.

After he got through filling the Blank Spaces with his John Hancock, he didn't have a Window to hoist or a Fence to lean on. He was simply sponging on Joel.

This went on for about a Month, and then Joel began to Fret.

"I don't think I am getting a Square Deal," said Joel. "Here is an Ancient Party without any Assets, who lives with me Week in and Week out and doesn't pay any Board. He is getting too Old and Wabbly to do Odd Jobs around the Place, and it looks to me like an awful Imposition."

So he went to the Old Gentleman and said: "Father, I know the Children must annoy you a good deal; they make so much Noise when they play House. Sometimes we want to use the Piano after it is your Bed-Time, and of course that breaks your Rest, so I have been thinking that you would be a lot better off in some Institution where they make a Specialty of looking after Has-Beens. I have discovered a nice, quiet Place. You will live in a large Brick Building, with a lovely Cupola on top. There is a very pretty Lawn, with Flower-Beds, and also an ornamental Iron Fence, so that the Dogs cannot break in and bite you. You will be given a nice Suit of Clothes, the same as all the others are wearing, and if you oversleep yourself in the Morning, a Man will come around and call you."

---

108. A person, especially a lawyer, who uses fraudulent or deceptive methods in business.

"In other Words, me to the Poor-House," said the Old Residenter.

"You need not call it that, unless you want to," said Joel. "If you choose, you may speak of it as the Home for Aged Persons who got Foolish with their Fountain Pens."

So Joel put his Father into the Spring Wagon and hauled him over the Hills to the Charity Pavilion, where all the Old Gentleman had to do was to sit around in the Sun looking at the Pictures in last year's Illustrated Papers and telling what a Chump he had been.

Over the Hills

But sometimes a Man is not all in, simply because he looks to be wrinkled and doddering. Joel's Father had a Few Thinks coming to him. Although he had been double-crossed and put through the Ropes, he still had a Punch left. He sent for a Lawyer who was even more Crafty than the one employed by Joel and he said to him: "There is a Loop-Hole in every Written Instrument, if one only knows how to find it. I want you to set aside that fool Deed."

Next day the Lawyer came for him in a double-seated Carriage and said, "They forgot to put on a Revenue Stamp and so the Transfer is off."

"And do I get all of my Property back again?" asked the Old Residenter.

"You get half and I get half," was the Reply of the Lawyer.

"Give me mine," said the Old Residenter. "I'm from Wisconsin and I want it in the Hand. Whatever I own from this time on, I carry right in my Clothes, and any Relative who separates me from it will have to set his Request to Music." Then he went to a Physician.

"Doc," he says, "they are counting nine on me, but I figure that before I cash in, I have time to spend all that I have. Look me over and tell me how long I would last on a Waldorf diet[109]. I want to gauge my Expenses so as to leave nothing behind for Joel except a Ha-Ha Message and a few Heirlooms."

"If you want to euchre your Family, why don't you leave it to an Orphan Asylum?" suggested the Lawyer.

"Nix the Orphan Asylum," said the Old Residenter. "They would bring a million witnesses to prove that I had been out of my Head for 20 years, and I wouldn't be there to contradict them. I learn that by a singular Coincidence, all the Old People who leave their Money to Hospitals and the like are Mentally Irresponsible. In order to prove that I am in my right Senses, I will Blow mine."

---

109. Food served at the Waldorf Astoria hotel in New York, renowned for being very rich and fattening.

So he went to Palm Beach and other Winter Resorts, at which they charge by the Minute, and wherever he went he gave a faithful Imitation of the Cowboy's first Night in Town.

He bought himself a hot Raglan[110] with a Surcingle[111] around it, and a very doggy line of Cravats, and when he went into the Dining-Room he picked out a Table which commanded a View of the Door at which the Girls came in.

All this time Joel was worried. It seemed a Sin and a Shame for an Old Man to go around spending his own Money.

The Residenter had so much Fun during his Second Time on Earth that he decided to make it a sure-enough Renaissance, so he

Second Time on Earth

---

110. An overcoat with sleeves that extend in one piece fully to the collar.
111. A wide strap or belt.

married a Type-Writer 19 years old, that he met in a Hotel Lobby, and then Joel did go up in the Air.

When she began to pick out Snake Rings, and Diamond Wish-Bones, the Old Gentleman saw that there was no longer any Hope for Joel.

MORAL: *When buncoing a Relative always be sure that the Knock-Out Drops are Regulation Strength.*

The Lesson:

This is one of my favorites of George Ade's stories. My father told me that it was based on a true story of a farmer and his son who lived near Earl Park, south of Kentland, Indiana. In that case the son kicked the father out of the house to live in an implement shed rather than the county poorhouse. In real life, the story had an ending similar to Shakespeare's *King Lear* or perhaps the movie *Hud*.

However, George was "the warm-hearted satirist" so instead of tragedy we get a comedy.

I posted this entire story on the TIGER 21 website forum on estate planning. It received more comments, downloads and hits than anything else on estate planning. Like so much of George's writing, it has stood the test of time.

George's best stories were about people, characterizations of how they behaved, should've behaved and might have behaved. People have not changed.

Of course, if you really are going to draw a lawyer like a gun, you should make certain that it's sure-fire and of sufficient caliber. As we will see later in this section, George was very adept in his use of the law and lawyers.

Don't hire a shyster!

A Chapter of French Justice as Dealt Out In the Dreyfus Case

From *In Pastures New*, 1906

A good many people do not understand the method of French courts of law. Take the Dreyfus case[112], for instance. It has been dragging along for years, and the more evidence accumulated by Captain Dreyfus to prove his innocence, the greater seems to be his portion of woe. He has been vindicated over and over again and the vindications simply make him more unpopular with those who prefer to regard him as a mysterious and melodramatic villain.

People living at home have never understood why Captain Dreyfus was convicted in the first place. That is because they are not familiar with the workings of a French court and cling to the Anglo-Saxon rule, that every man must be regarded as innocent until he is proven guilty. The French say that trials may be greatly simplified if the presumption of guilt is attached to every defendant

---

112. The Dreyfus case, or Dreyfus Affair, was a criminal justice scandal in France at the turn of the 20th century. See https://www.britannica.com/event/Dreyfus-affair, accessed November 27, 2023.

in a criminal case. When the presumption of guilt is combined with a personal unpopularity, the prisoner usually finds it advisable to throw himself on the mercy of the court and accept a life sentence.

In order to elucidate the rules of procedure in a French court and show how and why Captain Dreyfus was convicted, let us suppose that French methods could be transferred to the United States and applied to an ordinary criminal case—say the theft of a dog. Here is what would happen.

The Court—"Prisoner, you are accused of stealing a dog. Are you guilty or not guilty?"

Prisoner—"Not guilty."

Court—"Well, someone stole a dog, and if you refuse to acknowledge your guilt, we may be compelled to cast suspicion on gentlemen who would be deeply pained to have themselves interrogated.

The Prisoner—"How can I acknowledge my guilt when I didn't steal the dog?"

Court—"That isn't the point. The point is that a great many prominent and influential people have said at different times that you stole the dog. Now, if you come before the tribunal and prove that you didn't steal the dog you are going to humiliate a great many well known and sensitive persons and make the whole situation very distressing to me. It would simplify matters greatly if you would admit that you stole the dog."

The Prisoner—"But how can I admit stealing the dog when I am entirely innocent?"

The Court—"Did you ever see the dog said to have been stolen?"

Prisoner—"Yes, sir." (Profound sensation.)

Court—"And yet you have the audacity to stand there and say you didn't steal it?"

Prisoner—"A great many other people saw the dog."

Court—"Perhaps so; but they would make trouble if you or

A Chapter of French Justice

anyone else began insinuating against them, so I don't propose to have their names hauled in here. Of all the men who saw the dog and had a chance to steal it, you are the only one whose conviction would satisfy the general public."

Prisoner—"I can bring witnesses who saw another man steal the dog. I can prove that he confessed to stealing the dog and that he has fled to escape punishment."

Court—"You ought not to bring any such testimony into this court, for if you do so you are going to upset some theories held by very dear friends of mine, and if I permit the introduction of such testimony, there is no telling what they will say about me. If you didn't steal the dog isn't there something else you have done that is punishable in one way or another?"

Prisoner—"I can't think of anything just now."

Court—"Oh, pshaw! Aren't you guilty of something? Just think a moment. Nearly every man is guilty of something. If we can find you guilty of any old crime it will help some."

Prisoner—"I refuse to acknowledge any degree of guilt. I am innocent."

Court—"I don't see how you can be when so many estimable people think otherwise, but I suppose we shall have to give you a trial. Call the first witness."

First Witness—"Your Honor, I am a very high-minded and aristocratic person, and I have always disliked this defendant. (Sensation.) As soon as I had heard that someone had accused him of stealing a dog, I knew he must be guilty. I still hold to the opinion that he is guilty. I know that another man has confessed to stealing the dog, and has skipped out in order to avoid arrest, but these details have no weight with me. I am satisfied that if the defendant did not steal the dog mentioned in this affidavit, he must have stolen some other dog that we know nothing about. Ever since this wretched defendant was first accused of this crime I have been going around saying that he was guilty beyond the shadow of a doubt. Naturally I am not going to come here now and acknowledge his innocence. If he is acquitted, I'll be the subject of ridicule. That is why I urge the court to convict him. No matter what the testimony may show, you take my personal assurance that he is guilty. Remember one thing, that I have a large pull."

The Court—"Thank you very much for your testimony. Call the second witness."

Second Witness—"Your Honor, one day last spring I met a man whose friend told him that one day he saw the defendant pass the house from which the dog was stolen. From that moment I became convinced of the defendant's guilt. (Terrific sensation.) Another day a stranger walked into my office and told me that 'D' was the first letter of the name of the man who stole the dog. Although there are 100,000 persons in town whose names begin with 'D' I had no difficulty in coming to the conclusion that the particular 'D' who stole the dog was the scoundrel now on trial. The reason that I came to this conclusion was that he used to wear a red necktie, and I dislike any man who wears a red necktie. Also I attach great importance to the fact that the letter 'D,' which is the first letter in his name, is also the first letter in 'Dog,' thus proving that he stole the dog. (Profound sensation.) In conclusion I would like to request the court to bring in a verdict of guilty."

The Court—"We will now have some expert testimony."

First Expert—"Your Honor, I never saw the prisoner before, and I had no personal acquaintance with the dog, but I am convinced that he stole the dog, and I will tell you why. You know, of course, that another man has confessed to stealing the dog. My theory, evolved after much thought, is that the man who confessed did not steal the dog at all, but that the dog was stolen by the defendant, who disguised himself so as to resemble the man who has confessed. (Great sensation.) There seems to be a universal admission that the man who stole the dog was a brunette. Some people claim that this fact points to the innocence of the defendant, who is a blonde; but my theory is that the defendant dyed his hair and whiskers so as to cause them to resemble the hair and whiskers of a certain innocent man, then he borrowed a suit of the innocent man's clothes and went and stole the dog, and the resemblance was so perfect that even the innocent man and the dog were both deceived. The innocent man thought that he, and not the defendant, had stolen the dog, so he confessed and then ran away. But I am here to save him in spite of his confession. I maintain that if this defendant were to dye his hair and whiskers and put on a suit of clothes belonging to the man who has confessed to stealing the dog, then to anyone a short distance away he would bear a striking resemblance to the man who has confessed. Therefore the dog was not stolen by the man who has confessed, but by this infamous defendant cleverly disguised to resemble the man who has confessed."

The Court—"Then you think he is guilty?"

Expert Witness—"If there is anything in my theory, it is simply impossible for him to be innocent."

The Court—"Much obliged. Call the next witness."

Next Witness—"I would like to state to the court that the defendant is not very well liked down in our neighbourhood, where he formerly resided, and if the court will only convict him it will be a distinct personal favour to several of us."

The Court—"Do you think him guilty?"

Next Witness—"I haven't the slightest doubt of it. Neither has my wife. I have been convinced of his guilt ever since I heard him say one morning, 'I have something to do this afternoon.' It is evident to my mind that when he said, 'I have something to do this afternoon,' he meant, 'I am going to steal a dog this afternoon.'" (Sensation.)

The Court—"Then you are quite sure that he did steal the dog?"

Next Witness—"Of course."

The Court—"Are there any other witnesses?"

Prisoner—"I have several witnesses here who saw the other man steal the dog. I can prove that at the time of the stealing I was ten miles away, attending a picnic. I can prove, also, that I didn't need a dog; that I never liked dogs; that I had no earthly motive for stealing a dog; and that from the time of my first accusation I have consistently and emphatically denied any knowledge of the crime."

The Court—"Well, I don't see that the dog has anything to do with the case. I'll sentence you to six months in the bridewell[113] for being so blamed unpopular."

The Lesson:

We should never underestimate the importance of an independent judiciary, trial by jury and our constitution's checks and balances. Is our legal system perfect? Of course not. But the alternatives are all much worse. I have lived overseas and worked overseas for most of my adult life, and I have done this under many different legal jurisdictions and international law. By far the best available is American jurisprudence.

In the legal systems of communist China and Vietnam, the Communist party decides whatever it wants without any regard to the contract, the law or the evidence. That's it. Nothing else matters.

I have also experienced classical Third World law in Indonesia and the Philippines, where "crony capitalists" have everything set up so that the law is basically for sale, or pre-bought and paid for by the oligarchs.

I have worked under absolute monarchy in the Sultanate of Brunei. When I arrived in Brunei it was a British protectorate but by the time I left the Sultan had declared himself not only the legislature and the chief executive, but also the head of the Supreme Court. Whatever he said was law. Period.

---

113. A jail for petty offenders.

There are also some surprises in UK law. I found out to my detriment that although we share many principles of Anglo-Saxon law, under UK law an attachment is not automatically incorporated in a contract and can simply be ignored as if it wasn't there.

Which brings us back to the Dreyfus case and the Napoleonic Code under which the case was decided. Napoleon was a great man; his code is the law throughout most of Europe. Once I was a consultant to PetroFina, the Belgian company that is now part of Elf. The contract they offered me was under Belgian law, Code Napoleon, which is very much French law. I was a Singapore firm and as all the work would be done in Singapore, I requested that our contract be under Singapore Law, which is Anglo Saxon law—almost identical to the UK. PetroFina agreed.

The Attenuated Attorney Who Rang in the Associate Counsel

From *People You Know*, 1903

Once there was a sawed-off Attorney who had studied until he was Bleary around the Eyes and as lean as a Razor-Back. He knew the Law from Soup to Nuts, but much learning had put him a little bit to the Willies. And his Size was against him. He lacked Bellows.

He was an inconspicuous little Runt. When he stood up to Plead, he came a trifle higher than the Chair. Of the 90 pounds he carried, about 45 were Gray Matter. He had Mental Merchandise to burn but no way of delivering it.

When there was a Rally or some other Gabfest on the Bills, the Committee never asked him to make an Address. The Committee wanted a Wind-Jammer who could move the Leaves on a Tree 200 feet distant. The dried-up Lawyer could write Great Stuff that would charm a Bird out of a Tree, but he did not have the Tubes to enable him to Spout. When he got up to Talk, it was all he could do to hear himself. The Juries used to go to sleep on him. He needed a

Megaphone. And he had about as much Personal Magnetism as an Undertaker's Assistant.

The Runt lost many a Case because he could not Bark at the Jury and pound Holes in a Table. His Briefs had been greatly admired by the Supreme Court. Also it was known that he could draw up a copper-riveted Contract that would hold Water, but as a Pleader he was a Pickerel.

At one time he had an Important Suit on hand, and he was Worried, for he was opposed by a couple of living Gas Engines who could rare up and down in front of a yap Jury for further Orders.

"I have the Law on my Side," said the Runt. "Now if I were only Six-Feet-Two with a sole-leather Thorax, I could swing the Verdict."

While he was repining, in came a Friend of his Youth, named Jim.

This Jim was a Book-Agent. He was as big as the Side of a House. He had a Voice that sounded as if it came up an Elevator Shaft. When he folded his Arms and looked Solemn, he was a colossal Picture of Power in Repose. He wore a Plug Hat and a large Black Coat. Nature intended him for the U.S. Senate, but used up all the Material early in the Job and failed to stock the Brain Cavity.

Jim had always been at the Foot of the Class in School. At the age of 40 he spelled Sure with an Sh and sank in a Heap when he tried to add 8 and 7. But he was a tall Success as a Book Peddler, because he learned his Piece and the 218 pounds of Dignified Superiority did the Rest.

Wherever he went, he commanded Respect. He could go into a strange Hotel and sit down at the Breakfast Table and say: "Please pass the Syrup" in a Tone that had all the majestic Significance of an Official Utterance. He would sit there in silent Meditation. Those who sized up that elephantine Form and noted the Gravity of his Countenance and the fluted Wrinkles on his high Brow, imagined that he was pondering on the Immortality of the Soul. As a matter of fact, Jim was wondering whether he would take Ham or Bacon with his Eggs.

Jim had the Bulk and the awe-inspiring Front. As long as he held to a Napoleonic Silence he could carry out the Bluff. Little Boys tip-toed when they came near him, and Maiden Ladies sighed for an introduction. Nothing but a Post-Mortem Examination would have shown Jim up in his True Light. The midget Lawyer looked up in Envy at his mastodonic Acquaintance and sighed.

"If I could combine my Intellect with your Horse-Power, I would be the largest Dandelion in the Legal Pasture," he said.

Then a Happy Idea struck him amidships.

"Jim, I want you to be my Associate Counsel," he said. "I understand, of course, that you do not know the difference between a Caveat and a Caviar Sandwich, but as long as you keep your Hair combed the way it is now and wear that Thoughtful Expression, you're just as good as the whole Choate Family[114]. I will introduce you as an Eminent Attorney from the East. I will guard the Law Points and you will sit there and Dismay the Opposition by looking Wise."

So when the Case came up for Trial, the Runt led the august Jim into the Court Room and introduced him as Associate Counsel. A Murmur of Admiration ran throughout the Assemblage when Jim showed his Commanding Figure, a Law Book under his Arm and a look of Heavy Responsibility on his Face. Old Atlas, who carries the Globe on his Shoulders, did not seem to be in it with this grand and gloomy Stranger.

For two hours Jim had been rehearsing his Speech. He arose.

"Your Honor," he began.

At the Sound of that Voice, a scared Silence fell upon the Court Room. It was like the Lower Octave of a Pipe Organ.

"Your Honor," said Jim, "we are ready for Trial."

---

114. A prominent New England family, several of whom were graduates of Harvard and were lawyers, judges, ambassadors, politicians and doctors.

The musical Rumble filled the Spacious Room and went echoing through the Corridors. The Sound beat out through the Open Windows and checked Traffic in the Street. It sang through the Telegraph Wires and lifted every drooping Flag.

The Jurors turned Pale and began to quiver. Opposing Counsel were as white as a Sheet. Their mute and frightened Faces seemed to ask, "What are we up against?"

Learned Colleague

Jim sat down and the Trial got under way.

Whenever Jim got his Cue he arose and said, "Your Honor and Gentlemen of the Jury, I quite agree with my learned Colleague."

Then he would relapse and throw on a Socrates Frown and the Other Side would go all to Pieces. Every time Jim cleared his Throat, you could hear a Pin drop. There was no getting away from the dominating Influence of the Master Mind.

The Jury was out only 10 Minutes. When the Verdict was rendered, the Runt, who had provided everything except the Air Pressure, was nearly trampled under foot in the general Rush to Congratulate the distinguished Attorney from the East. The Little Man gathered up his Books and did the customary Slink, while the False Alarm stood in awful Silence and permitted the Judge and others to shake him by the Hand.

MORAL: *An Associate Counsel should weigh at least 200 Pounds.*

The Lesson:

This story is about lawyers, but it can apply to any business or investment situation where you are unable to do it all by yourself. The ancient Greeks inscribed "Know Thyself" on the temple of Apollo at Delphi, and George took it to heart.

When you know that you don't have the wherewithal, the physique, the education or the intellect to do something, it doesn't mean that you quit! By no means. Under those circumstances seek out and find someone who can fill your own deficiencies and press on! My most successful ventures have been those involving partners who complimented my skill set and vice versa—Bogue Hunt in particular. See *Wildcat Road Volume II* for more on that.

George's Business Contracts and Correspondence

George possessed a level of business and legal knowledge well above that of his peers, including his very rich brother-in-law, Warren T. McCray. Indeed, George paid a great deal of attention to his business and investment contracts and royalties. I can confirm his diligence because I have seen with my own eyes at the Purdue University Special Collections the archival evidence of the audits he conducted to determine whether he was being paid his fair share of royalties from his book sales and the box office proceeds from his plays. The following letters offer even more proof that George was anything but complacent when it came to protecting his business interests.

From *Letters of George Ade,* 1973

To Jan Wheelock[115]

Chicago
February 26, 1904

My dear Wheelock: -

   . . . I have a letter from Miss [Elisabeth] Marbury in which she says she has been talking with you in regard to getting an offer from a manager. I suggest that we do not become involved in any misunderstanding regarding Miss Marbury. I have no doubt that she is a very clever woman and that her services would be of great value to an author seeking to establish connections with managers but I cannot see that her services would be of any value to one who is seeking to avoid connections with managers; in other words, I have had more offers than I wish to entertain and have had several offers for the piece which I mentioned to you, the terms being fully as liberal as those suggested by Miss Marbury. There was nothing in my conversation with her which would justify her in believing that I wished her to approach any managers in my behalf and I have written Mr. Charles Frohman[116] to that effect. As I told you, I am not at all over-anxious to do any play writing for a long time to come and it would be nonsense for me to give Miss Marbury 10% of my royalties in order to induce her to make contracts for me when I don't want the contracts made. All that I want is to be let alone. You are the only man on earth that I have promised to talk business with at all for the next year. Because of my personal esteem for you and my faith in your abilities, I did tell you that I

---

115. AKA Joseph Wheelock Jr., a turn-of-the-century American stage actor.
116. An American theatre manager and producer.

would take up with your manager a proposition in regard to the piece we have discussed.[117]

Candidly, and without any reflection on our very clever friend I don't think we need the intervention of Miss Marbury. She would claim 10% of all the royalties that may ever come to me and I cannot figure out how she would be entitled to them since I already have two or three offers for the piece, some of them being much more liberal than those she mentioned in her letter. It is not so much a matter of terms with me as being associated with people in whom I have confidence and with whom I can work in sympathy.

There is no need of having any smash-up with Miss Marbury; simply let her know that I will be very busy on other matters for a time and then later on, if we decide to come down to cases with Mr. Frohman or anyone else, we can do so without referring the matter to her.

With best wishes,
George Ade

---

117. The play *The Bad Samaritan*.

To Herbert S. Stone & Co.[118]

Hazelden
Brook, Indiana
October 1, 1904

Gentlemen: -

I am informed that a literary agent in New York has been recently offering to various publishers all the publication rights in the five books of mine that you have got out. I have not my contract at hand, but I thought we had in our revised contract covering all of the books a clause concerning the transfer of publication rights.

I judge from your recent reports that all of these books have had their day but I should not like to see the publication rights hawked about, and if you are anxious to dispose of them I am willing to talk business with you, not because I expect to go into the publishing business myself but because I should like to protect the future of these books in case I should ever want to revise the stuff and bring a number of my books out in uniform edition.[119]

I shall be glad to hear from you at once concerning your intentions in regard to the books and I will entertain any reasonable proposition, but I do not think that under our present contract you have a right to transfer these books to publishers who will get them out in cheap form and from whom I may possibly have no guarantee of protection. I most certainly will not consent to any reduction of the royalties and I suggest that in fairness to all persons concerned you do not transfer these publication rights until you are sure that you have the legal right under our present contract.

For instance we have in our contract a clause declaring that

---

118. A Chicago-based publishing house that published some of George's works, namely *Artie, Pink Marsh, Doc' Horne, Fables in Slang* and *More Fables*.
119. This he did; George used this material for the new industry of motion pictures and reworked parts into new plays. In 1923 he revised many of his works in new collections.

the agreement shall be null and void if payments are not made at the time specified. This clause has been violated by you but I have not taken advantage of it to nullify the contract but shall do so if necessary to protect my rights.

Under the circumstances I think the reasonable thing to do would be to compromise and allow me to take back these books since you no longer find them salable. I shall be glad to hear from you regarding your views of the matter.

Yours truly,
George Ade

To Elsie Janis[120]

[Chicago, Illinois]
November 23, 1915

My dear Elsie Janis : -

Confirming my wire of last evening I am more than pleased to turn the play[121] over to you if I receive the royalty usually paid for regular union authors and can have some assurance that it will be prepared and produced by people who know their business. If you are on the job I think the piece will be protected. As I wired you, I could not undertake the immediate preparation of a scenario but I will be glad to go over the book and make suggestions and possibly revise the dialogue and subtitles.

Remember me to your mother.

Sincerely,
George Ade

---

120. An American actress-comedienne who starred in George's play *The Fair Co-Ed*.
121. The play is *The Fair Co-ed*. Janis had requested George's permission to make the play into a movie.

EDITOR'S NOTE: Warren T. McCray was married to George's sister, Ella, and was the Governor of Indiana. He ran into some serious financial difficulties—self-inflicted, by the way—and asked George to sign a guaranty which would have made him (George) personally liable for $600,000 plus legal fees should McCray default on his financial obligations. The following is George's response to his brother-in-law:

To Warren T. McCray

Hazelden
Brook, Indiana
July 5th, 1923

My dear Governor: -

    I have read over very carefully the document left here yesterday. It strikes me as very binding and obligatory and probably was framed by some enterprising attorney for the bank who wished to make everything air-tight. The sum of money involved is so large and the chances of marketing any kind of farm property within the next few years are so uncertain, not to say hazardous, that I cannot bring myself to the belief that the signing of this document will be a mere formality. If I have read the document in its true meaning I would be assuming an obligation equivalent to all of the assets that I could possibly command, even by a forced sale of all of my holdings. As I told you yesterday, I am operating in a small way now—I am not buying, selling, or speculating, but simply trying to live safely within my income and carry out some reasonable plans in connection with Purdue University and other institutions in which I am interested. I would not dare to guarantee any project of my own which involved the sale of large tracts of land within the next few years and I am just as reluctant to guarantee any projects for anyone else. In the matter of contracts I have found that the only safe plan is to submit all written instruments to my attorney,

Mr. [Carl] Meyer, of the firm of Mayor, Meyer, Austrian & Platt, of Chicago. I have sent in to him a copy of the proposed guarantee or surety and I am asking him to what extent I would be obligated and bound in case I signed my name. I am awaiting an opinion from him, but I think it is only fair to let you know, in the meantime, that probably I will be compelled to say that I cannot sign any document which would put into jeopardy everything that I possess. I would not do it for my own benefit and I cannot convince myself that it is my duty to assume what might develope into a large risk, however much I am desirous of granting a favor.

I shall write you again when I hear from Mr. Meyer.

I am, with best wishes,

Sincerely,
George Ade

The Lesson:

George's brother-in-law Warren T. McCray was over leveraged, and George recognized this. He astutely and tactfully refused to be pulled down in what would become one of the most spectacular bankruptcies in Indiana history.

After McCray was sentenced to the federal penitentiary for fraud, George quietly and anonymously supported his sister, Mrs. Ella Ade McCray, and put her son through college at his own expense.

Tariffs

An excerpt from George's play *The County Chairman*, 1903

Act III

SCENE: *Interior of Hackler and Wheeler's Law Office. Plain, shabby room, large table with books, writing materials, papers, and open box of cigars C. Large windows, three at back, looking out of second story toward houses on street drop at back. Door R.U. leading into small Ante-room like the top landing of a flight of stairs. Door L.U. leading to supposed front stairs of building. Plain old book shelves up C. with shabby books and pamphlets. Old desk down L. of it. Shelf above it with books. Large office chair back of table C., also chair R. and L. of table C. Tall stool R. of chair, back of table. Old-fashioned wood stove on a six-inch platform R. A long stovepipe runs up the R. wall to pipe hole near ceiling. Wood box R. of stove. Large brown cuspidors in front of stove. Old fashioned rocker with shabby cushions in front of stove, between it and C. table; small washstand with tin basin, a water pitcher with water R. against wall of Ante-room. Small mirror in plain frame hung over wash-stand. Long dirty roller towel on wall R. of wash-stand. Chair R. of wood box. Tall waste-basket up L. of door L.U. Broom up R. by door. Maps and prints of Washington and Wheeler R. and L. walls respectively.*

At the rise, Chub *is seated on stool back of table C., reading dime novel.* Uncle Eck *sits L. of table C.* Prewitt *in chair at window up L.C.*

Jimmison *sits on corner of C. table.* Henry, Whitney, Barcus *and* Montgomery, *with two or three character men, seated round office.* Jimmison *talking earnestly as curtain rises.*

JIMMISON. (*To* Prewitt) What I claim is this. If we open our ports we come into direct competition with the pauper labor of Europe. (Prewitt *nods his head. All others listen intently, but* Chub, *who is buried in his book*) Now, then, the point I make is that we've got to protect American labor. (*All nod their heads and say ad lib.,* "That's right." "No gittin' round that," *etc.*)

PETTAWAY. Say, Vance, where is all this American labor we hear so much about? I don't see very much of it here in Antioch.

UNCLE ECK. I remember the tariff question come up in 1836, when I was livin' in Syracuse, New York, and I—

PREWITT. There's one thing to be remembered. We could buy goods cheaper under free trade. (*All nod assent*)

PETTAWAY. I don't see what the tariff's got to do with electin' a Prosecutin' Attorney. I'm in favor of anything that'll pull Till Wheeler through.

PREWITT. We'll never pull him through unless Jim Hackler attends to business. I've been waitin' here an hour to see him. (*Rises, calls to* Chub.) Chub! Chub!

CHUB. Leave me alone, can't you? They're just goin' to scalp the heroine.

PREWITT. You'll ruin your mind readin' them yellow-backs.

CHUB. If I ruin my mind, I can always git a job as editor. (*All laugh at* Prewitt)

PETTAWAY. (*At his L.*) Editor? Why, Chub, I thought you was goin' to be a railroad man.

CHUB. Maw wouldn't let me run on the road, or be a clown in the circus, so I'm going to be a lawyer. (*All laugh.* Jimmison *gives* Eck *a cigar from box on table*)

PETTAWAY. Well, that's a fair compromise.

PREWITT. (*Looks at watch*) What time do you figure Hackler'll be here?

CHUB. (*Still reading*) Some time next week.

(Cleaver *and* Briscoe *enter L.U.*)

CLEAVER. Good morning, gentlemen. (*Looks round at* Briscoe) Well, he ain't here. (*Enter Sassafras R.U. with paste bucket, paste brush and roll of campaign bills under his arm, wears a campaign hat and several campaign badges. Puts bucket, etc., R.C. To* Chub) Where's Hackler?

CHUB. (*Without looking up*) Gone fishin'.

CLEAVER. Where's Wheeler?

CHUB. (*Without looking up*) Over to the Court House. (*Looks up at* Sassafras) Sass—go over and tell Mr. Wheeler an old friend wants to see him. (*Reads*)

SASSAFRAS. (*Indignantly*) Look heah, juvenile child, I'm the official bill-posteh of this heah campaign. I ain't no errand boy. (*R.C.*)

CHUB. Well, I'm studyin' law. I ain't goin' to do no chores. You go ahead.

SASSAFRAS. Nothin' but wohk. (*Disgusted, starts to go L.U., stops, goes back, picks up bucket, etc.*) I ain't goin' to leave my propehty here—a lot of politicians settin' 'round. (*Exit L.U.* Briscoe *and* Cleaver *at L. of C. table. Tries to pump* Chub)

BRISCOE. (*To* Chub) I understand Hackler's gone over to Illinois?

CHUB. (*Does not look up during any of the speeches*) That's so?

CLEAVER. What do you s'pose he's doin' over there?

CHUB. Didn't tell me.

BRISCOE. When'll he be back?

CHUB. If he comes back as fast as he went, he ought to be here now.

CLEAVER. When did he go?

CHUB. Go where?

CLEAVER. Illinois.

CHUB. Is he in Illinois?

CLEAVER. Ain't he?

Tariffs

CHUB. (*Puts finger to side of nose, winks broadly, reads from book*) "At that moment a rifle shot rang out upon the frosty air and another redskin bit the dust."

BRISCOE. (*Disgusted*) Aw—w— (*Turns angrily away and starts to go to L.U. as* Wheeler *enters L.U., followed by* Sassafras)

JIMMISON and PREWITT. Hello, Till!

WHEELER. (*C. back of table, sees* Cleaver *and* Briscoe *L.*) Cleaver, what do you want here?

CLEAVER. (*Embarrassed tone*) I came over to get the monthly school report. We always publish it.

WHEELER. (*Sarcastically*) I am glad to observe, Mr. Cleaver, that even in the heat of a campaign you take such deep interest in educational matters. Miss Rigby, of the second grade, hasn't turned in her report yet. (*To* Sassafras) Sass, go down to the schoolhouse and tell Miss Rigby to leave her report here on her way home this afternoon.

SASSAFRAS. (*Angrily*) Why don't you let somebody else do some wohk once in a while? I'm the official bill-posteh.

WHEELER. (*Waves his hand at him*) Go on—go on. (Sassafras *exits L.U., muttering to himself. To* Briscoe *and* Cleaver) You needn't wait. (*They look at each other and start to exit L.U. He calls after them*) And don't come back. I'll send it over. (*They exit L.U.* Wheeler *is back of C. table, picks up pamphlet. Others all crowd up to table and begin to talk ad lib. Two or three pull out memos and thrust them to him*) One at a time, gentlemen. Mr. Hackler, who is running this campaign—

OMNES. Yes, yes.

WHEELER. (*Pointedly*) —and who has charge of the funds— (*Bus. "Yes, that's what we mean."*)

(Omnes, *showing him the memos, etc.*)

WHEELER. —is not here. Don't know where he is! (*Men drop back, quieting down, and go to former places. Sit*)

UNCLE ECK. They claim you ain't right on the tariff question.

WHEELER. (*Sitting back of C. table*) Well, I believe in high wages for the working man, and low prices for the consumer. Can you find any fault with that?

OMNES. No, that's all right, etc.

UNCLE ECK. (*Gravely*) I remember Henry Clay advocated the same thing in 1824. (*All show signs of irritation*)

The Lesson:

George set the play *The County Chairman* in the 1870s. The debate on the tariff issue was as hot then as it has become now. Even before and especially following the Great Depression, almost all economists agreed that the Smoot-Hawley Tarriff Act of 1930 was what made the Great Depression truly great. It was a tariff on the free market.

Today the issue is not so much consumer goods as it is the threat of the free market countries versus an authoritarian combine of Russia, China, Iran, and North Korea. I do not see any case for enacting a tariff upon countries that are free market democracies such as we are. However, faced with increasingly hostile totalitarian and authoritarian threats, a tariff on their products makes good sense.

> MORAL: *There are always two sides to every issue and the circumstances always matter.*

For more on the tariff issue, see *Mr. Kakyak Decides to Become a Republican* and the articles about tariffs in the Recommended Reading section.

On Philanthropy and Estate Planning

Two Philanthropic Sons

From *Knocking the Neighbors*, 1912

Two Boys sallied forth from a straggling Village in search of an irrational Female known as Dame Fortune.

It was a sad Jolt to the Walking Vegetables back in the Stockade when they heard, on Good Authority, that Ezra and Bill were slamming it over the Plate and batting above .400.

They simply wagged the ossified Domes and hoped the Boys were getting it Honestly.

Ezra and Bill, up among the inflammatory Posters and the nervous Electric Signs, kept on playing Tag with the Sherman Act until they had it in Oodles and Bundles and Bales and Stacks.

Finally when they became so prosperous that they had to wear Shoes specially made, with Holes in the top, they began to be troubled with Tender Recollections of Humble Birthplace.

Through the Haze of Intervening Years they saw the Game of Two-Old-Cat in the Vacant Lot back of the M. E. Church and forgot all about sleeping in the refrigerated Attic and going down in the morning to thaw out the Wooden Pump.

They yearned to elbow out from the Congested Traffic of the cold and heartless City and renew Sweet Associations.

They wanted to wander once more down the Avenues of

Rhubarb and clasp hands with Old Friends whose simple Hearts averaged about 14 Throbs to the Minute.

It is the regulation Dream of every Financial Yeggman[122] to go back to his Old Town wearing a Laurel Wreath and have the School Children throw Moss Roses in his Pathway.

So Ezra sent on a Proposition.

He wanted to build a Library at the corner of Fifth and Main, thereby making it easy for his old Neighbors to read the Six Best Sellers without plugging the Author's Game.

He offered to give 20,000 Bucks if the Citizens would raise 5,000 more and maintain the Thing.

Ezra had not been in the Habit of reading anything except the Tape and he cared about as much for George Bernard Shaw as George Bernard Shaw cared for him.

Nevertheless, he wanted to be remembered, 50 Years hence, as the Man who built the Library and not as the Guy who dealt from the Bottom of the Deck, utilizing the Sleeve Device and the Bosom Hold-Out.

By the use of Anaesthetics and Forceps the 5,000 was secured.

Then the Building was erected and the only Criticism made was that the Location was poor and the dod-blasted Concern looked like a Barn and it was arranged wrong inside and nobody didn't want no Library nohow.

When Ezra came down to the Dedication to face an outraged and tax-burdened People, he was just as popular as Tonsilitis or Sciatica ever dared to be.

Bill came back also.

He floated into Town one day and appeared in Jimison's General Store and called for a Good Cigar.

He told Mr. Jimison to take one and called up the Boys around the Stove.

---

122. A person who breaks open safes; a burglar.

When the Word got out that Bill was Buying over at the Bee Hive, representative Citizens came on the Jump from the Harness Shop and the Undertaking Parlors and the Elite Bowling Alley.

Every Man that showed up got a Lottie Lee with a Band around it, and when Bill left on the 3:40 a Mob followed him to the Train.

Ever after that the Word was freely passed around that Bill was a Prince.

MORAL: *In scattering Seeds of Kindness, do it by Hand and not by Machinery.*

The Lesson:

George is well known for his public philanthropy. He collaborated with another Purdue alum, David E. Ross, to build the Ross-Ade Stadium at Purdue. He donated money for construction of Purdue's Memorial Gymnasium and its Memorial Union building, and was a major supporter of his fraternity, Sigma Chi. He raised funds for the American Red Cross during World War I, and spearheaded veterans assistance efforts in Indiana and nationwide.

Less recognized are the countless private acts of charity that George quietly performed "by hand."

My favorite story of George's clandestine philanthropy is the tale of "Little Buck the Trapper", which I previously published in Volume I of my memoir, *Wildcat Road*.[123] Long story short, George once executed an elaborate, secretive and very funny scheme involving Buffalo Bill Cody in an effort to elevate the social standing of Kentland's most disparaged town drunk. George would go to just about any lengths to make things right. He set a wonderful example for anyone wishing to be an effective hands-on benefactor.

---

123. William C. Ade, *Wildcat Road, Vol I* (Brook, Indiana: Ade Royalties and Publishing, 2020), 50-55.

The Fable of the Good Fairy with the Lorgnette, and Why She Got It Good

From *Fables in Slang*, 1899

Once Upon a Time there was a Broad Girl who had nothing else to do and no Children to look after, so she thought she would be Benevolent.

She had scared all the Red Corpuscles out of the 2 by 4 Midget who rotated about her in a Limited Orbit and was known by Courtesy as her Husband. He was Soft for her, and so she got it Mapped out with Herself that she was a Superior Woman.

She knew that when she switched the Current on to herself she Used up about 6,000 Ohms an hour, and the whole Neighborhood had to put on Blinders.

She had read about nine Subscription Books[124] with Cupid and Dove Tail-Pieces[125] and she believed that she could get away with any Topic that was batted up to her and then slam it over to Second in time to head off the Runner.

---

124. Popular in the 18th and 19th centuries, these were books "lent" to readers for a fee (by subscription).
125. Fancy finishing details.

Her clothes were full of Pin-Holes where she had been hanging Medals on Herself, and she used to go in a Hand-Ball Court every Day and throw up Bouquets, letting them bounce back and hit Her.

Also, She would square off in front of a Camera every Two Weeks, and the Man was Next, for he always removed the Mole when he was touching up the Negative. In the Photograph the Broad Girl resembled Pauline Hall[126], but outside of the Photograph, and take it in the Morning when she showed up on the Level, she looked like a Street just before they put on the Asphalt.

But never you Fear, She thought She had Julia Arthur[127] and Mary Mannering[128] Seventeen up and One to play, so far as Good Looks were concerned; and when it came to the Gray Matter—the Cerebrum, the Cerebellum, and the Medulla Oblongata—May Wright Sewell[129] was back of the Flag and Pulled up Lame.

The Down-Trodden Man, whom she had dragged to the Altar, sized Her all right, but he was afraid of his Life. He wasn't Strong enough to push Her in front of a Cable Car, and he didn't have the Nerve to get a Divorce. So he stood for Everything; but in the Summer, when She skated off into the Woods to hear a man with a Black Alpaca Coat lecture to the High Foreheads about the Subverted Ego, he used to go out with a few Friends and tell them his Troubles and weep into his Beer. They would slap him on the Back and tell him she was a Nice Woman; but he knew better.

Annyhow, as Bobby Gaylor used to say, she became restless around the House, with nothing to do except her Husband, so she made up her mind to be Benevolent to beat the Band. She decided that she would allow the Glory of her Presence to burst upon the Poor and the Uncultured. It would be a Big Help to the Poor and Uncultured to see what a Real Razmataz Lady was like.

---

126. A popular turn-of-the-century prima donna in America.
127. A Canadian stage and screen actress.
128. An English actress.
129. An American reformer, who was known for her service to the causes of education, women's rights, and world peace.

She didn't Propose to put on Old Clothes, and go and live with Poor People and be One of Them, and nurse their Sick, as they do in Settlements. Not on Your Previous Existence! She was going to be Benevolent, and be Dead Swell at the Same Time.

Accordingly, she would Lace Herself until she was the Shape of a Bass Viol[130], and put on her Tailor-Made, and the Hat that made her Face seem longer, and then she would Gallop forth to do Things to the Poor. She always carried a 99-cent Lorgnette[131] in one Hand and a Smelling-Bottle in the Other.

"Now," she would say, feeling Behind to make sure that she was all strung up, "Now, to carry Sunshine into the Lowly Places."

As soon as she struck the Plank Walks, and began stalking her Prey, the small Children would crawl under the Beds, while Mother would dry her Arms on the Apron, and murmur, "Glory be!" They knew how to stand off the Rent-Man and the Dog-Catcher; but when 235 pounds of Sunshine came wafting up the Street, they felt that they were up against a New Game.

The Benevolent Lady would go into a House numbered 1135A with a Marking Brush, and after she had sized up the front room through the Lorgnette, she would say: "My Good Woman, does your Husband drink?"

"Oh, yes, sir," the grateful Woman would reply. "That is, when he's working. He gets a Dollar Ten."

"And what does he do with all his Money?" the Benevolent Lady would ask.

"I think he plays the Stock Market," would be the Reply.

Then the Benevolent Lady would say: "When the Unfortunate Man comes Home this Evening you tell him that a Kind and Beautiful Lady called and asked him please to stop Drinking, except a

---

130. Also called a *church bass* or *Yankee bass viol*, this is a type of bowed string instrument which enjoyed popularity in early 19th century New England. Essentially George is saying that the woman was shaped like an hourglass.

131. A pair of spectacles with a handle used to hold them in place rather than fitting over the ears or nose.

Glass of Claret at Dinner, and to be sure and read Eight or Ten Pages from the *Encyclopedia Britannica* each Night before retiring; also tell him to be sure and save his Money. Is that your Child under the Bed?"

"That's little William J."

"How Many have you?"

"Eight or Nine—I forget Which."

"Be sure and dress them in Sanitary Underwear; you can get it for Four Dollars a Suit. Will you be good enough to have the Little Boy come from under the Bed, and spell 'Ibex' for the Sweet Lady?"

"He's afraid of you."

"Kindly explain to him that I take an Interest in him, even though he is the Offspring of an Obscure and Ignorant Workingman, while I am probably the Grandest Thing that ever Swept up the Boulevard. I must go now, but I will Return. Next time I come I hope to hear that your Husband has stopped Drinking and is very Happy. Tell the Small Person under the Bed that if he learns to spell 'Ibex' by the time I call again I will let him look at my Rings. As for you, bear in mind that it is no Disgrace to be Poor; it is simply Inconvenient, that's all."

Having delivered herself of these Helpful Remarks she would Duck[132], and the Uplifted Mother would put a Nickel in the Can and send Lizzie over to the Dutchman's.

In this manner the Benevolent Lady carried forward the Good Work, and Dazzled the whole Region between O'Hara's Box Factory and the City Dump. It didn't Cost anything, and she derived much Joy from the Knowledge that Hundreds of People were Rubbering at her, and remarking in Choked Whispers: "Say, ain't she the Smooth Article?"

But one day a Scrappy Kid, whose Mother didn't have any Lorgnette or Diamond Ear-Bobs, spotted the Benevolent Lady. The

---

132. Leave hurriedly.

Benevolent Lady had been in the House telling his Mother that it was a Glorious Privilege to wash for a Living.

After the Benevolent Lady went away the Kid's Mother sat down and had a Good Cry, and the Scrappy Kid thought it was up to him. He went out to the Alley and found a Tomato Can that was not working, and he waited.

In a little while the Benevolent Lady came out of a Basement, in which she had been telling a Polish Family to look at her and be Happy. The Scrappy Kid let drive, and the Tomato Can struck the Benevolent Lady between the Shoulder Blades. She squawked and started to run, fell over a Garbage Box, and had to be picked up by a Policeman.

She went Home in a Cab, and told her Husband that the Liquor League had tried to Assassinate her, because she was Reforming so many Drunkards. That settled it with her—she said she wouldn't try to be Benevolent any more—so she joined an Ibsen Club[133].

The Scrappy Kid grew up to be a Corrupt Alderman, and gave his Mother plenty of Good Clothes, which she was always afraid to wear.

MORAL: *In uplifting, get underneath.*

The Lesson:

George was well acquainted with Chicago's Hull-House—a settlement house established to aid recently-arrived European immigrants—and possibly its founder Jane Addams, the Mother Theresa of her age. As it is in contemporary times with Mother Theresa, there were many who wished to put on the airs of a Jane Addams without really doing anything remotely useful. Hence George's

---

133. An organization devoted to the promotion of the works of the Norwegian dramatist and poet Henrik Ibsen.

satire against those who wanted to be seen as important reformers and social workers without actually doing any of the work.

Jane and George shared enthusiasm for Theodore Roosevelt, being two of the first public figures to support the Bull Moose Party. George's hero Mark Twain was one of the original founders of the Anti-Imperialist League along with Jane Addams. Although George never formally joined the Anti-Imperialist League, his "Stories of Benevolent Assimilation" certainly puts him firmly in the company of Addams and Twain. However, by no means did George and Jane agree on all things. She was anti-alcohol and George was no teetotaler; George was no pacifist and supported WWI and WWII ardently.

The Samaritan Who Got Paralysis of the Helping Hand

From *People You Know*, 1903

O nce there was a moving Target who was strong on the Brotherhood of Man. He ran a little Sunshine Factory all of his own. When it came to scattering Seeds of Kindness, the Farm Drill was a Poor Second.

Every time he started down Town he would have to zigzag so as to cover both sides of the Street and glad-hand all of his Acquaintances.

From time to time he joined Fraternal Organizations and took blistering Oaths that he would always love his Fellow-Man and stand for any Touch within Reason. Consequently a good many People found it cheaper to send for him than to hire a Professional Nurse. He would travel Miles in order to have the Pleasure of sitting up with a Corpse. And he was one of the handiest Pall-Bearers in the Business.

Any one who happened to be nursing a Hard-Luck Story would hunt up sympathetic Jasper and give him the Grip and then weep on his Shoulder. Usually he promised to do what he could to square Matters, even though he had to cut in where he wasn't wanted. In flying around, trying to re-instate No-Goods who had lost their

Jobs and secure Salaried Positions for Nice Fellows who were willing to do anything except Work, he got many a Jolt, but he was not discouraged.

One of his regular Assignments was to arbitrate a Domestic Scrap, merely out of the Goodness of his Heart.

In this way he managed to re-unite quite a number of Couples who were afterward sorry that they had been reuned, and what they said about him would get the Blue Pencil[134] if inserted at this Point.

When a kind-hearted Herring starts out to be a Relief Bureau and First Aid to the Injured and a portable Home for the Friend-less, nobody tries to take the Job away from him. His Acquaintances do what they can to boost his Game.

Therefore when any one in that Community sought out a Busy Man of Affairs and began to unwrap his Tale of Woe and offer to exhibit his wounds, the B. M. of A. would say, "Here, I'll give you a Letter of Introduction to my old friend Jasper. He is a Samaritan from away back."

It came about that Jasper's Outer Office was frequently co-agulated with a Choice Assortment of Pan-Handlers, and all the short-winded Brothers who want to hitch on to somebody's else Pull, as they say in Boston.

At times Jasper would become weary of having Folks come along and turn their Private Griefs over to him, but he did not want to become a Cynic and lose his Faith in Human Nature. He was frequently Stung, but still he could not resist any Appeal that was backed up by a few Weeps.

In the Course of Time he came into quite a Bundle of Money, and then all the Bread that he had cast on the Waters came back to him, a Bakery at a time. Those whom he had succored came around to Sucker him.

---

134. Censored out.

A Promoter whose Schemes he had guaranteed, because the Man's Children needed Shoes, now had a Chance to show his Gratitude. He let Jasper in on the Ground Floor of a Company organized to manufacture an Automobile that could be turned out of the Shop for $35 and would run 90 Miles on a pint of Gasoline.

Gentlemen who were getting along without Overcoats came in to see him about Mining Stock that was sure to touch Par by January 1st. The only Reason they came to him first, instead of tackling John W. Gates[135], was that he had always been a True Friend and they wanted to put him next to a Good Thing.

The Promoter

---

135. John Warne Gates, also known as "Bet-a-Million" Gates, was an American Gilded Age industrialist and gambler. A native of the Chicago area, he was a pioneer promoter of barbed wire. He was also the business partner of George's mentor in business and finance, Ort Wells.

After one or two of these Gift Enterprises had been slipped to him, he began to back water and be a trifle Sore. Yet he found it very Hard to be discourteous to one who came in and did the Brother Act. Besides, the Bunk who has the Joint Note already made out and ready to be signed, usually has a Talk calculated to make a Heart of Stone mellow to the Consistency of a Baked Apple.

What really did more than any other one Thing to cure him of his Innate Goodness was an Experience with a Sweet Girl who was being courted by a Hound quite unworthy of her.

The unselfish Benefactor who tries to sidetrack Weddings that are sure to turn out unhappily is always a Candidate for the Hospital, with a Long Shot at the Morgue.

The Sweet Girl in Question was the daughter of an Old Friend, for whose Funeral Expenses he had been landed. She was a Confiding Thing, and did not know that the Bachelor who had started in to Rush her seven nights a Week was a Rounder and a Poker-Player and somewhat of a Lush.

Every one who knew the Sweet Girl said it was too Bad and that some one ought to go to her and warn her. After the Old Ladies and the Elders had talked the Matter over on the side, it was decided that Jasper was It. He was known to be kind and disinterested and was accustomed to dealing out Good Advice. Anything that he said would go a long Way to head off the Deal.

Accordingly he did a Fatherly Talk to the Daughter of his Old Friend, giving her a Straight Line on the Conduct of the High-Roller who was trying to warm up to her.

She thanked him right from the Bottom of her heart. Then she sent a Messenger Boy to hunt up the High-Roller, because she wanted to know if it was all True or merely a Cruel Slander.

When she sprung his Record on him he leaned right over against her and cried and said that no matter what he had been, she was the one to make him a Good Man. Then she stroked his Hair and begged Forgiveness and he asked her who had been Knocking and she gave the whole Snap away and begged him not to do anything Desperate. He said that whatever he did, he would do out of Love for her.

After which he went home to oil up his Pocket Hardware.

Next Morning the Man who wanted to help Everybody did a Flying Leap down the Back Stairway of his Office. Just as he ducked a Bullet and cut into the Alley back of the Post-Office, it occurred to him that the True Friend Gag had its Drawbacks.

He escaped with his Life, but there was always more or less Dark Talk of his being mixed up in a Woman Case.

He is now what is known in Obituary Notices as a Practical Philanthropist. That is, he refers all Hard-Luck Tales to a Society which was never known to give up. The Office Boy has Instructions to admit only those who are listed in Bradstreet[136]. And, of course, he is never called in to smooth out Family Fights because of the Blot on his Character.

> MORAL: *To be a successful Benefactor, wait and put the whole Lump Sum into Libraries.*

The Lesson:

Making money—especially a lot of money—is very hard, but not nearly as hard as doing meaningful philanthropy that doesn't result in negative ramifications. I can personally attest to this, but decline to go into detail here . . .

Having a good heart is not enough to succeed in philanthropy. Often, having a good heart simply results in the philanthropist being used.

---

136. This later became Dunn & Bradstreet, the publishers of the Who's Who of the corporate world and corporations.

Vacations

From *Single Blessedness*, 1922

When the days are long, get ready to file off the ball and chain. Wait until the asters are blooming and then, no matter where you are, go somewhere else. Only an oyster remains forever at the old homestead.

If the all-wise Arranger had meant for you to look out of the same window all the time, he wouldn't have given you legs.

The planet you are now visiting may be the only one you ever see. Even if you get a transfer, the next one may not have any Grand Canyon or Niagara Falls.

Move around before the ivy begins to climb up your legs. It is true that a rolling stone gathers no moss, but it gets rid of the rough corners and takes on a lovely polish. Besides, who wants to be covered with moss?

Go on a journey every year so that you may jolt out of your brittle head-piece the notion that our home township is the steering-gear of the universe.

Some hermits have learned, but only the travelers are wise. If you have earned a vacation, take it. The time has come to exchange your cold currency for some new sensations. You are due to accept a reward for all the years of sacrifice and denial. But you worry, if you splurge around and have a good time, maybe the children will not have all the funds they need, fifteen years hence, to keep them in red touring cars and squirrel coats.

You are afraid to make a will reading as follows:

Dear offspring:

Go out and get it—the same as I did.

Think of the thousands of worthy old people now penned up at home who ought to be scooting around in Henrys[137] and lake steamers and Pullman cars, rounding out the long day of toil with a late afternoon of gleeful enjoyment! It wouldn't cost them a cent. The heirs would pay all the bills.

We need in this country many Night Schools for Old People. It is time to declare for the rights and privileges of the passing generation.

The world and the fullness thereof do not belong entirely to the flapper with the concealed ears and the dancing tadpole whose beltline is just below the shoulder-blades.

Take your vacations while you can get them. Eventually you may not be able to name the spots you are going to visit next.

The Lesson:

Why did I put this essay about vacations under estate planning? Because many first-generation wealth creators are like the old pioneers and often times forego their vacations.

George wrote this for his parents' generation . . . the pioneer society in Newton County in which he grew up just after the Civil War. A generation that was self-sacrificing for the next generation to the degree that they would never take a vacation. He was certainly not writing to his own father, who was very well travelled.

---

137. The Henry was a car built by the Henry Motor Car Company in Muskegon, Michigan from 1910 to 1912. It debuted in Chicago to great fanfare; perhaps George even witnessed the parade in which it was introduced to the masses.

The Fable of the Never-to-be Benefactor Who Took a Brand-New Tack

From *True Bills*, 1904

Once there was a Multi-Millionaire who felt jealous when he saw Carnegie throwing Twenty-Dollar Gold Pieces at the Squirrels, while Coal-Oil Johnny Rockefeller was handing his pet University another Million every time a new Student came in out of the Tall Grass and Matriculated.

He saw that a very Rich Man who wishes to be Respected must fill his Clothes with Currency and go out and slather it around, and holler for everybody to have Something on him and keep the Change. He decided to follow the prevailing Fashion and spend his Money before he died[138], thereby giving the Ha-Ha to the Legal Profession.

But when this would-be Philanthropist got ready to cut the Strings on his Bundle he struck a Snag. The Philanthropy Business

---

138. In George's time, philanthropy was led by Andrew Carnegie. In his famous book *The Gospel of Wealth*, Carnegie's goal was to give away 100% before he died. Today's "billionaire pledge" is more modest—to give away 50% of their wealth before they die. However, it's practically equivalent, because in Carnegie's day there was no income tax!

had been overworked. Every Town large enough to be indicated on the Map had a Carnegie Library. He found that the Orphans were receiving more Care and Attention than the Children of Club-Women. About the only Little Ones who got into the Country in the Summer were the Homeless Waifs. As for Colleges, they had multiplied so rapidly that all through the Middle West it was practically impossible to get Harvest Hands. The Poor Working-Man showed no inclination to go against the Free Reading-Room and the Cheap Lectures on Astronomy, for he had the Price in his Pocket and preferred to play Seventy-Seven in some German Place where they served a Hot Lunch.

It began to look as though the benevolent Millionaire would have to burn his Money or else leave it to the usual Nephew who lives on High Balls and Musical Comedy.

"Surely there is Suffering somewhere in this World," said the perplexed Millionaire. "Some one is waiting for a Helping Hand. Now to find him."

He began a careful Study of Social Conditions and soon discovered that the real Sufferer, the mute and patient Victim who was getting the Hooks oftener than any one else, was the Gentleman who wore the High Collar and carried in his Hip Pocket a little Work on Etiquette and Good Behavior.

The poor Reptile whose Wife got up in the Morning and grabbed the Paper to see if the Family was mentioned, he was the banner Patsy of all Creation and he was the Boy that was praying for some one to come along and throw him a Life-Line.

By further Investigation the Multi-Millionaire was horrified to learn that here in this smiling Land of Plenty, where the Roses bloom in June and the Editorial Writer calls attention to the prevalent Peace and Happiness, there were thousands of sad-eyed Men and Women who put on their Good Clothes when they would rather not do so, who went out when they would rather stay at Home, who Ate when they were not Hungry, Drank when they were not Thirsty, Conversed by the hour with People who bored them, listened to Speeches they did not want to hear, applauded Vocal Music that was too fierce for words, fondled the Infants that they wanted to throttle, and read Historical Romances that caused them to have Charley-Horse Dreams.

"Oh, why should we send Relief Ships to India when there is so much Misery right here in our own principal Residence Streets?" asked the philanthropic Millionaire.

So he founded and endowed a Society for the Relief of those who are Invited Out. The Purpose of this glorious Organization was to prove that Entertainments should entertain.

As a first Move, the Benefactor invited all the well-known Citizens to a Formal Dinner in honor of a Statesman who wore Medals for talking against Time. All the Local Orators who were accustomed to paying for their Plates by telling the same Stories that used to go so well in the Primrose and West Days were up at the Head Table. A feeling of Sadness seemed to brood over the large Assemblage until it was discovered that in front of each Plate was a Card saying that any one attempting to make a Speech would be thrown out on his Neck. Three or four of the Spell-Binders were temporarily stunned, but the Main Bunch laid their Faces down among the Cut Flowers and wept for Joy. The Dinner proceeded with tremendous Enthusiasm. There were no Dark Clouds on the Horizon threatening a Wind-Storm. No one was wondering how long the Mayor or the Congressman was going to Spout, or whether they had Manuscripts concealed on their Persons. The Orchestra played Coon Songs[139] without any Interruption from the Chairman. No one said anything about the Feast of Reason and the Flow of Soul. The Man with the Megaphone Voice cut no Ice whatsoever, for they had him sewed up. Every one went home feeling good.

---

139. A genre of music by Black people, or that presented a stereotype of Black people.

The Fable of the Never-to-be Benefactor

Next Day no less than forty grateful Persons stopped the Reformer on the Street and bade him Godspeed in his Noble Work.

The next Thing the Society did was to offer a Cash Bonus to any one giving a Reception at which there would be no standing in Line and shaking Hands. Also it offered annual Salaries to all Celebrities who refrained from reading long-winded Papers to helpless Clubs.

A special Fund was set aside for the purpose of having Children in the Public Schools taught, by means of Charts, the Deadly Effects of the Lap Supper.

Then the Society offered a Bounty of Two Dollars for the Scalp of any Person guilty of Amateur Theatricals, and a Reward of $100 for the Body, dead or alive, of any one proposing a Lady Minstrel Show.

A diamond-encrusted Brooch was offered to every Young Woman who would pledge herself never to sing anything that she learned at the Conservatory.

Special Endowments were offered to Colleges on condition that Graduates should not be permitted to arise on a Hot Day and quote from Emerson.

A large Sum was set aside to secure the passage of a Law prohibiting the sale of Flutes to any one except a German employed in an Orchestra.

Society Leaders were quietly bribed to circulate the Report that Party Calls were no longer fashionable.

A Hall of Fame was established for Bridal Couples that refused to take Presents and cut out the Reception at the Home of her Parents.

Then the Multi-Millionaire inaugurated a Grand Movement for the final Emancipation of those who wear Dress Clothes. He worked on the Legislature to set aside three Days in every Week for the private use of those who want to do as they please without being pulled and hauled. Any one who broke in on these days with Invitations was liable to Prosecution, the Penalty being a Fine or Imprisonment, or both.

By the time this practical Reformer had spent a couple of Millions helping the unfortunate Upper Classes to throw off the Shackles, he was the most popular Character in the Country.

His heroic Example induced many weak and faltering Souls to swear off on the Entertainments that had been slowly but surely leading them towards the Foolish House.

After he passed away, his Statue was set up in every Park and his Birthday was observed in the Public Schools with a Half-Holiday instead of a Programme of Recitations and Speeches.

MORAL: *Some People are too Polite to call for Help.*

The Lesson:

In George's very short autobiography, he wrote, " . . . I do not choose to make speeches or listen to speeches." Back in the day, dinners with speeches could be long rambling affairs that undoubtedly could be boring to the point of pain.

George's Legacy

At the end of the story "Two Philanthropic Sons", I touched upon a few of George's most public philanthropy efforts—his contributions to the creation of Ross Ade Stadium, the Memorial Gymnasium and the Memorial Union at Purdue; Sigma Chi; the American Red Cross and veterans assistance. He also gave of his time, serving on Purdue's Board of Trustees and as a member of Purdue's Alumni Association. He was a member of National Institute of Arts and Letters, an executive committee member of the Authors Guild, and president of the Mark Twain Association of America. His aforementioned work on behalf of the Red Cross and veterans led to a World War II liberty ship being named the *SS George Ade* in his honor.

The fact is, after accumulating his farms, George spent the rest of his lifetime income on philanthropy and international travel. He did a lot of his philanthropy anonymously "by hand" rather than "by machine," as evidenced by a letter he received from his sister Ella thanking him for his quiet contributions to her family during the imprisonment of her husband, Warren T. McCray, for his financial crimes.

The Great Depression devastated almost everyone's finances, including George's. The stock market fell by 90% and dividends were mostly eliminated. The royalties from his books, plays and movies dried up. His farmland could not produce enough income to pay the local property taxes. The three strong pillars of his finances had been pulled down by the Samson of the Great Depression.

What do you do when you suffer a 90% loss of all income, a similar drop in equities and a 40-60% drop in farm prices? George answered that question correctly. Rather than panic and liquidate his assets, he called literary agents in New York and committed himself once more to the assembly line of producing magazine articles on demand, monthly. He picked up his No. 2 pencil and yellow notepad and went to work. He was, as my father put it, an old man at the start of the Great Depression, however his mind was still keen and his copy sold. Thus he was not forced to sell his assets. George survived—nay, thrived—by the pencil.

George's estate at his death in 1944

- Farms 2500ac: ($37,500,000 at today's $15,000/ac)
- Stocks and bonds valued at $100,000 in 1944 ($1,712,713 in 2023 dollars)
- Royalties (According to heir George Ade Davis, these were worth less than $10,000 then, or circa $176,822 in today's money).

It was an estate worth circa $39,400,000 in today's money. George gave much of his wealth to charity during his lifetime and also in his last will (see the Appendix for Geoge's complete Last Will and Testament). To his sisters or their descendants, his nieces and nephews, he bequeathed most of his farmland.

At the beginning of George's will he talks about how he does not want his estate to be one large estate, and speaks to the importance of having several small holdings. There is an excellent case to be made for the toxic effects of too much inheritance. Of course, there are those who will squander anything and there are those who will be good stewards and advance even the largest of estates. But it is on the whole that these things must be judged. There is a limit.

According to Warren Buffett, "You should leave your children enough so they can do anything, but not enough so they can do nothing." Exactly what that is in practice he never specified . . . perhaps because it depends upon the person.

Ayn Rand wrote in *Atlas Shrugged*:

> *Only the man who does not need it is fit to inherit wealth—the man who would make his own fortune no matter where he started. If an heir is equal to his money, it serves him; if not, it destroys him.*

It's very difficult to know this when writing a Last Will.

The brilliant businessman and author Robert Townsend wrote in his 1970 book *Further Up the Organization*:

> MONEY AT THE TOP. *The best boss to work for—if you can find him—is one who's made enough keeping money (over $1,000,000[140] after taxes) by his own efforts so that he can walk out the door if he gets pushed too hard from upstairs in a direction he knows is wrong. He runs his outfit like he owns it.*
>
> *Too much inherited keeping money (over $5,000,000[141]) is a birth defect. It produces high and visible insecurity. When concentrated in outrageous amounts, it tempts Daddy to buy control of U.S. Environment Corporation for Sonny to play with. That's not all bad, because it makes a bleeding genius out of whoever follows Sonny. But, in a way, it's unfair. Edgar Bronfman, for example, may be a great chief executive at Seagrams. Nobody'll ever find out.*

---

140. According to the CPI calculator, $1 million in 1970 is circa $7,919,665 today.
141. According to the CPI calculator, $5 million in 1970 is circa $39,648,325 today—by coincidence exactly George's estate at the time of his death, which he said he wanted broken up!

So, using Robert Townsend's metrics, in today's money an inheritance of $8 million would be enough to do anything, while an inheritance of $40 million would be enough to do nothing. Of course, this is subjective and very much depends upon the person and the professional pursuit. For instance, $8 million would certainly not be enough to get into farming today.

So how did George stack up against these ideas?

His bequests were circa 220 to 700 acres (and the 700 acres were mortgaged). At roughly $15,000/ac in 2023 dollars, each bequest would amount to between $3 million and $10 million. Of course at the very high end of the inheritance scale was George Ade Davis, who was by his own efforts President and Chairman of the Board of Oklahoma Gas & Electric. He was undoubtedly the most accomplished of George's heirs.

By this metric, George anticipated the rules of thumb of Ayn Rand, Robert Townsend, and perhaps Warren Buffett himself. No one received such a large inheritance that they could do nothing (circa $39 million today). And the one who received the largest inheritance, George Ade Davis, had already proven that he did not need any inheritance at all!

On Life, Family and Success

The Set of Poe

From *In Babel: Stories of Chicago*, 1906

r. Waterby remarked to his wife: "I'm still tempted by that set of Poe. I saw it in the window to-day, marked down to fifteen dollars."

"Yes?" said Mrs. Waterby, with a sudden gasp of emotion, it seemed to him.

"Yes—I believe I'll have to get it."

"I wouldn't if I were you, Alfred," she said. "You have so many books now."

"I know I have, my dear, but I haven't any set of Poe, and that's what I've been wanting for a long time. This edition I was telling you about is beautifully gotten up."

"Oh, I wouldn't buy it, Alfred," she repeated, and there was a note of pleading earnestness in her voice. "It's so much money to spend for a few books."

"Well, I know, but—" and then he paused, for the lack of words to express his mortified surprise.

Mr. Waterby had tried to be an indulgent husband. He took a selfish pleasure in giving, and found it more blessed than receiving. Every salary day he turned over to Mrs. Waterby a fixed sum for household expenses. He added to this an allowance for her spending money. He set aside a small amount for his personal expenses and deposited the remainder in the bank.

He flattered himself that he approximated the model husband.

Mr. Waterby had no costly habits and no prevailing appetite for anything expensive. Like every other man, he had one or two hobbies, and one of his particular hobbies was Edgar Allan Poe. He believed that Poe, of all American writers, was the one unmistakable "genius."

The word "genius" has been bandied around the country until it has come to be applied to a long-haired man out of work or a stout lady who writes poetry for the rural press. In the case of Poe, Mr. Waterby maintained that "genius" meant one who was not governed by the common mental processes, but "who spoke from inspiration, his mind involuntarily taking superhuman flight into the realm of pure imagination," or something of that sort. At any rate, Mr. Waterby liked Poe and he wanted a set of Poe. He allowed himself not more than one luxury a year, and he determined that this year the luxury should be a set of Poe.

Therefore, imagine the hurt to his feelings when his wife objected to his expending fifteen dollars for that which he coveted above anything else in the world.

As he went to his work that day he reflected on Mrs. Waterby's conduct. Did she not have her allowance of spending money? Did he ever find fault with her extravagance? Was he an unreasonable husband in asking that he be allowed to spend this small sum for that which would give him many hours of pleasure, and which would belong to Mrs. Waterby as much as to him?

He told himself that many a husband would have bought the books without consulting his wife. But he (Waterby) had deferred to his wife in all matters touching family finances, and he said to himself, with a tincture of bitterness in his thoughts, that probably he had put himself into the attitude of a mere dependent.

For had she not forbidden him to buy a few books for himself? Well, no, she had not forbidden him, but it amounted to the same thing. She had declared that she was firmly opposed to the purchase of Poe.

Mr. Waterby wondered if it were possible that he was just beginning to know his wife. Was she a selfish woman at heart? Was she complacent and good-natured and kind only while she was having her own way? Wouldn't she prove to be an entirely different sort of woman if he should do as many husbands do—spend his income on clubs and cigars and private amusement, and gave her the pickings of small change?

Nothing in Mr. Waterby's whole experience as a married man had so wrenched his sensibilities and disturbed his faith as Mrs. Waterby's objection to the purchase of the set of Poe. There was but one way to account for it. She wanted all the money for herself, or else she wanted him to put it into the bank so that she could come into it after he—but this was too monstrous.

However, Mrs. Waterby's conduct helped to give strength to Mr. Waterby's meanest suspicions.

Two or three days after the first conversation she asked: "You didn't buy that set of Poe, did you, Alfred?"

"No, I didn't buy it," he answered, as coldly and with as much hauteur as possible.

He hoped to hear her say: "Well, why don't you go and get it? I'm sure that you want it, and I'd like to see you buy something for yourself once in a while."

That would have shown the spirit of a loving and unselfish wife.

But she merely said. "That's right: don't buy it," and he was utterly unhappy, for he realised that he had married a woman who did not love him and who simply desired to use him as a pack-horse for all house-hold burdens.

As soon as Mr. Waterby had learned the horrible truth about

his wife he began to recall little episodes dating back years, and now he pieced them together to convince himself that he was a deeply wronged person.

Small at the time and almost unnoticed, they now accumulated to prove that Mrs. Waterby had no real anxiety for her husband's happiness. Also, Mr. Waterby began to observe her more closely, and he believed that he found new evidences of her unworthiness. For one thing, while he was in gloom over his discovery and harassed by doubts of what the future might reveal to him, she was content and even-tempered.

The holiday season approached and Mr. Waterby made a resolution. He decided that if she would not permit him to spend a little money on himself he would not buy the customary Christmas present for her.

"Selfishness is a game at which two can play," he said.

Furthermore, he determined that if she asked him for any extra money for Christmas he would say: "I'm sorry, my dear, but I can't spare any. I am so hard up that I can't even afford to buy a few books I've been wanting a long time. Don't you remember that you told me that I couldn't afford to buy that set of Poe?"

Could anything be more biting as to sarcasm or more crushing as to logic?

He rehearsed this speech and had it all ready for her, and he pictured to himself her humiliation and surprise at discovering that he had some spirit after all and a considerable say-so whenever money was involved.

Unfortunately for his plan, she did not ask for any extra spending money, and so he had to rely on the other mode of punishment. He would withhold the expected Christmas present. In order that she might fully understand his purpose, he would give presents to both of the children.

It was a harsh measure, he admitted, but perhaps it would teach her to have some consideration for the wishes of others.

It must be said that Mr. Waterby was not wholly proud of his revenge when he arose on Christmas morning. He felt that he had accomplished his purpose, and he told himself that his motives had been good and pure, but still he was not satisfied with himself.

He went to the dining-room, and there on the table in front of his plate was a long paper box, containing ten books, each marked "Poe." It was the edition he had coveted.

"What's this?" he asked, winking slowly, for his mind could not grasp in one moment the fact of his awful shame.

"I should think you ought to know, Alfred," said Mrs. Waterby, flushed, and giggling like a school-girl.

"Oh, it was you—"

"My goodness, you've had me so frightened! That first day, when you spoke of buying them and I told you not to, I was just sure that you suspected some-thing. I bought them a week before that."

"Yes—yes," said Mr. Waterby, feeling the salt-water in his eyes. At that moment he had the soul of a wretch being whipped at the stake.

"I was determined not to ask you for any money to pay for your own presents," Mrs. Waterby continued. "Do you know I had to save for you and the children out of my regular allowance. Why, last week I nearly starved you, and you never noticed it at all. I was afraid you would."

"No, I—didn't notice it," said Mr. Waterby, brokenly, for he was confused and giddy.

This self-sacrificing angel—and he had bought no Christmas present for her!

It was a fearful situation, and he lied his way out of it.

"How did you like *your* present?" he asked.

"Why, I haven't seen it yet," she said, looking across at him in surprise.

"You haven't? I told them to send it up yesterday."

The children were shouting and laughing over their gifts in the next room, and he felt it his duty to lie for their sake.

"Well, don't tell me what it is," interrupted Mrs. Waterby. "Wait until it comes."

"I'll go after it."

He did go after it, although he had to drag a jeweller away from his home on Christmas-day and have him open his great safe. The ring which he selected was beyond his means, it is true, but when a man has to buy back his self-respect, the price is never too high.

The Lesson:

If jumping to conclusions was an Olympic sport, Mr. Waterby would be the gold medal winner. While it may be tempting to assume the worst when assessing another person's actions or motives, it is rarely helpful to you or to them—especially when that other person is a loved one. Suspicion and mistrust lead to bitterness and instability in our relationships. Nobody enjoys being wrongly accused, which is why I'm all for giving family members the benefit of the doubt. So, the next time someone's behavior puzzles you, remember Mr. and Mrs. Waterby and these four words: *Be curious, not judgmental*. Investigate and/or ask for clarification from the source before you jump to a negative conclusion. In doing so you'll retain your self-respect—and the respect of the other person.

The Galloping Pilgrim

From *Knocking the Neighbors*, 1912

A certain affluent Bachelor happened to be the only Grandson of a rugged Early Settler who wore a Coon-Skin Cap and drank Corn Juice[142] out of a Jug. Away back in the Days when every Poor Man had Bacon in the Smoke House, this Pioneer had been soaked in a Trade and found himself loaded up with a Swamp Subdivision in the Edge of Town.

Fifty years later the City had spread two miles beyond the Swamp and Grandson was submerged beneath so much Unearned Increment that he began to speak with what sounded to him like an English Accent and his Shirts were ordered from Paris.

On the 1st of every Month the Agents would crawl into the Presence of the Grandson of the mighty Muskrat Hunter and dump before him a Wagon-load of Paper Money which had been snatched away from the struggling Shop-Keepers, who, in turn, had wheedled it from the People who paid a Nickel apiece for Sunday Papers so as to look at the Pictures of the Decorations in the Supper Room at the Assembly Ball graced by the Presence of the aforesaid Bachelor whose Grandfather had lifted the original Catfish out of the Chicago River.

---

142. Whiskey made from corn.

Then the Representative of the Old Family would take a Garden Rake and pattern all this hateful Currency into a neat Mound, after which a milk-fed Secretary would iron it out and disinfect it and sprinkle it with Lilac Water and tie it into artistic Packets, using Old Gold Ribbon.

After that, it was Hard Lines for the Bachelor, because he had to sit by a window at the Club and dope out some new Way of getting all that Coin back into Circulation.

As a result of these Herculean Efforts to vaporize his Income, he found himself at the age of 40 afflicted with Social Gastritis. He had gorged himself with the Pleasures of this World until the sight of a Menu Card gave him the Willies and the mere mention of Musical Comedy would cause him to break down and Cry like a Child.

He had crossed the Atlantic so often that he no longer wished to sit at the Captain's Table. He had rolled them high at Monte Carlo and watched the Durbar[143] at Delhi and taken Tea on the Terrace at Shepheard's[144] in Cairo and rickshawed through Japan and ridden the surf in Honolulu, while his Name was a Household Word among the Barmaids of the Ice Palace in London, otherwise known as the Savoy.

Occasionally he would return to his provincial Home to raise the Rents on the Shop-Keepers and give out an Interview criticising the New School of Politicians for trifling with Vested Interests and seeking to disturb Existing Conditions.

Any time his Rake-Off was reduced from $10 a Minute to $9.98 he would let out a Howl like a Prairie Wolf and call upon Mortimer, his Man, for Sympathy.

After Twenty Years of getting up at Twilight to throw aside the Pyjamas and take a Tub and ease himself into the Costume made

---

143. British Indian word for any official meeting of importance. The most famous was the Delhi Durbar, an Indian imperial-style mass assembly organized by the British in Delhi, India to mark the succession of an Emperor or Empress of India.
144. The leading hotel in Cairo and one of the most celebrated hotels in the world from the middle of the 19th century.

famous by John Drew[145], the Routine of buying Golden Pheasants and Special Cuvee Vintages for almost-Ladies, preserved by Benzoate of Soda and other Chemical Mysteries, began to lose its Sharp Zest.

In other Words, he was All In.

He was Track-Sore and Blasé and full of Ongway. He had played the whole String and found there was nothing to it and now he was ready to retire to a Monastery and wear a Gunny-Sack Smoking Jacket and live on Spinach.

The Vanities of the Night-World had got on his Nerves at last. Instead of sitting 8 Feet away from an Imported Orchestra at 2 A. M. and taunting his poor old Alimentary System with Sea Food, he began to prefer to take a 10-Grain Sleeping Powder and fall back in the Alfalfa.

About Noon the next Day he would come up for Air, and in order to kill the rest of the Day he would have to hunt up a Game of Auction Bridge with three or four other gouty old Mavericks.

When the Carbons begin to burn low in the sputtering Arc Lights along the Boulevard of Pleasure and the Night Wind cuts like a Chisel and the Reveler finds his bright crimson Brannigan[146] slowly dissolving itself into a Bust Head, there is but one thing for a Wise Ike to do and that is to Chop on the Festivities and beat it to a Rest Cure.

That is just what the well-fixed Bachelor decided to do.

He resolved to Marry and get away from the Bright Lights and lie down somewhere in a quilted Dressing Gown and a pair of Soft Slippers and devote the remainder of his Life to a grand clean-up of the Works of Arnold Bennett[147].

He selected a well-seasoned Senorita who was still young

---

145. An Irish-American actor who was considered a matinee idol at the turn of the 20th century.
146. A drinking spree, especially Irish style.
147. A prolific English author.

The Galloping Pilgrim

enough to show to your Men Friends but old enough to cut out all the prevalent Mushgush about the Irish Drama and Norwegian Art and Buddhism and the true Symbolism of Russian Dancing.

Best of all, she had a spotless Reputation, holding herself down to one Bronx at a Time and always going behind a Screen to do her Inhaling.

They were Married according to the new Ceremonies devised by the Ringling Brothers. As they rode away to their Future Home, the old Stager leaned back in the Limousine and said: "At last the Bird has Lit. I am going to put on the Simple Life for an Indefinite Run. I have played the Hoop-La Game to a Standstill, so it is time for a Haven of Rest."

As soon as they were safely in their own Apartments, the beautiful Bride began to do Flip Flops and screech for Joy.

"At last I have a License to cut loose!" she exclaimed. "For years I have hankered and honed to be Dead Game and back Excitement right off the Cards, but every time I pulled a Caper the stern-faced Mater[148] would be at Elbow, saying: 'Nix on the Acrobatics or you'll lose your Number.' Now I'm a regular honest-to-goodness Married Woman and I don't recognize any Limit except the Sky-Line. I grabbed you because I knew you had been to all the Places that keep Open and could frame up a new Jamboree every day in the Year. I'm going to plow an 8-foot Furrow across Europe and Dine forevermore at Swell Joints where famous Show Girls pass so close to your Table that you can almost reach out and Touch them. I'm going to Travel 12 months every Year and do all the Stunts known to the most imbecile Globe-Trotter."

A few Weeks after that, a Haggard Man with tattered Coat-Tails was seen going over the old familiar Jumps.

---

148. From the Latin for Mother.

MORAL: *Those who Marry to Escape something usually find Something Else.*

The Lesson:

Some of the best marriage advice I've ever heard came not from a therapist but from a couple of excellent investors, namely Warren Buffett and his late partner, Charlie Munger. Why **not** take marriage and general partnership advice from successful investors? After all, marriage is one of the biggest investments you'll ever make, and you certainly want to be sure you're going into it with your eyes wide open. Here's what Munger and Buffett had to say on the topic:

> *"If you want to ruin your life, spend it trying to change your spouse,"* Munger said. *"It's really stupid."*
>
> *"Marrying somebody to change them is crazy,"* Buffett chimed in. *"And I would say hiring somebody to change him is just as crazy, and becoming partners with them to change them is crazy."*[149]

So sayeth the Oracle of Omaha and his Right-Hand Man. George would undoubtedly approve this message.

So too would he approve the thinking of Lee Kuan Yew, late Prime Minister of Singapore. When picking a spouse, you're doing more than just picking someone you think you can live with happily. Lee had this to say on the topic of marriage:

> *You marry a non-graduate, then you are going to worry if your son or daughter is going to make it to the university.*

---

149. Jane Thier, "Why Charlie Munger and Warren Buffett refused to buy companies with bad managers," https://fortune.com/2023/11/29/charlie-munger-warren-buffett-bad-managers/, accessed November 30, 2023.

Very often, Lee was on the radio or television talking about why he broke with Chinese custom and married a woman older than himself. He said it was because she was smarter than he was. He constantly hit home on the importance of marrying an educated, intelligent person. I was in Singapore when he gave a speech at the 1983 National Day Rally about the growing trend of highly educated women delaying or vetoing altogether marriage and children in favor of having a career. He was afraid that the trend would lead to a dilution of the gene pool and have an adverse effect on Singapore's economy. Thus he proposed a bold measure:

> *We must . . . amend our policies, and try to reshape our demographic configuration so that our better-educated women will have more children to be adequately represented in the next generation . . . Equal employment opportunities, yes, but we shouldn't get our women into jobs where they cannot, at the same time, be mothers . . . You just can't be doing a full-time heavy job like that of a doctor or engineer and run a home and bring up children.*[150]

I agree wholeheartedly. Your choice of a spouse dictates the genetics of your children and your society. Choose wisely.

---

150. Straits Times, "PM's National Day Rally Speech", August 15, 1983.

Mr. Payson's Satirical Christmas

From *In Babel: Stories of Chicago*, 1906

Mr. Sidney Payson was full of the bitterness of Christmas-tide. Mr. Payson was the kind of man who loved to tell invalids that they were not looking as well as usual, and who frightened young husbands by predicting that they would regret having married. He seldom put the seal of approval on any human undertaking. It was a matter of pride with him that he never failed to find the sinister motive for the act which other people applauded. Some of his pious friends used to say that Satan had got the upper hand with him, but there were others who indicated that it might be Bile.

Think of the seething wrath and the sense of humiliation with which Mr. Sidney Payson set about his Christmas-shopping! In the first place, to go shopping for Christmas-presents was the most conventional thing that any one could do, and Mr. Payson hated conventionalities. For another thing, the giving of Christmas-presents carried with it some testimony of affection, and Mr. Payson regarded any display of affection as one of the crude symptoms of barbarous taste.

If he could have assembled his relatives at a Christmas-gathering and opened a few old family wounds, reminding his brother and his two sisters of some of their youthful follies, thus shaming them before the children, Mr. Sidney Payson might have managed to make out a rather merry Christmas. Instead of that, he was condemned to go out and purchase gifts and be as cheaply idiotic as the other wretched mortals with whom he was being carried along. No wonder that he chafed and rebelled and vainly wished that he could hang crape[151] on every Christmas-tree in the universe.

Mr. Sidney Payson hated his task and he was puzzled by it. After wandering through two stores and looking in at twenty windows he had been unable to make one selection. It seemed to him that all the articles offered for sale were singularly and uniformly inappropriate. The custom of giving was a farce in itself, and the store-keepers had done what they could to make it a sickening travesty.

"I'll go ahead and buy a lot of things at haphazard," he said to himself. "I don't care a hang whether they are appropriate or not."

At that moment he had an inspiration. It was an inspiration which could have come to no one except Mr. Sidney Payson. It promised a speedy end to shopping hardships. It guaranteed him a Christmas to his own liking.

He was bound by family custom to buy Christmas-presents for his relatives. He had promised his sister that he would remember every one in the list. But he was under no obligation to give presents that would be welcome. Why not give to each of his relatives some present which would be entirely useless, inappropriate, and superfluous? It would serve them right for involving him in the childish performances of the Christmas-season. It would be a burlesque on the whole nonsensicality of Christmas-giving. It would irritate and puzzle his relatives and probably deepen their hatred

---

151. Old-fashioned spelling of crepe: thin wrinkled paper for making decorations. In this case, black crepe for a funeral.

of him. At any rate, it would be a satire on a silly tradition, and, thank goodness, it wouldn't be conventional.

Mr. Sidney Payson went into the first department store and found himself at the book-counter.

"Have you any work which would be suitable for an elderly gentleman of studious habits and deep religious convictions?" he asked.

"We have here the works of Flavius Josephus[152] in two volumes," replied the young woman.

"All right; I'll take them," he said. "I want them for my nephew Fred. He likes Indian stories."

The salesgirl looked at him wonderingly.

"Now, then, I want a love-story," said Mr. Payson. "I have a maiden sister who is president of a Ruskin club[153] and writes essays about Buddhism. I want to give her a book that tells about a girl named Mabel who is loved by Sir Hector Something-or-Other. Give me a book that is full of hugs and kisses and heaving bosoms and all that sort of rot. Get just as far away from Ibsen and Howells and Henry James as you can possibly get."

"Here is a book that all the girls in the store say is very good," replied the young woman. "It is called 'Virgie's Betrothal; or, the Stranger at Birchwood Manor.' It's by Imogene Sybil Beauclerc."

"If it's what it sounds to be, it's just what I want," said Payson, showing his teeth at the young woman with a devilish glee. "You say the girls here in the store like it?"

"Yes; Miss Simmons, in the handkerchief-box department, says it's just grand."

"Ha! All right! I'll take it."

He felt his happiness rising as he went out of the store. The joy shone in his face as he stood at the skate-counter.

---

152. A Roman-Jewish historian and military leader born in 37 AD.
153. The Ruskin Art Clubs, founded in 1888, promoted the arts and culture, and furthered women's causes.

"I have a brother who is forty-six years old and rather fat," he said to the salesman. "I don't suppose he's been on the ice in twenty-five years. He wears a No. 9 shoe. Give me a pair of skates for him."

A few minutes later he stood at the silk-counter.

"What are those things?" he asked, pointing to some gaily coloured silks folded in boxes.

"Those are scarfs."

"Well, if you've got one that has all the colours of the rainbow in it, I'll take it. I want one with lots of yellow and red and green in it. I want something that you can hear across the street. You see, I have a sister who prides herself on her quiet taste. Her costumes are marked by what you call 'unobtrusive elegance.' I think she'd rather die than wear one of those things, so I want the biggest and noisiest one in the whole lot."

The girl didn't know what to make of Mr. Payson's strange remarks, but she was too busy to be kept wondering.

Mr. Payson's sister's husband is the president of a church temperance society, so Mr. Payson bought him a buckhorn corkscrew.

There was one more present to buy.

"Let me see," said Mr. Payson. "What is there that could be of no earthly use to a girl six years old?"

Even as he spoke his eye fell on a sign: "Bargain sale of neckwear."

"I don't believe she would care for cravats," he said. "I think I'll buy some for her."

He saw a box of large cravats marked "25 cents each."

"Why are those so cheap?" he asked.

"Well, to tell the truth, they're out of style."

"That's good. I want eight of them—oh, any eight will do. I want them for a small niece of mine—a little girl about six years old."

Without indicating the least surprise, the salesman wrapped up the cravats.

Letters received by Mr. Sidney Payson in acknowledgment of his Christmas-presents:

1.

"Dear Brother: Pardon me for not having acknowledged the receipt of your Christmas-present. The fact is that since the skates came I have been devoting so much of my time to the re-acquiring of one of my early accomplishments that I have not had much time for writing. I wish I could express to you the delight I felt when I opened the box and saw that you had sent me a pair of skates. It was just as if you had said to me: 'Will, my boy, some people may think that you are getting on in years, but I know that you're not.' I suddenly remembered that the presents which I have been receiving for several Christmases were intended for an old man. I have received easy-chairs, slippers, mufflers, smoking-jackets, and the like. When I received the pair of skates from you I felt that twenty years had been lifted off my shoulders. How in the world did you ever happen to think of them? Did you really believe that my skating-days were not over? Well, they're *not*. I went to the pond in the park on Christmas-day and worked at it for two hours and I had a lot of fun. My ankles were rather weak and I fell down twice, fortunately without any serious damage to myself or the ice, but I managed to go through the motions, and before I left I skated with a smashing pretty girl. Well, Sid, I have you to thank. I never would have ventured on skates again if it had not been for you. I was a little stiff yesterday, but this morning I went out again and had a dandy time. I owe the renewal of my youth to you. Thank you many times, and believe me to be, as ever, your affectionate brother,

"WILLIAM."

2.

"Dear Brother: The secret is out! I suspected it all the time. It is needless for you to offer denial. Sometimes when you have acted the cynic I have almost believed that you were sincere, but each time I have been relieved to observe in you something which told me that underneath your assumed indifference there was a genial current of the romantic sentiment of the youth and the lover. How can I be in doubt after receiving a little book—a love-story?

"I knew, Sidney dear, that you would remember me at Christmas. You have always been the soul of thoughtfulness, especially to those of us who understood you. I must confess, however, that I expected you to do the deadly conventional thing and send me something heavy and serious. I knew it would be a book. All of my friends send me books. That comes of being president of a literary club. But you are the only one, Sidney, who had the rare and kindly judgment to appeal to the woman and not to the club president. Because I am interested in a serious literary movement it need not follow that I want my whole life to be overshadowed by the giants of the kingdom of letters. Although I would not dare confess it to Mrs. Peabody or Mrs. Hutchens, there are times when I like to spend an afternoon with an old-fashioned love story.

"You are a bachelor, Sidney, and as for me, I have long since ceased to blush at the casual mention of 'old maid.' It was not for us to know the bitter-sweet experiences of courtship and marriage, and you will remember that we have sometimes pitied the headlong infatuation of sweethearts and have felt rather superior in our freedom. And yet, Sidney, if we chose to be perfectly candid with each other, I dare say that both of us would confess to having known something about that which men call *love*. We might confess that we had felt its subtle influence, at times and places, and with a stirring uneasiness, as one detects a draught. We might go so far as to admit that sometimes we pause in our lonely lives and wonder what might have been and whether it would not have been better, after all. I am afraid that I am writing like a sentimental school-girl, but you must know that I have been reading your charming little book, and it has come to me as a message from you. Is it not really a confession, Sidney?

"You have made me very happy, dear brother. I feel more closely drawn to you than at any time since we were all together at Christmas, at the old home. Come and see me. Your loving sister,

"GERTRUDE."

3.

"Dear Brother: Greetings to you from the happiest household in town, thanks to a generous Santa Claus in the guise of Uncle Sidney. I must begin by thanking you on my own account. How in the world did you ever learn that Roman colours[154] had come in again? I have always heard that men did not follow the styles and could not be trusted to select anything for a woman, but it is a libel, a base libel, for the scarf which you sent is quite the most *beautiful* thing I have received this Christmas. I have it draped over the large picture in the parlour, and it is the envy of every one who has been in to-day. A *thousand, thousand* thanks, dear Sidney. It was perfectly sweet of you to remember me, and I call it nothing less than a stroke of genius to think of anything so appropriate and yet so much out of the ordinary.

"John asks me to thank you—but I must tell you the story. One evening last week we had a little chafing-dish party after prayer-meeting, and I asked John to open a bottle of olives for me. Well, he broke the small blade of his knife trying to get the cork

---

154. The bright colors favored by Ancient Romans in clothing and décor.

out. He said: 'If I live to get downtown again, I'm going to buy a corkscrew.' Fortunately he had neglected to buy one, and so your gift seemed to come straight from Providence. John is very much pleased. Already he has found use for it, as it happened that he wanted to open a bottle of household ammonia the very first thing this morning.

"As for Fred's lovely books, thank goodness you didn't send him any more story-books. John and I have been trying to induce him to take up a more serious line of reading. The Josephus ought to help him in the study of his Sunday-school lessons. We were pleased to observe that he read it for about an hour this morning.

"When you were out here last fall did Genevieve tell you that she was collecting silk for a doll quilt? She insists that she did not, but she must have done so, for how could you have guessed that she wants pieces of silk above anything else in the world? The perfectly lovely cravats which you sent will more than complete the quilt, and I think that mamma will get some of the extra pieces for herself. Fred and Genevieve send love and kisses. John insists that you come out to dinner some Sunday very soon—next Sunday if you can. After we received your presents we were quite ashamed of the box we had sent over to your hotel, but we will try to make up the difference in heart-felt gratitude. Don't forget—any Sunday. Your loving sister,

"KATHERINE."

It would be useless to tell what Mr. Sidney Payson thought of himself after he received these letters.

The Lesson:

The lesson here is self-evident.

Away From Home (An Excerpt)

From *Single Blessedness*, 1922

..."**D**on't Worry" should be painted on every piece of luggage. Travelling together through the dark woods of an unfamiliar region is the supreme test of compatibility. Prolonged propinquity induces irritability. Solitary confinement with another person present is a terrible punishment. The greatest risk of travel arises from too much forced companionship. Happy and much out of the ordinary is the wanderer who doesn't get fed up on his playmates.

We feel compelled to travel in groups, and the members of the party are literally thrown upon each other for hours and hours at a time. Someone has to manage and be spokesman, and if he can hold the job to the satisfaction of all the persons concerned, he is a seven-times wonder . . .

. . . If travellers act loony (and they do) probably two thirds of the afflictions which threaten to unhinge reason are wished upon them by friends and relatives. Every day a hundred petty problems present themselves. They are of no importance whatever except to an overchafed imagination. Regard them with smiling indifference, and you ride over without a bump. Keep on tearing the hair and wringing the hands and, after a while, every mole hill will look like the Himalaya Mountains.

The happy pilgrims are those who do not attempt to move in a herd all of the time. The thing to do is to go bravely up to your good friend and travel mate and say, "Comrade, I have inspected you at close range until your well-known personality has lost all the charm of novelty. I could write a book on the technique which you employ in opening eggs. The slightly audible effects which you originate when gathering coffee from the cup have ceased to be music to my ears. I know that your character is still unimpeachable and you have lost none of the rugged virtues which give you a high standing in our golf club at home, but I am dead weary of seeing your Adam's apple in action. In other words, dear friend, you have got on my nerves, and I have no doubt whatever that you would be happy to gaze at a landscape once in awhile without discovering me in the foreground wearing the same old suit of clothes. Therefore I suggest that, at the next stop, you go to the Continental and I will go to the Bristol and each will do as he blame pleases for three days, and then, when we get together again, we can look at each other without shuddering."

The tantrums which the amateur traveller exhibits when he is far from home could be headed off if he would take a short course in Christian Science before booking his passage. Drench your spirit with a don't-care attitude. Acknowledge, with a smile, that the biggest fool job in the world is to attempt to reconstruct the inevitable according to your private plans and specifications. If you have become so ossified by habit that you cannot put up with the manners and customs and transportation facilities and cooking and cocktails of the older civilizations, the thing for you to do is to stay at home and watch the trains go through.

Once I heard a man, standing in front of the Café de Paris, say that he couldn't get anything to eat in Paris. He meant that he couldn't get thin beefsteak that had been pounded with a potato masher and then rolled in flour and fried with onions.

Have you ever met the family that went to Europe in search of culture and came back with the news that all the coffee had chicory in it?

Seeing the outside world is the most diverting and profitable of all employments, after one has learned the simple recipe of sitting back relaxed; refusing to be frightened by imaginary pitfalls, and declining to worry over some experience that is rapidly sliding into the past tense.

Beyond every frontier lies a country which has spent many centuries in arranging its own domestic affairs to suit the resident population. When you drop in from Missouri or Michigan, the clever thing to do is to accept the local arrangements and not try to be a missionary.

Also, remember that you are on a visit and not attending a vaudeville performance. There is no need of exploiting the far-famed nasal accent. You can't get rid of it, but you can omit the tin megaphone. Many of the ladies living in Europe twitter instead of talk. We haven't many of the twittering kind here at home. Our women-folks converse. It sounds all right until you hear it shattering the deathly stillness of the *salle à manger* somewhere on the Continent, and then it sounds just like a billboard advertisement of the U.S.A.

Travellers cease to be painfully abnormal in their habits when they learn that all the beaten paths are smooth, and all the arrangements foolproof, and the ticket which secures kind treatment is the friendly spirit, with unfailing courtesy attached as a coupon . . .

The Lesson:

This wise advice was of great use to me during the decades that I lived and worked overseas. While so many of my fellow Americans,

Australians and Europeans succumbed to culture shock in Asia, I did not. There are many books written about culture shock—what it is, how to avoid it, what to do if you get it. The best and simplest advice is that which is given here by George. It worked for me.

Effie Whittlesey

From *In Babel: Stories of Chicago*, 1906

rs. Wallace assisted her husband to remove his overcoat and put her warm palms against his red and wind-beaten cheeks.

"I have good news," said she.

"Another bargain sale?"

"Pshaw, no! A new girl, and I really believe she's a jewel. She isn't young or good-looking, and when I asked her if she wanted any nights off she said she wouldn't go out after dark for anything in the world. What do you think of that?"

"That's too good to be true."

"No, it isn't. Wait and see her. She came here from the intelligence office about two o'clock and said she was willing to 'lick right in.' You wouldn't know the kitchen. She has it as clean as a pin."

"What nationality?"

"None—that is, she's a home product. She's from the country—and *green!* But she's a good soul, I'm sure. As soon as I looked at her, I just felt sure that we could trust her."

"Well, I hope so. If she is all that you say, why, for goodness sake give her any pay she wants—put lace curtains in her room and subscribe for all the story papers on the market."

"Bless you, I don't believe she'd read them. Every time I've looked into the kitchen she's been working like a Trojan and singing 'Beulah Land.'"

"Oh, she sings, does she? I knew there'd be some draw-back."

"You won't mind that. We can keep the doors closed."

The dinner-table was set in tempting cleanliness. Mrs. Wallace surveyed the arrangement of glass and silver and gave a nod of approval and relief. Then she touched the bell and in a moment the new servant entered.

She was a tall woman who had said her last farewell to girlhood.

Then a very strange thing happened.

Mr. Wallace turned to look at the new girl and his eyes enlarged. He gazed at her as if fascinated either by cap or freckles. An expression of wonderment came to his face and he said: "Well, by George!"

The girl had come very near the table when she took the first overt glance at him. Why did the tureen sway in her hands? She smiled in a frightened way and hurriedly set the tureen on the table.

Mr. Wallace was not long undecided, but during that moment of hesitancy the panorama of his life was rolled backward. He had been reared in the democracy of a small community, and the democratic spirit came uppermost.

"This isn't Effie Whittlesy?" said he.

"For the land's sake!" she exclaimed, backing away, and this was a virtual confession.

"You don't know me."

"Well, if it ain't Ed Wallace!"

Would that words were ample to tell how Mrs. Wallace settled back in her chair blinking first at her husband and then at the new girl, vainly trying to understand what it meant.

She saw Mr. Wallace reach awkwardly across the table and shake hands with the new girl and then she found voice to gasp: "Of all things!"

Mr. Wallace was confused and without a policy. He was wavering between his formal duty as an employer and his natural regard for an old friend. Anyway, it occurred to him that an explanation would be timely.

"This is Effie Whittlesy from Brainerd," said he. "I used to go to school with her. She's been at our house often. I haven't seen her for—I didn't know you were in Chicago," turning to Effie.

"Well, Ed Wallace, you could knock me down with a feather," said Effie, who still stood in a flustered attitude a few paces back from the table. "I had no more idee when I heard the name Wallace that it'd be you, though knowin', of course, you was up here. Wallace is such a common name I never give it a second thought. But the minute I seen you—law! I knew who it was, well enough."

"I thought you were still at Brainerd," said Mr. Wallace, after a pause.

"I left there a year ago November, and come to visit Mort's people. I s'pose you know that Mort has a position with the street-car company. He's doin' *so* well. I didn't want to be no burden on him, so I started out on my own hook, seein' that there was no use of goin' back to Brainerd to slave for two dollars a week. I had a good place with Mr. Sanders, the railroad man on the north side, but I left becuz they wanted me to serve liquor. I'd about as soon handle a toad as a bottle of beer. Liquor was the ruination of Jesse. He's gone to the dogs—been off with a circus somewheres for two years."

"The family's all broken up, eh!" asked Mr. Wallace.

"Gone to the four winds since mother died. Of course you know that Lora married Huntford Thomas and is livin' on the old Murphy place. They're doin' about as well as you could expect, with Huntford as lazy as he is."

"Yes? That's good," said Mr. Wallace.

Was this an old settlers' reunion or a quiet family dinner. The soup had been waiting.

Mrs. Wallace came into the breach.

"That will be all for the present, Effie," said she.

Effie gave a startled "Oh!" and vanished into the kitchen.

"What does this mean?" asked Mrs. Wallace, turning to her husband, who had lain back in his chair to relieve himself with silent laughter.

"It means," said Mr. Wallace, "that we were children together, made mud pies in the same puddle and sat next to each other in the old school-house at Brainerd. She is a Whittlesy. Everybody in Brainerd knew the Whittlesys. Large family, all poor as church mice, but sociable—and freckled. Effie's a good girl."

"Effie! *Effie!* And she called you Ed!"

"My dear, there are no misters in Brainerd. Why shouldn't she call me 'Ed'? She never heard me called anything else."

"She'll have to call you something else here. You tell her so."

"Now, don't ask me to put on any airs with one of the Whittlesys, because they know me from away back. Effie has seen me licked at school. She has been at our house, almost like one of the family, when mother was sick and needed another girl. If my memory serves me right, I've taken her to singing-school and exhibitions. So I'm in no position to lord it over her, and I wouldn't do it any way. I'd hate to have her go back to Brainerd and report that she met me here in Chicago and I was too stuck up to remember old times and requested her to address me as 'Mister Wallace.' Now, you never lived in a small town."

"No, I never enjoyed that privilege," said Mrs. Wallace, dryly.

"Well, it is a privilege in some respects, but it carries certain penalties with it, too. It's a very poor schooling for a fellow who wants to be a snob."

"I wouldn't call it snobbishness to correct a servant who addresses me by my first name. 'Ed' indeed! Why, I never dared to call you that."

"No, you never lived in Brainerd."

"And you say you used to take her to singing-school?"

"Yes, ma'am—twenty years ago, in Brainerd. You're not surprised, are you? You knew when you married me that I was a child of the soil, who worked his way through college and came to the city in a suit of store clothes. I'll admit that my past does not exactly qualify me for the Four Hundred[155], but it will be great if I ever get into politics."

"I don't object to your having a past, but I was just thinking how pleasant it will be when we give a dinner-party to have her come in and address you as 'Ed.'"

Mr. Wallace patted the table-cloth cheerily with both hands and laughed.

"I really don't believe you'd care," said Mrs. Wallace.

"Effie isn't going to demoralise the household," he said, consolingly. "Down in Brainerd we may be a little slack on the by-laws of etiquette, but we can learn in time."

Mrs. Wallace touched the bell and Effie returned.

As she brought in the second course, Mr. Wallace deliberately encouraged her by an amiable smile, and she asked, "Do you get the Brainerd papers?"

"Yes—every week."

"There's been a good deal of sickness down there this winter. Lora wrote to me that your uncle Joe had been kind o' poorly."

"I think he's up and around again."

"That's good."

And she edged back to the kitchen.

With the change for dessert she ventured to say: "Mort was wonderin' about you the other day. He said he hadn't saw you for a long time. My! You've got a nice house here."

---

155. A term created by Ward McAllister (the 1880s version of an influencer) who said that there were only 400 people in fashionable New York society. "If you go outside that number," McAllister said, "you strike people who are either not at ease in a ballroom or else make other people not at ease."

After dinner Mrs. Wallace published her edict. Effie would have to go. Mr. Wallace positively forbade the "strong talking-to" which his wife advocated. He said it was better that Effie should go, but she must be sent away gently and diplomatically.

Effie was "doing up" the dishes when Mr. Wallace lounged into the kitchen and began a roundabout talk. His wife, seated in the front room, heard the prolonged murmur. "Ed" and Effie were going over the family histories of Brainerd and recalling incidents that may have related to mud pies or school exhibitions.

Mrs. Wallace had been a Twombley, of Baltimore, and no Twombley, with relatives in Virginia, could humiliate herself into rivalry with a kitchen girl, or dream of such a thing, so why should Mrs. Wallace be uneasy and constantly wonder what Ed and Effie were talking about?

Mrs. Wallace was faint from the loss of pride. The night before they had dined with the Gages. Mr. Wallace, a picture of distinction in his evening clothes, had shown himself the bright light of the seven who sat at the table. She had been proud of him. Twenty-four hours later a servant emerges from the kitchen and hails him as "Ed"!

The low talk in the kitchen continued. Mrs. Wallace had a feverish longing to tip-toe down that way and listen, or else go into the kitchen, sweepingly, and with a few succinct commands, set Miss Whittlesy back into her menial station. But she knew that Mr. Wallace would misinterpret any such move and probably taunt her with joking references to her "jealousy," so she forbore.

Mr. Wallace, with an unlighted cigar in his mouth (Effie had forbidden him to smoke in the kitchen), leaned in the doorway and waited to give the conversation a turn.

At last he said: "Effie, why don't you go down and visit Lora for a month or so? She'd be glad to see you."

"I know, Ed, but I ain't no Rockefeller to lay off work a month at a time an' go around visitin' my relations. I'd like to well enough—but—"

"O pshaw! I can get you a ticket to Brainerd to-morrow and it won't cost you anything down there."

"No, it ain't Chicago, that's a fact. A dollar goes a good ways down there. But what'll your wife do? She told me to-day she'd had an awful time gettin' any help."

"Well—to tell you the truth, Effie, you see—you're an old friend of mine and I don't like the idea of your being here in my house as a—well, as a hired girl."

"No, I guess I'm a servant now. I used to be a hired girl when I worked for your ma, but now I'm a servant. I don't see as it makes any difference what you call me, as long as the work's the same."

"You understand what I mean, don't you? Any time you come here to my house I want you to come as an old acquaintance—a visitor, not a servant."

"Ed Wallace, don't be foolish. I'd as soon work for you as any one, and a good deal sooner."

"I know, but I wouldn't like to see my wife giving orders to an old friend, as you are. You understand, don't you?"

"I don't know. I'll quit if you say so."

"Tut! tut! I'll get you that ticket and you can start for Brainerd to-morrow. Promise me, now."

"I'll go, and tickled enough, if that's the way you look at it."

"And if you come back, I can get you a dozen places to work."

Next evening Effie departed by carriage, although protesting against the luxury.

"Ed Wallace," said she, pausing in the hallway, "they never will believe me when I tell it in Brainerd."

"Give them my best and tell them I'm about the same as ever."

"I'll do that. Good-bye."

"Good-bye."

Mrs. Wallace, watching from the window, saw Effie disappear into the carriage.

"Thank goodness," said she.

"Yes," said Mr. Wallace, to whom the whole episode had been like a cheering beverage, "I've invited her to call when she comes back."

"To call—here?"

"Most assuredly. I told her you'd be delighted to see her at any time."

"The idea! Did you invite her, really?"

"Of course I did! And I'm reasonably certain that she'll come."

"What shall I do?"

"I think you can manage it, even if you never did live in Brainerd."

Then the revulsion came and Mrs. Wallace, with a full return of pride in her husband, said she would try.

The Lesson:

How deeply ingrained are Hoosier, small town and country cultural norms? On my first overseas assignment to Manila, Philippines we needed to hire a household staff. It was near impossible to run a small mansion in the Third World without servants. The modern conveniences of dishwashers, washers, dryers, vacuum cleaners, etc. etc. were not generally in use. And even when they were the electricity was so unreliable that they were ineffective closet ornaments much of the time. Or they blew out the electricity if used for more than a couple minutes. Air conditioning? One window rattler in our bedroom. If we were lucky enough it ran all night.

So we began to staff our house: maids, cook, gardener and security guards (this last position was mandatory and required by our employer, Phillips Petroleum). The company had a roster of household staff that had been vetted by other company employees. One of the higher-level executives was rotating out as we rotated in and gave an enthusiastic recommendation for his housekeeper, Priscilla.

We had no experience with household staff whatsoever. Priscilla had been a licensed high school teacher in the Philippines, but she had given it up because working as a maid for expatriate Americans paid much better. She had a daughter aged seven, and working as a housekeeper allowed her to spend more time with her daughter. She said she could also do the cooking as well as the housekeeping if we would allow her to use the extra space in the servants quarters for her daughter. It was a great deal . . . room and board plus what amounted to about $5 per day in 2023 dollars.

My wife Laurel was working on her master's degree at the University of the Philippines during the day, while I was working downtown with Phillips. I'll always remember coming home to our first meal prepared by our new cook and housekeeper. Everything was set up beautifully. Dinner was served on our patio outside the kitchen by the swimming pool. As Priscilla brought the food out, we invited her and her daughter to sit at the table and join us for dinner.

"Oh no! No, no!" she cried. "We cannot eat at the table. It is not permitted." And our Filipina teacher with a master's degree carefully explained to us how class structure operated in the Philippines. Under no condition whatsoever was she permitted to sit in our presence. She was not even allowed to eat the same food that she prepared for us. Priscilla had at her command the entire Philippines compendium of Emily Post etiquette. (The reader might recall virtually any scene in the movie *Gone with the Wind* when Mammy would object to any change of class traditions by saying, "It just ain't fittin'.")

It took us a while to absorb what Priscilla said. But it was the culture, and there was no use trying to change it or we would lose our housekeeper and cook! I thought back on George's "Effie Whittlesey" story and realized how much of a cultural Hoosier from Newton County I really was.

Surrounding our lovely mansion in the Manila suburb of

Greenhills were cinderblock walls topped with broken glass and barbed wire. Every mansion in the subdivision was a small fort and the gate into our private community had armed guards. We had a day guard on patrol at our house and a night guard. Security was tight because of crime and the threat from the New People's Army, a communist guerilla group. Priscilla saw to it that our guards were very well fed.

George Ade was known to never lock the doors to his house at Hazelden. My parents also never locked their doors. When they passed away my sisters and I were unable to find the key to the door of the old farmhouse.

Yes, I learned a lot from reading George's writings. They helped me with my life and my career. I also learned to value very much the traditional American Hoosier culture that I grew up in.

Chicago High Art Up to Date

From *Stories of the Streets and of the Town*, 1941

The epidemic at present raging among art students of Chicago made its appearance in a virulent form about one year ago. [circa 1890s]

There had been a few scattered cases before that time, but the malady had not taken a firm hold and the bacilli were not yet generally distributed.

The disease should be known as "Beardsley-ism," although its victims generally regard it as high art, up to date. Aubrey Beardsley[156], a young Englishman, deliberately started the trouble and succeeded in having himself talked about and imitated, which is practically the same as being successful.

Something like his pictures had been carved on the walls of the temple of Luxor many centuries ago. Japanese artists who decorated fans and vases had anticipated his style to a degree and generations of amateurs in all ages and countries made pictures of men with necks too long and bodies too short and whiskers done in scroll-work—little suspecting how near they had come to greatness.

---

156. Beardsley was an English author and illustrator who was active in the 1890s. He was associated with Aestheticism, the British equivalent of Decadence and Symbolism. Interestingly, he founded what was known as "The Yellow Book", a quarterly illustrated literary magazine. See the next chapter for insight into what George thought of that!

. . .

The old-fashioned way of learning to draw pictures was to study perspective, light and shade, exact form, anatomy and a few other things. Students went to the Art Institute and sketched for hours at a time to get Hercules absolutely correct, with every tracery of muscle shown.

They studied the ancient models of statuary and the paintings which revealed the speaking likenesses of men and women.

That was before the malady appeared. Mr. Beardsley's pictures came along and the traditions of thirty centuries were shattered.

The new kind of art demonstrated that a woman's neck is shaped like the letter S, that the waist may be thin to nothingness, that the hair may be of the outline of pruning hooks.

Mr. Beardsley's strongest "things" consisted of great dashes of circling black lines with a pair of frightened eyes peering through the bubbling mass of spaghetti.

There were hands which had three tines each, like a fork, and there were figures which careened sidewise in violation of all known laws of gravity and had apparently been dried over a barrel.

This is not an art criticism. It is a simple account of the kind of pictures that allured the amateurs. They found that to be great they must forget all about anatomy, proportion or laws of light and shade, and let their imagination run amuck in circles and streaks of black.

The amateur who had despaired of becoming an illustrator suddenly learned that he or she could be a genius. In the new school it was possible for any student to draw things which were perfectly unintelligible.

One young man in Chicago adopted the boldness of the style, eliminated the utter insanity, utilized the decorative effect of striking contrast, and, by reason of the fad, made a reputation as a designer, bringing some good out of the mess of evil.

Sketching from a Model

But the ordinary victim of the epidemic was content to follow the weird suggestions of Mr. Beardsley. If it were an ear to be drawn he made it come to a point on top. Why? Because an ear isn't shaped like a Bartlett pear, and to draw it so suggests original conception. Besides, do the critics know that when the artist looks at the human ear it doesn't appear to him to be shaped like a pear?

Those stricken by the epidemic love to make pictures of cats—cats with bodies too long, with black pegs for legs and fish-spears for tails. Of course no cat ever had a fish-spear where the tail should be and probably is. The fish-spear notion is a flash of genius.

Be different. That's the motto of all who are taken down. At all times be so different that people laugh at your pictures. Then you have not only genius, but genius persecuted for art's sake.

"They'll come around in time," said an instructor. "Just now they're drawing shell-eyed women with worms in their hair, but they'll get over that all right. Most of them will. Others will have to be cared for. We had something of the same trouble when Oscar Wilde came over here."

The Lesson:

Since joining TIGER 21 and R360 I have encountered many art festivals and met many artists. Based on my own experiences most of what my friends and associates buy as art is no more than autograph collecting. Without the signature even the so-called professional art critics can't tell the real from the fake, the original from the copy. The so-called *avant garde* or modern art or stream of consciousness movements in literature all leave me cold, as do the Cubists and abstract artists who appear to me to be merely lazy.

One artist, who has asked that his name be withheld, demonstrated this by throwing paint over his shoulder onto a canvas and then signing it. He then sold it via an art auction house together with his bona fide work. It brought near the same amount as his serious paintings, circa $100,000. Caveat emptor.

I have a better collection of art than most of my peers; I have several of my grandchildren's superb pieces. Side by side with Picasso, no one can tell which is which unless they look at the autograph.

Yellow! Yellow! The Poet of the New School Speaks

From *Verses and Jingles*, 1911

I'm great and
I know it.
People can't understand me.
I can't understand myself.
I don't want to.
If I did understand myself
I wouldn't be great.
Listen now:
—*The moon reels and the*
Phantom passes twice and thrice
The death damp hand
Across my brow.
O what of joy?
O what of grief?
Darkness—blank—a sob in the throat.
O phantom, phantom, phantom!—
Pretty good, eh?
Especially if it has
Some little, smudgy, inky

Pictures strung along the edges.
I used to write about
Men and women, back yards,
Plain courtships, flowers and other things
That people understood.
Now I write lines that have
No meaning, because they are
Fragments of dreams that
Were never dreamt.
—*A soul writhed long*
In its purple belongings.
O *drip of blood!*
O *drip of blood!*
Caught up in the wan hand of sleep
And clotted with the dawn.—
Do you notice the "O"—
The upper-case "O"?
I use that a great deal.
If anyone will tell me
What I am writing about
I will let him smoke my
Opium pipe all afternoon.
These little, twisted,
Ugly, whirligig pictures
Have nothing to do with
The lines I am writing.
If I tell about a midnight trance,
I have a picture of a sunrise.
If the lines mention something
About a maiden with snaky hair
The picture is that of a demon
With a forked tail.

This is genius.
The world didn't find it out
Until last year.
There are but two colors
In all this world—yellow
And another shade of yellow.
I am very yellow myself,
But people say I am great.
I write my stuff on yellow paper
And use yellow ink.
Excuse me for awhile,
I'm full of hop.[157]

The Lesson:

Stephen Hawking once said, "The fact that no one understands you doesn't mean you're an artist." I am certain that George would have agreed with that statement, as evidenced by the preceding essay on "Chicago High Art" and this poem. George was of the realist school of literature. His fiction fit into reality and could have happened. He came up into literature through journalism and investigative reporting.

Unlike the fictional poet above, George was not a fan of pretentiousness, posturing and self-importance. He did not take himself too seriously. He did, however, take his relationships, integrity, education and work seriously. Those he guarded with all his might.

O, but what a fine way to be!

Figuring out how to enjoy the pleasures of life while still adhering to your values . . . exhibiting the type of self-confidence that never makes the leap to pompousness . . . learning how to make

---

157. Slang for "full of nonsense." Also slang for opium, heroin, or other narcotic or psychoactive drugs.

light of your foibles without lowering yourself . . . these are the marks of a mature, well-adjusted person.

My final word on this subject, Dear Reader: if I ever change my mind on this so-called high art and literature, I intend to seek psychiatric care.

Whirligigs

From *Single Blessedness*, 1922

The boy you knew back in grammar school, the one locally groomed for the U. S. Senate—what became of him? Driving a taxi right back there in the old home town.

And silent Edgar, who was not good enough for the ball team? Merely president of the J. P. and H.

We live in a land of opportunity—and blow-ups.

Did any other part of the globe, at any time, ever witness such meteoric flashes across the open firmament or such cataclysmal collapses into the soft mud?

In older regions, where usages have petrified, each individual may find himself wedged and locked into a numbered social stratum and destined to remain there.

Over here, the facilities for going up in balloons and falling down elevator shafts are glorious and unexcelled.

The well-known team of Presto and Change is doing legerdemain[158] in every centre of population. Now you see them and now you don't see them!

If you want to check up on the sensational upsets and sky-rocket ascensions, do not figure a man merely from one birthday to

---

158. Deceit, trickery.

another. Invoice him at twenty and, after that, leave him alone until he is fifty. Then add him up. Compare the ratings.

Youth is heedless and cannot be warned, because it commands no perspective of the years. It never has seen towering notables peter away to wilted remnants, while plodding yokels grew into giants and sat on their thrones as if they had been born under purple hangings.

It isn't the start that counts, here in the land of whirligigs. It's the finish.

Trunk lines heading for the most important destinations go through a lot of scrubby waystations.

The traveller picked up by an avalanche and carried to nameless depths of oblivion passes a lot of superior scenery on the way down.

The point being that our immediate background this afternoon doesn't matter so much, but it is most important to know which way our little solitaire special is headed.

A most revealing occupation is to get out the family album and review the biographies of those dudes and debutantes who were in bud about the time of the World's Fair in Chicago.

Discover, if you can, why Fate seems to work with a dice-box instead of a T-square.

Try to explain why the most theatrical matrimonial alliances finish on the rocks, wrecked to a fare-ye-well.

Regard the painful smash-ups which waited for young people who inherited money and were supposed to be "lucky."

Learn by deduction that money doesn't care to whom it belongs.

Good repute can be switched on and off, like an electric current.

Why call it a melting-pot? It's a churn.

The Lesson:

So very true. So very American.

In the Philippines and many countries overseas the class you are born into is almost certainly the class you will die in. Not so here.

One of the interesting things in the chapters of TIGER 21 and R360 where I am partner is the number of recent immigrants who are members of these ultra-high net worth societies. Many of them are children of parents who arrived penniless in the United States, especially from Cuba and other communist countries.

They come to America, because here they have freedom. If they work hard, they can make and save a lot of money, and be free of degradation, poverty and want under communism and other authoritarian dictatorships.

It works the other way too. One of the founding partners of R360, Michael Cole, wrote a book called *More Than Money* in which he outlines how the typical wealthy family goes through three phases—"shirt sleeves to shirt sleeves in three generations", "rice paddies to rice paddies in three generations", "clogs to clogs in three generations", and so on. Losing the family fortune is a trait that transcends all cultures and all nations. Certainly this has been true in my family. Our farm was facing bankruptcy in 1984 when I assumed the debts.

About the same time that George was writing "Whirligigs" Theodore Roosevelt wrote his famous "Man in the Arena" speech and the British poet Rudyard Kipling wrote "If." The freedom to succeed and the freedom to fail; it seems you can't have one without the other. Frank Borman, former chairman of the now extinct Eastern Airlines, once said, "Capitalism without bankruptcy is like Christianity without hell."[159] A very pithy observation indeed.

---

159. *Forbes*, June 8, 1981.

The Married Couple That Went to Housekeeping and Began to Find Out Things

From *People You Know*, 1903

Once there was a Happy Young Pair, each of whom got stuck on the Photograph of the other and thereupon a Marriage was arranged by Mail.

Shortly after taking the Life Risk, they started in to get acquainted. Up to the time that they moved into the Arcadian Flats and began to take Orders from the Janitor, he never had seen little Sunshine except in her Evening Frock.

He had a sort of sneaking Suspicion that she arose every Morning already attired in a Paris Gown and all the Diamonds.

And she supposed that he went to the Office every Day in his regular John Drew effect with the Folding Hat.

After she began to see Hubby around the Flat in his Other Clothes the Horrible Truth dawned upon her that he was not such a Hot Swell as he had looked to be in the Bunko Photograph.

Sometimes, on Rainy Sundays, he would cut out the Morning Service and decide not to Shave, and then when she got a good long Look at him, she would begin to doubt her own Judgment.

And so far as that is concerned, there were Mornings, after they had been out Late to a Welsh Rabbit Party, when she was a little Lumpy, if any one should ask.

Love's Young Dream was handed several goshawful Whacks about the Time that they started in to get a Line on each other.

For instance, the first Morning at Breakfast it came out that her Idea of a Dainty Snack with which to usher in the Day was a Lettuce Sandwich, a Couple of Olives and a Child's Cup full of Cocoa, while he wanted $35 worth of Ham and Eggs, a stack of Griddle Cakes and a Tureen of Coffee.

She was a case of Ambrosia and Nectar and he was plain old Ham and Spinach.

Inhaling It

It used to give her Hysterics to see him bark at an Ear of Green Corn, at the same time making a Sound like a Dredge.

For Dinner she liked a little Consommé en Tasse and then a Nice Salad, while he insisted on a Steak the size of a Door Mat and German Fried to come along.

They did not Mocha and Java at all on their Reading Matter. She liked Henry James and Walter Pater[160] and he preferred Horse Papers and the Comic Supplement. Sometimes when she would wander off into the Realms of Poesy he would follow her as far as he could, and then sit down and wait for her to get through rambling and come back.

If they took in a Show she was always plugging for Mrs. Fiske[161] or Duse[162], while he claimed that Rogers Brothers were better than Booth and Barrett had been in their Prime.

She could weep over a Tosti Serenade, and he would walk a Mile at any time to see a good Buck Dance[163].

When they got around to fixing up Invitation Lists, there was more or less Geeing and Hawing.

All of his Friends belonged to the Hit-emup Division. Their only Conception of a Happy Evening was to put the Buck in the Centre of the Table, break a fresh Pack and go out for Blood.

Wifey found her most delirious Joy in putting passionate Shades on all the Lamps, and sitting there in the Crimson Glow to discuss Maeterlinck[164] and Maarten Maartens[165] and a few others that were New Ones on the he-end of the Sketch.

When they had an Evening At Home up in the Flat, it was

---

160. An English essayist, art and literary critic, and fiction writer, regarded as one of the great stylists.
161. Minnie Maddern Fiske, billed simply as Mrs. Fiske, was one of the leading American actresses of the late 19th and early 20th century.
162. Eleonora Giulia Amalia Duse, often known simply as Duse, was an Italian actress, rated by many as the greatest of her time.
163. A type of folk dance, like clogging, where the dancer's footwear is used percussively.
164. A Belgian playwright.
165. A Dutch writer.

usually a two-ring Affair. She would have the Cerebellums in the Front Room looking at the New Books and eating Peppermint Wafers, while he and the other Comanches would be out in the Dining-Room trying to make their House Rent and tossing off that which made Scotland famous. Sometimes it would take half the Night to get the Smoke out of the House.

Although she feared that she had turned up the wrong Street while searching for her Affinity, the Partnership Arrangement had to stand.

They came to the Conclusion that Married Life is a Series of Compromises. If he did well while sitting in with some of his Friends, he would divide up with her and she would take the Money and buy Art Pastels.

He would spot the Afternoons on which the Ethical Researchers were due at his Premises and he would go to a Dutch Restaurant.

She permitted him to have a Room and call it his Den, so that he and his Friends could do the Escape in case somebody in the Parlor started a Reading.

He put up the Coin to enable her to attend State Conventions, and when she was elected Recording Secretary of the Society for trying to find out what Browning was up to, he took her Picture around to all the News-papers and told every one that he had a little Woman up at the House who was as Keen as a Hawk, as Swift as an Eagle, and Sharper than Chained Lightning.

He fumbled a great many of her In-Shoots, but that did not prevent him from admiring her Delivery.

Finally they arranged their separate Schedules so that they did not see much of each other and they began to get along all right. Occasionally they had a slight Difference, but they could always patch it up. For instance, she selected Aubrey De Courcey as a Name for the First Born, while he held out for Bill, so they had to compromise on Aubrey De Courcey.

Aubrey is now ten years of age. Mother is teaching him to Crochet and Father is showing him how to Draw without tipping off his Hand, while all the Friends are sitting around, waiting to see Aubrey's Finish.

MORAL: *The Two of a Kind is not always the Strongest Combination.*

The Lesson:

This is one of my cousin James Ade Kurfess's favorite stories. I recall him reading it to his whole family after dinner during one of my visits in 1974.

Truly, sometimes the best business partner, law partner or marriage partner can be an opposite.

The Fable of The Last Day at School & The Tough Trustee's Farewell to the Young Voyagers

From *Forty Modern Fables*, 1901

A High-Grade Heeler who had helped divvy the Campaign Fund and round up the Barrel-House Vote and get the Hoboes into Line for Good Government, was so beloved by his Party that he was made a Member of the Board of School Trustees and set up as an Example to the Young.

Whenever the High School Graduates put on their White Organdies and Dark Cutaways and got ready to up the Gang-Plank and embark on Life's Voyage, it was the Custom to have a Representative Member of the School Board on hand to give them a Send-Off. One Year the Political Boss was chosen for this Honor. He had been putting up Flat Buildings and buying Bonds on a Salary of $1,800, and it was believed that he was just the one to tell the Young Folks how to Succeed in Life. He wanted to know what he was expected to Talk about, and they told him about Ten Minutes, and be sure and tell the Class how to shin up the Ladder and get their Death-Grip on the Top Round. For it must be known, Reader, that when the Gentle Youth break out of High School they not only Launch on the Tempestuous Sea, but they also begin to climb the ladder of Fame and hike up the toilsome Mountain-Side and go into the waiting Harvest Field, all at the same time.

The Boss was no Albert J. Beveridge[166]. Oratory was not his Long Suit. He was better on a Still Hunt than on the Stump. He did his most effective Work with a Dark Lantern and a pair of Goloshes. Fortunately he had a Talented Stenographer, and he told her to draw up to her Machine and beat out about 500 Words of South Wind. She wrote the customary Josh—the kind that has been passed out to Graduating Classes since the Year One.

She said they were standing on Life's Threshold, getting ready to put Rosem on their hands and do the Ladder Act. All those who had been Studious and had loved Teacher and got 98 in Botany were dead sure to be Useful and Respected Citizens if they continued to be Honest and Industrious and Persevering. When the Trustee looked it over he said there couldn't be any possible Kick on such Advice, because it had been used on Thousands of Children and never seemed to affect them one way or the other. So he put it in his Pocket.

On Commencement Day he went up to the High School. He wore a Black Suit that was meant for a Polar Expedition. It was a Hot, Sticky Day. The Exercises struck him as being very Yellow.

Two Scared little Girls, with gas-pipe Underpinning, played one of those hurry-up Duets. Then a tow-headed Boy stood on one Foot and told why Greece and Rome had Petered out. He offered a few husky Suggestions in regard to Educating the Masses and edged back to his Seat, falling over himself on the Way.

Then a fat little girl, who seemed to have a rush of Blood to the

---

166. An orator, historian and United States Senator from Indiana.

The Fable of The Last Day at School

Head, told all about "Ambition." She said there were several kinds of Ambition, and those who overplayed it would surely get a good hard Toss sooner or later.

She said the Trouble was that some People were Ambitious to make Money and control Legislation. She didn't think it was right.

A pale Boy with high-water Trousers and a recent Hair-Cut, pulled out the Tremolo Stop[167] and sang a low Refrain about "Life's Duties." He said that no one should accumulate Wealth or try to get the Bulge on Honest Toil or put on any toppy Lugs with Silks and Broadcloth. He advised every one to give up the mad Race for Wealth and be a Philanthropist, drying the Widow's Tears, jollying up the Orphans and planting sweet Flowers along Life's Rugged Pathway.

"Our Country" was the Subject chosen by another Boy. He said we had Europe and Asia crowded off the Map and nothing could head us off, unless we forgot the Flag in our desire to grab off the Money. He gave the Politicians a hard Larruping and said he wanted to see the pure-minded Patriots put in charge of Things.

There were other Clarion Calls to Duty, and then a panicky Miss, whose Voice sounded like some one standing too close to the 'Phone, read the Valedictory. She claimed that the Class was all Broken Up at the Prospect of bolting away from the kind Principal and the Dear Teachers, but the time had come for them to tackle the Ladder and get on the Boat and start up the Mountain, etc., etc. She hoped that the whole Class was ready to Scatter into the Great World and pull for Success, and she said that Success was measured by Good Deeds and not by Dollars and Cents.

Then the Principal made one of these We-have-with-us-this-Afternoon Introductions, whereupon the Member of the Board unfolded himself and worked out into the Clearing. He felt in his inside Coat Pocket for the MSS.[168], but it was not there. He fanned

---

167. A piece sometimes added to a guitar to enhance the tone.
168. An abbreviation for manuscripts.

his clothes and Patted himself, but nary a Sound of Legal Cap. Then he remembered that in changing to the Pall-Bearer's Make-Up he had neglected to transfer the Speech.

For a few Seconds he was Non-Plussed. Then he braced himself and decided to introduce a Positive Novelty at Commencement Exercises and speak what was on his Mind. So he said: "Little People, I have been in a kind of Trance for a couple of Hours. You have been handing over a few that were too High for your Uncle Fuller. I have been around more or less in my Time, and I thought I had bumped up against several hefty Intellects, but when it comes to being there with the Gray Matter you have got all of us Old People left at the Post. When I look up at these 16-story Minds I feel like a Discarded Deuce. You ought to be proud of the Fact that you have more Knowledge than the School Board and all of your Relatives put together. I happen to know that when the President of the Board wants to find out the interest on $175 for one year and nine months at Six Per Cent, he wears out a Pencil or two and gets all Balled Up, and finally has to go over to the First National Bank and have the Man work it out for him. I have told myself at times that I was a fairly Hot Potato, but if any one asked me to define Algebra, I couldn't make a Sound. I'll tell you, a rusty old Wheel Horse hasn't got the Nerve to try and show any speed when you enter him against a Juvenile Phenom.

"I think it is a Safe Bet that you Young Folks are better Posted now than you ever will be again. In the Years to come, your Steady Job will be to Forget what you learned in High School. When you get thrown out of Employment you can always sit down and work at that. I am predicting that 20 odd Years from now, when almost any one of you will be trying to raise two or three Children with one Hand and lift a Mortgage with the other, if some one came along and asked you to tell the difference between Syntax and Prosody you would tell him to Brush By.

"Far be it from me to Knock the Benefits of High School

training. Although I received my Mental Discipline in a Brick Yard, I have always been Sore because I didn't get to wear Class Colors and learn one of these Siss-Boom-Ah Yells. I have worried along without a Diploma, and although shy on Latin and History, I have picked up a few points on doing the Other Fellow, which reminds me: I notice that nearly all of you take a long Run and Jump at the Almighty Dollar and the Machine in Politics. There seems to be a general Determination not to go out after the Shekels. What you want is Culture, and not the Coin. If you feel that way about it, you can Gamble that you will never have enough of it to make you Proud and Overbearing. Nobody is going to force it on you; in fact, my Experience is that it is pretty hard to Rake Up, even when you want it and want it Bad. Probably you have given more Thought to this Matter than I have, but if you don't mind being steered a little, I would suggest that you get what you can of the Long Green and afterwards arrange for a little Culture on the Side. In most Households now-a-days the Husband Rustles around and gets the Stuff and lets his Wife work the Culture End of the Game. Any time that he provides her with the Spondulix, she will bring Home enough Culture for Two, all right, all right.

"It seems, too, that the whole Bunch is going out to Root for Purity in Politics. I would be a Reformer Myself if I could find any one who would pay me a Salary for Kicking. As soon as I find a Reform Party compactly Organized and Cornering the Spoils, I will declare for it good and strong, and I hope you will all be with me. As nearly as I can find out, Politicians are not with the Machine because they are Stuck on it, but because they need the Money. They would be perfectly willing to Plug for the General Good if they could see Anything in it. As you grow older and get more Light on the Subject and some of your Friends begin to run for Office, probably you will take a more charitable View of Party Management.

"I will now ask you to come up and get your Sheepskins. Take this precious Certificate home and put it in a Dark, Cool Place. A few Years hence when you are less Experienced, it will give you a Melancholy Pleasure to look at it and Hark back to the Time when you knew it all. Just one Word in Parting. Always count your Change, and if you can't be Good, be Careful."

And he sat down.

MORAL: *To avoid dealing with Facts, always have your Speech in your Pocket.*

The Lesson:

No doubt George sat through many commencement ceremonies and speeches. His observations are spot on common sense: although perpetually out of fashion, making money and practical politics are necessary. This is perhaps the best commencement speech ever written.

The New Fable of the Marathon in the Mud and the Laurel Wreath

From *Ade's Fables*, 1914

A Stub-Nosed Primary Pupil, richly endowed with old-gold Freckles, lived in a one-cylinder Town, far from the corroding influences of the Stock Exchange. He arrived during the age of Board Sidewalks, Congress Gaiters, and Pie for Breakfast.

The Paper Collar, unmindful of the approaching Celluloid, was still affected by the more tony Dressers. Prison-made Bow Ties, with the handy elastic Fastener, were then considered right Natty.

Limousines, Eugenics, Appendicitis, and the regulation of Combines were beyond the rise of the Hill, so the talk was mostly about the Weather and Married Women.

The baptismal Cognomen[169] of the mottled Offspring was Alexander Campbell Purvis, but on account of his sunny Disposition he was known to the Countryside as Aleck.

One morning the Lad did his crawl from under the Quilt at an

---

169. Name or nickname.

hour when our Best People of the new Century are sending away the empty Siphons.

He was acting on a Hunch.

The far-famed Yankee Robinson show, with the Trick Mule and the smiling Tumblers, had exhibited the day before on the vacant Lot between the Grist-Mill and the Parsonage.

Aleck was familiar with the juvenile Tradition that Treasure could be discovered at or near the trampled Spot on which the Ticket-Wagon had been anchored.

It was known that the agitated Yahoos from up in the Catfish Country were likely to fumble and spill their saved-up Currency, thereby avoiding the trouble of handing it over to the Grafters later on.

Aleck was the first Prospector to show. He got busy and uncovered a Silver Buck.

It looked about the size of a Ferris Wheel.

While beating it for the parental Roof he began laying out in his Mind all the Pleasures of the Flesh that he could command with the Mass of Lucre.

The miscue he made was to flash his fortune in the Family Circle.

After breakfast he found himself being steered to the Farmers & Merchants' Bank.

He was pried away from the Cart-Wheel and given a teeny little Book which showed that he was a Depositor.

"Now, Alexander C.," said his Ma, "if you will shin up the ladder and pick Cherries every day this week at two cents per Quart, by nightfall of Saturday you will have another Case-Note to put into Cold Storage."

"But, if I continue dropping the proceeds of my Labor into the Reservoir, what is there in it for me?" asked the inquisitive Chick.

His mother replied, "Why, you will have the Gratification of moving up to the Window at the Bank and earning a Smile of Approbation from old Mr. Fishberry with the Throat Whiskers."

So the aspiring Manikin clung to the perilous Tree-Tops day after day, dropping the ruby Cherries into the suspended Bucket, while all of the Relatives stood on the ground and applauded.

One day there was a Conference and it was discovered that little Aleck was solvent to the extent of $2.80.

"Would it not be Rayzorius?" queried the Sire of Alexander; "would it not be Ipskalene if Aleck kept on and on until he had assembled five whole Dollars?"

Thus spurred to Endeavor by a large and rooting Gallery, the Urchin went prowling for Old Iron, which he trundled off to the Junkman.

Also for empty Bottles, which he laboriously scoured and delivered at the Drug Store for a mere dribble of Chicken Feed.

The sheet of Copper brought a tidy Sum, while old Mrs. Arbuckle wondered what had become of her Wash-Boiler.

With a V to his Credit, Aleck put a Padlock on every Pocket in his Store Suit and went Money-Mad.

He acquired a Runt and swilled it with solicitude until the Butcher made him an offer.

It was a proud Moment when he eased in the $7.60 to T. W. Fishberry, who told him to keep on scrounging and some day he would own a share in the Building & Loan.

Our Hero fooled away his time in School until he was all of eleven years old, when he became associated with one Blodgett in the Grocery Business, at a weekly Insult of Two Bones.

All the time Aleck was cleaning the Coal-Oil Lamps or watching the New Orleans Syrup trickle into the Jug, he was figuring how much of the Stipend he could segregate and isolate and set aside for the venerable Mr. Fishberry, the Taker-In up at the Bank with the Chinchilla on the Larynx.

For ten long years the White Slave tested Eggs and scooped the C Sugar.

When Aleck became of Age, Mr. Blodgett was compelling him to take $30 the first of every month.

He lived on Snowballs in the Winter and Dandelions in the Summer, but he had paid $800 on a two-story Brick facing Railroad Street.

His name was a Byword and Hissing among the Pool-Players. Nevertheless, he stood Ace High with the old Two-per-cent-a Month up at the Abattoir[170] known as the Farmers & Merchants' Bank.

The Boys who dropped in every thirty Days came to know him as a Wise Fish and a Close Buyer. They boosted at Headquarters, so the first thing you know Aleck was a Drummer, with two Grips[171] bigger than Dog-Houses and a chance to swing on the Expense Account.

A lowly and unsung Wanamaker would be sitting in his Prunery, wearing Yarn Wristlets to keep warm and meditating another Attack on the Bottle of Stomach Bitters in the Safe, when Aleck would breeze in and light on him and sell him several Gross of something he didn't need.

The Traveling Salesman dug up many a Cross-Roads overlooked by the Map-Makers.

He knew how to pin a Rube[172] against the Wall and make him say "Yes."

He rode in Cabooses, fought the Roller-Towels, endured the Taunts of Ess, Bess, and Tess who shot the Sody Biscuit, and reclined in the Chamber of Horrors, entirely surrounded by Wall-Paper, but what cared he?

He was salting the Spon.

---

170. Slaughterhouse.
171. Slang for suitcases.
172. A country bumpkin.

He was closing in on the Needful.

For a term of years he lived on Time-Tables and slept sitting up.

Day after day he dog-trotted through a feverish Routine of unpacking and packing, and then climbing back to the superheated Day Coach among the curdled Smells.

Every January 1st he did a Gaspard[173] Chuckle when he checked up the total Get, for now he owned two Brick Buildings and had tasted a little Blood in the way of Chattel Mortgages.

One of the partners in the Jobbing Concern happened to die. Before Rigor Mortis could set in or the Undertaker had time to flash a Tape Measure, Aleck was up at the grief-stricken Home to cop out an Option on the Interest.

Now he could give the Cackle to all the Knights of the Road who had blown their Substance along the gay White Ways of Crawfordsville, Bucyrus, and Sedalia.

He was the real Gazook with a Glass Cage, a sliding Desk and a whole Battery of Rubber Stamps.

In order to learn every Kink of the Game, freeze out the other Holders of Stock and gradually possess himself of all the Money in the World, Aleck now found it necessary to organize himself into both a Day and a Night Shift and have his Lunches brought in.

The various Smoothenheimers who were out on the Road had a proud chance to get by with the padded Expense Account. Aleck could smell a Phoney before he opened the Envelope, because that is how he got His.

With a three-ton Burden on his aching Shoulders, he staggered up the flinty Incline.

Away back yonder, while sleeping above the Store, a vision had come to him. He saw himself sitting as a Director at a Bank Meeting—an enlarged and glorified Fishberry.

Now he was playing Fox and pulling for the Dream to work out.

---

173. The man in charge of royal treasure.

The cold-eyed Custodians up at the main Fortress of Credit began to take notice of the Rustler.

He was a Glutton for Punishment, a Discounter from away back, and a Demon for applying the Acid Test to every Account.

He was a Sure-Thinger, air-tight and playing naught but Cinches. No wonder they all took a slant at him and spotted him as a Comer.

The Business Associates of Alexander liked to see Europe from the inside every summer and investigate the Cocktail Crop of Florida every winter, so they allowed him to be the Works.

He began building the Skids which finally carried them to the Fresh Air and left only one name on the Gold Sign.

Up to his Chin in Debt and with a Panic looming on the Horizon, it behooved Alexander to be on the job at 7:30 A. M. and hang around to scan the Pay-Roll until 9:30 P. M.

Ofttimes while galloping from his Apartment to the Galleys or chasing homeward to grab off a few wasteful hours of Slumber, he would see People of the Lower Classes going out to the Parks with Picnic Baskets, or lined up at the Vaudeville Palaces, or watching a hard-faced Soubrette[174] demonstrate something in a Show Window.

It got him to think Dubs could frivol around and waste the golden Moments when they might be hopping on to a Ten-Cent Piece.

His usual Gait was that of a man going for the Doctor, and he talked Numbers to himself as he sped along and mumbled over the important Letters he was about to dictate.

Those who were pushed out of his way would overhear a scrap or two of the Raving and think he was Balmy.

The answer is that every hard-working Business Guy acts as if he had Screech-Owls in the Tower.

---

174. A flirtatious young woman.

Aleck had his whole Staff so buffaloed that the Hirelings tried to keep up with him, so that Life in the Beehive was just one thing after another, with no Intermission.

The Whip cracked every five minutes, and the Help would dig in their toes and take a fresh lean-up against the Collars, for the Main Squeeze was trying to be a Bank Director, and Rockefeller had stolen a long start on him.

With a thousand important Details claiming his attention, Aleck had no time to monkey with side issues such as the general State of his Health or the multifarious plans for uplifting the Flat-Heads that he could see from his Window.

Those who recommended Golf to him seemed to forget that no one ever laid by anything while on the Links.

As for the Plain People, his only Conviction when he surveyed them in the Mass was that every Man-Jack was holding back Money that rightfully belonged to him (Alexander).

Needless to say, the battling Financier was made welcome at the Directors' Table and handed a piece of a Trust Company and became an honored Guest when any Melon was to be sliced.

All that he dreamt while sleeping in the cold room over the Store had eventuated for fair.

The more Irons in the Fire, the more flip-flops he turned.

He never paused, except to weep over the fact that some of the rival Procurers were getting more than he could show. It was an unjust World.

Brushing away the salty Tears, he would leap seven feet into the Air and spear a passing Dollar.

By the time he had the Million necessary for the support of a suitable and well-recommended Lady, he was too busy to go chasing and too foxy to split his Pile with a rank Outsider.

His Motor-Car squawked at the Sparrow Cops when they waved their Arms.

The engineer who pulled the Private Car always had his Orders to hit it up.

Sometimes the Private Secretary would drop out from Exhaustion, but the Human Dynamo never slowed up. He would shout his General Orders into the Cylinder of a Talking Machine.

He reposed at Night with a Ticker on his Bosom and a Receiver at his Ear.

When he finally flew the Track and blew out the Carburetor, they had to use a Net to get him under Control so that he could be carted away to the Hospital.

Then the Trained Nurse had to practise all the Trick Holds known to Frank Gotch[175] to keep him from arising to resume the grim Battle against his Enemies on the Board.

He fluttered long before calming down, but finally they got him all spread out and as nice a Patient as one could wish to see.

When he was too weak to start anything, Doc sat down and cheered him along by telling what Precautions should have been taken, along about 1880.

"And now, I have some News for you," said the Practitioner, holding in his Grief so well that no one could notice it. "You are going away from here. Owing to the total absence of many Organs commonly regarded as essential, it will be impossible for you to go back to the Desk and duplicate any of your notable Stunts. No doubt we shall be able to engage Six Men of Presentable Appearance to act as Pall-Bearers. It is our purpose to proceed to the Cemetery by Automobile so as not to impede Traffic on any of the Surface Lines in which you are so heavily interested. I congratulate you on getting so far along before being tripped up, and I am wondering if you have a Final Request to make."

---

175. A champion professional wrestler.

"Just one," replied the Great Man. "I'd like to have you or somebody else tell me what it's all been about."

The only remaining Fact to be chronicled is that the original Dollar, picked up on the Circus Lot, was found among the Effects.

A Nephew, whom Alexander Campbell Purvis never had seen, took the Dollar and with it purchased two Packs of Egyptian Ciga-roots, Regal size, with Gold Tips.

> MORAL: *A pinch of Change, carefully put by, always comes in handy.*

The Lesson:

Money is just a tool. As the protagonist in this story learned too late, without a purpose there is no point to adding more and more hammers to your tool belt.

The Fable of Almost Getting Back to Nature

From *Handmade Fables*, 1920

Mr. and Mrs. Fortescue motored to their Camp up in the Wilderness. The Corps of Servants and a vast Cargo of Supplies preceded by Rail.

That is, they were supposed to precede by Rail, but a Bridge burned and the Streak of Rust that wound through the Woods and up into the Hills went Blooey.

So the First Cook and the Second Cook and the Door-Opener and the Superintendent of Collar-Buttons and the Feather-Duster Twins and the imported Hair-Fixer were all laid out at a Whistling Post, miles from their Destination.

They could not get the Terrible News to the Fortescues, because the Latter were off the Earth some-where, speeding along in the Big Balloon.

Thus it befell that a couple of Fortescues landed in at the gloomy Fortress which some one, in a Spirit of Levity, had labelled a Camp, but no trembling Menials poured forth to meet them.

There they were, Leagues and Leagues from Nowhere, facing the grim Necessity of waiting on themselves.

Thus it befell that a couple of Fortescues landed in at the gloomy Fortress...

They had a Chauffeur with them, but his Contract read that he should drive the Car.

He could not be expected to start the Fires and prepare 8 kinds of Food for every Meal and arrange the Flowers and turn down the Beds and Lay out the Corduroys for Master, because these Duties were outside of his Department.

Now, the Skeleton in Mr. Fortescue's Family Closet was that Grandfather built a Log House with his own Hands.

As for Mrs. Fortescue, it is not generally known that her Mommer was born on a Canal Boat.

Both had tried hard to eradicate all Family Traits and Standardize themselves according to English Models, but they must have made a Mess of the Job.

For Mr. Fortescue found himself out in the Woods collecting Chunks for the Fireplaces, and Mrs. F. began to drag Stuff out of

Cedar Chests and run down a Strip of Bacon and bust an Egg into the Coffee, taking it all up just where Ma had left off in 1898, when the first Dividend came in.

They found that they could put Skillets on the Fire rather than starve to Death and, Oh, the Lark they had next morning!

For Mr. Fortescue learned that he could still lace his Shoes, and Mrs. Fortescue was as proud as Punch after combing her own Hair.

It was really a postponed Honeymoon.

After three days they were almost Chummy.

Then the delayed Train pulled in and they had to starch up and Climb back on the Pedestals.

MORAL: *Full many a good Farm-Hand is hiding behind a Plaited Shirt.*

The Lesson:

Perhaps 80% of the members of TIGER 21 and R360 are first generation. Yes, today it's as true as it was 100 years ago: "Full many a good Farm-Hand is hiding behind a Plaited Shirt." Too often by generation three it's no longer true and as they say in Asia "rice paddies to rice paddies in three generations."

George on America's "Spiritual Awakening"

From *Letters of George Ade*, 1973

To George Vaughn[176]

Hazelden
Brook, Indiana
Oct. 29, 1936

Dear Professor Vaughn: -

    I have postponed replying to your letter of inquiry because I doubt very much if I am qualified to speak with any authority regarding the need of a "spiritual awakening." I think our greatest national handicap at present is the willingness and the desire of so many people to live at government expense and get money from the government on any sort of pretext. If you would define a spiritual awakening as a renewed enthusiasm for the activities of the orthodox churches, and especially those of Protestant persuasion, I must say frankly that I do not discover any tendencies in that direction. I think we need a revival of the spirit of independence and unselfish patriotism and a return to the old-fashioned virtues of economy and saving. I fear that we are suffering from a lack of

---

176. Professor of Law at University of Arkansas.

moral fibre and have taken the wrong slant on what our government really should undertake to do for us. Frankly I have no recipe for insuring a return to the cardinal virtues.

I am, with best wishes,

Sincerely,
George Ade

The Lesson:

A generation after this letter was written, Lee Kuan Yew lectured the citizens of Singapore on how the Western welfare state would lead to its decline and to the rise of Asia. George voted for FDR once and then recoiled at his policies, spending the rest of his life writing against the New Deal and socialism. Nothing saps the spirit of a man more than taking away his role as the breadwinner.

The Fable of how Wisenstein did not Lose out to Buttinsky

From *The Girl Proposition*, 1902

Once there was a Steady who overplayed his Standing and came within an Ace of losing his Home.

It happened thuswise. He was a Daylight Performer and loved to parade his Attractions. If he had a Duchess on his Staff he would lead her along the main-travelled Streets and show her off. But he held her by the Arm just the same for fear that some one would run out of an Alley and grab her.

When he had a Beaut wearing his Photo in her Locket he wanted all the World to know about it.

Furthermore, he was the kind that would take a Friend with him when he went calling on No. 1. He wanted the Friend to see for him-self that the Girl thought the World of Papa. It was Fine Business for the Friend to sit over on the Far Side of the Room and watch them hold Hands, now and then stealing a little Old Hug. The Friend must have enjoyed every Minute of it.

Once in a While the busy Lover would look over at Friend and tip him the Wink as if to say, "Oh, I suppose this little Party fairly hates me."

But one Evening when he went out Hand-Holding and carried his own Gallery with him he ran into Bunches of Trouble. The Friend belonged to the Buttinsky Family and refused to stay on the Far Side of the Room. He was a clever two-handed Boy and had practiced a few Holds of his Own. He pulled his chair over and made it a Threesome. In about 8 Minutes he had the Regular Fellow stymied and Hazel was leaning against him so as to make his Conversation a Short Carry.

Before he left that Evening he had himself all dated up for a Return Engagement. It looked as though the other Young Gentleman had the Casters under him.

Wisenstein

The Fable of how Wisenstein did not Lose out to Buttinsky

From that time on it was Nip and Tuck. They took all of her Open Time in one Chunk and divided it up between them.

Sometimes they got on the Reservation together and then the only one who had a Good Time was the Girl.

The Original Gentleman Friend was a Wisenstein. As soon as he saw himself losing out, he began to lay deep and shifty Plans to head off the new Entry. A two-by-four chinless Intellect would have tried to put the Rival into the Nine-Hole by opening up on him and telling where he spent some of his Evenings, but Wisenstein had read on a sign somewhere that every Knock is a Boost. He knew that no Fellow ever landed a real Princess by talking Scandal about the other Candidates. Accordingly, he played a deep System. He became Press Agent for his Friend. He touted Mr. Buttinsky as the real Essence of Allygazam. He painted him in four bright Colors and put his Picture in every Window.

When he got the Girl aside he would tell her that dear old Buttinsky was one of the most charming Chaps in the World and claimed to have a lot of Women spreading their Nets for him. He said that Buttinsky was a great Singer, having been known up in the Country where he came from as the Village Thrush. He advised her to have Buttinsky tell a number of his Stories, because as an After-Dinner Wit he had Chauncey M. Depew[177] churned to a Froth and was commonly known as the Life of the Party. Then he asked her if she had seen Buttinsky cut loose in a Ball-Room. He said that all the Girls who saw Buttinsky move across the gleaming Floor in the Two-Step began to look Glassy out of the Eyes and sank back in a Stupor. If she ever found time she ought to talk Books with Buttinsky because he knew them from A to Izzard and could get rid of Literary Talk in a Style calculated to charm a Bird out of a Tree. And as for dear old Art, he was supposed to be the Man who had written it.

---

177. A U.S. senator from 1899 to 1911, best remembered as an orator and storyteller.

Buttinsky did not know that he was being Lithographed as a Phenom. When the Princess urged him to trot out his Accomplishments he thought she was so Sticky on him that everything he did looked good to her. So he squared up to the Piano and sang, "Because" in a Tenor that came from right between his Eyes. He chucked in a few Minors. They were these naughty Witch-Hazel Fellows, and after he had turned a few of the Tonsorials loose in the Parlor, he had the Princess straightened out as stiff as a Board and biting at the Doilies. When she led him around to the Subject of the late Novels he got all balled up, for he thought that Gertrude Atherton wrote "Mary MacLane." And one Night when she teased him out on the Dancing Floor and he missed Step and tried to walk up one side of her, she began to have a dim and twinkling Suspish that this Boy Wonder was a Two-Spot[178].

Buttinsky

---

178. An unimportant person or thing.

Buttinsky helped Matters a lot by trying to undermine Mr. Wisenstein, who had been saying all the Nice Things about him. Every time he got the Princess backed on a Sofa he did a Hammer Solo. For instance, he advised her to have no Dealings with a Man who drank. He said that Wisenstein was a Nice Fellow, But—. Then for about 30 Minutes the absent Wisenstein would get his.

About the time that the Princess began to class Buttinsky as a False Alarm so far as Accomplishments went, she started in to be Indignant because he roasted one who always spoke so Lovely of him.

As for Wisenstein, when she came right out and asked him about his Habits, he owned up and leaned on her Shoulder and said his only Hope was to get a Good Woman to Reform him. Which, probably, was a very foolish Move.

Then when she remembered how Magnanimous he had been, always speaking well of a Certain Person who had tried to sew Buttons on him, she perceived that Wisenstein was one of Nature's Noblemen. He contradicted her at first, but finally let her have her own Way. And Mr. Buttinsky did not seem to be One-Two-Seventeen.

> MORAL: *Beware of the Friend who tells how Good you are.*

The Lesson:

It is a matter of legend that George's father, John Ade, never said a disparaging word about anyone. I chronicled this in my book *A Pioneer in the Fullest Sense: The Wit and Wisdom of George Ade's Father*:

> *The enduring values that John taught his sons extended throughout George's life. Near the end of his career George formed a close collaboration with Will Rogers, at the time the highest paid star in Hollywood. Rogers famously said, "I never met a man I didn't like."*

*John shared that philosophy. He was widely known for never saying anything bad about anyone. The story goes that upon the death of the town's meanest drunk, a few of the townsfolk approached John for some fun, placing bets as to whether he would be able to say anything good about the not-so-dearly departed. When pressed, John replied, "Well, he **was** a pretty good whistler..."*

It is indeed wise never to run down a fellow man, even if they are a competitor.

The Fable of the Father Who Jumped In

From *Ade's Fables*, 1914

Once there was a leading Citizen with only one Daughter, but she was Some Offspring.

Bernice was chief Expense Account and Crown Jewel of a Real Estate Juggler who had done so well that all the Strap-Hangers regarded him as an Enemy to Society.

Papa was foolish, even as a Weasel.

He was what you might call Honest, which signified that all of his Low Work had been done by Agents.

A Person of rare judgment, withal. He never copped a piece of bulky Swag unless he had a Wheelbarrow with him at the time.

He had been going East with the Green Goods ever since the Party in Power precipitated the first Panic.

He had Stacks of the Needful, and his Rating was AA Plus 1, to say nothing of a Reserve cached in the little Tin Box.

Daughter alone could induce him to unbuckle, and melt, and jar loose, and come across, and kick in, and sting the Check-Book.

One day Bernice was a Little Girl, and the next she was head Flossie among the Debutantes, with a pack of Society Hounds pursuing in Full Cry, each willing to help count the Bank Roll.

Father was scared pink when he sized up the Field.

He still wore box-toed Boots and carried Foliage on the Sub-Maxillary[179] so that those who came ringing the Front Bell didn't look very lucky to him.

Sometimes he would dream that he had been pushed into a Mausoleum and that a slender Cyril with a Lady's Watch strapped on his wrist was spending all of that Money for Signed Etchings.

Whereupon he would awake in a Cold Sweat and try to think of a safe Recipe for poisoning Boulevard Blighters.

One day Bernice went out into the Sunshine and found something and brought it home with her and put it on a Rug in the Elizabethan Room.

Father came in and took one look and said: "Not for Mine! I won't stand for any Puss Willow being grafted on to our Family Tree."

His name was Kenneth, and he reduced his Percentage on the first day by having the hem-stitched Mouchoir[180] tucked inside of the Cuff.

Also, it was rumored that he put oil on his Eye-Brows and rubbed Perfumery on the backs of his Hands.

Father walked around the He-Canary twice, looking at him over the Specs, and then he rushed to the Library and kicked the Upholstery out of an $80 chair.

He could see the love-light glinting in the Eyes of Bernice. She had fallen for the Flukus.

Kenneth was installed as Steady.

When Bernice saw him turn the Corner and approach the House, he looked to her like Rupert, the long lost Heir—while Father discerned only an insect too large to be treated with Powder.

Kenneth was the kind of Sop that you see wearing Evening Clothes on a Colored Post-Card.

---

179. Facial hair beneath the lower jaw; chin whiskers.
180. Handkerchief.

If his private Estate had been converted into Pig Iron[181], he could have carried it in his Watch Pocket.

He was re-fined and had lovely Teeth, but those who knew him well believed the Story that when he was a Babe in Arms, the Nurse had let him fall and strike on the Head.

He wore his Hair straight back and used Patent Leather dressing.

He was full of Swank and put on much Side and wore lily-colored Spats[182] and was an awful Thing all around, from Pa's point of view.

In a crowd of Bank Directors he would have been a cheap Swivel[183], but among the Women Folks he was a regular Bright Eyes.

When you passed through the Archway of his Intellectual Domain you found yourself in the Next Block.

But—he could go into a Parlor and sprinkle Soothing Syrup all over the Rugs.

He had a Vaudeville Education and a small Tenor Voice, with the result that many a fluttering Birdie regarded him as the bona-fide Ketchup.

Bernice thought she was lucky to have snared him away from the others, and she had slipped him the whispered Promise, come Weal, come Woe.

She had no Mother to guide her, and it looked as if the Family was about to have a Bermuda wished on to it.

No wonder Father was stepping sideways.

He would come home in the evening and find the Mush perched on a Throne in the Spot Light, shooting an azure-blue Line of desiccated Drool, with Bernice sitting out in front and Encoring.

Then he would retire to the back part of the House to bark at the Butler and act as if he had been eating Red Meat.

He knew that if he elbowed in and tried to break up the Clinch,

---

181. Crude iron, an intermediate good used by the iron industry in the production of steel.
182. A type of footwear accessory for outdoor wear, covering the instep and the ankle.
183. Strength of mind or character.

it would mean a Rope Ladder, a piece in the Papers, and a final Reconciliation, with Parent playing the usual role of Goat.

He was resolved not to put in the remainder of his Days being panhandled by a Souffle who wore Dancing Pumps in the Daytime. The problem was to get shut of the Rodent without resorting to any Rough Stuff.

Father never had heard tell of the Perils of Propinquity, and he thought Psychology had something to do with Fish.

Just the same, he remembered about a Quail a day for 30 days, and he knew that the most agreeable Perfumery would not smell right if applied with a Garden Hose.

Likewise, he suspected that many a Quarter-Horse would blow, if put into a two-mile Handicap.

So he blocked out a Program which proved that Solomon had nothing on him.

Instead of grilling young Kenneth and holding him up to Contumely[184] and forbidding him the use of Cozy Corner, he started in to boost the Love Match.

Kenneth all but moved in his Trunk.

Father had a chance to weigh him, down to the last Ounce, and study the simple Mechanism of his transparent Personality.

Father classified the would-be Child-in-Law as a Gobbie, which means a Home-Wrecker who is still learning his Trade.

The Candidate became a regular Boarder.

Kenneth would sit right up close to old Cash-in-Hand, who would egg him on to tell Dialect Stories and, after that, show how to make a Salad.

The Stories were some that Marshall Wilder[185] stopped using in 1882 and since then have been outlawed on the Kerosene Circuit[186].

---

184. Insulting language or treatment.
185. An American actor, monologist, humorist and sketch artist.
186. Villages and small towns where obscure opera companies played one-night-stands in the late 1800s/early 1900s, thus named because the opera houses were lit with kerosene lamps. A step down from electric lights and limelights.

After Bernice had heard these Almanac Wheezes 26 or 28 times, she would sit still and look at the Center-Piece while Lover was performing.

The Gags didn't sound as killing as they had at first, and sometimes she wished the Dear Boy would chop on them.

No chance. Father had him kidded into believing that all the old ham-fat Riddles were simply Immense.

As for that Salad Specialty, the poor Gink[187] who calls loudly for English Mustard and thinks he is a Genius because he can rub a Bowl with a sprig of Garlic, may have his brief Hour of Triumph, but no man ever really got anywhere by doping Salad, when you stop to add it all up.

Father would put the two young people together in the back of the Touring Car and ride them around for Hours at a time.

Anybody who has cut in on one of those animated Automobile Conversations, while the salaried Maniac from France is hitting up 42 miles an Hour, will tell you that the hind end of a Motor Vehicle is no good Trysting Place for an Engaged Couple.

Bernice would get home after one of these wild swoops into the realm of the Death Angel, and totter to her room and lie down, and murmur: "I wonder what ailed Kenneth to-day. He seemed Preoccupied."

That Same Evening, just when she needed Smelling Salts and Absolute Quiet, her enthusiastic Father would have Fiancé up to Dinner to pull the same stale Repertoire and splash around in the Oil and Vinegar.

If any Guests were present, then Father would play Introducer and tell them beforehand how good Kenneth was.

When given his Cue, the Lad would swell up and spring a hot One about the Swede and the Irishman, while Bernice would fuss

---

187. An odd man or boy.

with the Salt and wonder dimly if the Future had aught in store for her except Dialect Stuff.

Father had read on a Blotter somewhere that Absence makes the Heart grow fonder, so he played his System with the Reverse English.

He arranged a nice long trip by Land and Water and took the male Sweetheart along, so that the Doting Pair could be together at Breakfast.

His cunning had now become diabolical. He was getting ready to apply the Supreme Test.

Every Morning, when Bernice looked over her Baked Apple she saw nothing in this wide World except Kenneth, still reeking of Witch Hazel and spotted with Talcum Powder, and not very long on Sparkling Conversation.

When he was propped up in the cold Dawn, with his eyes partially open, he did not resemble a Royal Personage nearly as much as he had in some of his earlier Photographs.

Father would order soft-boiled Eggs to be Eaten from the Shell. When Kenneth got around to these, he would cease to be a Romantic Figure for at least a few Minutes. Bernice would turn away in dread and look out at the swaying Trees and long to see some of her Girl Friends back home.

After Kenneth had been served to her, three meals a day, for two Weeks and they had ridden together for Ages and Ages, in Pullman Compartments, she made certain horrible Discoveries.

One of his Ears was larger than the other.

He made a funny noise with his Adam's Apple when drinking Hot Coffee.

When he was annoyed, he bit his nails.

When suffering from a Cold, he was Sniffy.

The first time she became aware of the slight discrepancy in Ears, she suffered only a slight Annoyance. It handed her a tiny Pang to find a Flaw in a Piece of Work that she had regarded as Perfect.

After she had seen nothing else but those Ears for many, many Days, it became evident to her that if Kenneth truly loved her, he would go and have them fixed.

Likewise, every time her Heart's Delight lifted the Cup to his Ruby Lips, she would grip the Table Cloth with both Hands, and whisper to herself, "Now we get the Funny Noise."

Kenneth, in the mean while, had found out that her Hair did not always look the same, but one who is striving to get a Meal Ticket for Life cannot be over-fastidious.

He was Game and stood ready to obey all Orders in order to pull down the Capital Prize.

He had been such a Hit in the Maple-Sundae Set that he could not conceive the possibility of any Female becoming satiated with his Society.

The poor Loon never stopped to figure out that the only way to keep a Girl sitting up and interested is to stay away once in a while and give her a Vacation.

Father was right on the Job to see that Bernice had no Vacation. He framed it up to give her a Foretaste of Matrimony every Day in the Week.

If the Future Husband wandered more than thirty feet from her side, Father would nail him and Sic him on to her again.

She would look up and say: "Oh, Fury! Look who's here again!"

This was no way for a true-hearted Maiden to speak of her Soul Mate.

Father put the Cap Sheaf[188] on his big Experiment by accepting an invitation to go Yachting.

He put them side by side on Deck and told them to comfort each other, in case anything happened.

They never could have been quite the same to each other after that Day.

---

188. The top sheaf of a stock or stack of grain; the crowning point, the climax.

Bernice wanted to get back on Shore and hunt her Room and peel down to a Kimono and refuse any Callers for a Month.

Even the accepted Swain was beginning to slow up. He could remember the time when he used to sit around with members of his own Sex.

Father had no Mercy. He took the two Invalids back to Land and rounded them up for Breakfast next morning.

When Kenneth appeared, he was slightly greenish in Color.

One Ear was three times as large as the other. He had caught a Sniffy Cold.

In partaking of his Coffee he made Sounds similar to those coming through the Partition when the People in the adjoining Flat have trouble with the Plumbing.

He saw Bernice glaring at him and bit his Nails in Embarrassment.

Father felt the Crisis impending and laid on the last Straw.

"I was trying to recall that Story," said he—"the One about the German and the Dog."

Bernice gave one Shriek and then dashed from the Room, making hysterical Outcries along the Corridor.

Father told Kenneth to check all the Trunks for Home and then catch an early Train.

Bernice was squirming about on the Hotel Sofa when Father entered the Room.

She threw herself into his Arms and passionately demanded, "Why, oh, why are you trying to force me into marrying that Creature?"

MORAL: *Don't get acquainted too soon.*

The Fable of the Father Who Jumped In

The Lesson:

If one has dedicated much of one's life to the accumulation of financial capital, then it is of great importance to make sure the next generation has picked up enough intellectual, social, human, emotional and spiritual capital to recognize a suitable mate. It's much easier to make a fortune than to find a good partner. The Father who Jumped In was late, but perhaps not too late.

Looking Back From Fifty

From *Single Blessedness*, 1922

So far as I can testify, and as I do verily believe, nothing much happened previous to 1870. The world at that time was all prairie and cornfields, except for the white houses of the county seat and a dark line of timber against the horizon.

There was a railway in front of our house at the edge of town. Beyond the railway ran a country lane—gray and rutty in dry weather, black porridge every spring.

As for the railroad, the soft metal of the rails was dreadfully snagged, and the locomotive was mostly smokestack.

Wagons, canopied with white, toiled through the mud, all headed for Kansas and Populism.

It was only a short cut across the fields to unbroken prairie that had never been touched by plough.

Every township in the Middle West should have reserved and parked one square mile of the prairie, leaving it just as the settlers found it. It was a grassy jungle matted with flower gardens. Tall perennials shot up their gummy stalks and waved broad, fibrous leaves. A traveller leaving the beaten road found himself chin-high in a rank growth of blue and yellow blooms.

We have gasolene chariots now, and clothes ordered from the catalogue, but the glory of the open country has departed, save for the vivid patch here and there at some neglected corner.

When I was a boy, the explorer could start from anywhere out on the prairie and move in any direction and find a slough. In the centre, an open pond of dead water. Then a border of swaying cat-tails; tall rushes; reedy blades, sharp as razors, out to the upland, spangled with the gorgeous blue and yellow flowers of the virgin plain.

A million frogs sang together each evening, and a billion mosquitos came out to forage when the breeze died away.

Did you ever try to elude the man-eating gallinipper[189] by sitting in the smoke of a "smudge"? A smudge was an open fire, smothered with damp leaves or fresh grass.

The Anopheles mosquito, purveyor of malaria, went along unrestricted and unsuspected. Chills and fever entered into the programme of every life; but those who chattered thought they were being jounced by the hand of Providence.

The "smudge" is gone, and quinine is no longer a staple.

The sloughs have gone, and after years of tile drainage and the levelling processes of cultivation, the five-acre pond on which we skated is just a gentle swale in a dry and tidy cornfield.

Thirty dollars an acre is no longer a boom price. Offer the man two hundred[190], and you fail to interest him.

Geese and brant, mallards and red-heads, prairie chickens and quail—so plentiful that hunters brought in wagon loads. We used to tire of quail potpie and long for meat from the butcher's.

This is not Saskatchewan or Oklahoma that we are describing. This country of croaking frogs and black mud and myriad flocks of wild fowl was so near Chicago that one night in October, just as far back as I can reach into the past, we sat on the fence and looked

---

189. Large mosquito.
190. $15, 000 today.

at a blur of illumination in the northern sky and learned that the city which we had not seen was burning up in a highly successful manner.

The Lesson:

Eventually, George's dream of restoring a bit of the prairie to Newton County came true. Today the Kankakee Sands is over 8,000 acres of wild prairie with the largest buffalo herd east of the Mississippi River. Together with other nature reserves, the total area is over 20,000 acres.

Kankakee Sands Tallgrass Prairie Preserve

George's Mile Posts

From *Letters of George Ade*, 1973

To Josephine Crowder

Hazelden
Brook, Indiana
Aug. 29th, 1926

Dear Miss Crowder: -

I have been some what under the weather lately and my regular work has been so interrupted that I simply cannot undertake to dictate a long article for you this morning and it must be understood that I am not writing and signing any article for a syndicate. I have not your letter at hand but I think you wanted me to say something about the turning point in my career. I don't think that any man determines his whole career by any single performance. He is constantly changing the program. Of course, a very important day for me was the one on which my father told me that I might go to Purdue University. If I had not gone to Purdue it is probable that I would not have broken into the centers of population and had all the interesting experiences which came to me as a newspaper man and a playwright and a traveler.

In 1890 when I went up to Chicago and joined John McCutcheon I was simply carrying out a plan which had been in the back of my head all of the time. I became a newspaper worker. The day in 1894 when the editor put me in charge of a department was an important mile post because I was given a chance to write the kind of stuff which could be put into books and my long service as a story writer prepared me for writing dialogue and inventing situations and so in time I found myself writing for the stage. The money which permitted me to travel and sort of map out my own timetable every year came from the theater. So I suppose the day on which Henry Savage induced me to submit a play to him was another turning point. Going back to that, the day on which John McCutcheon and I decided to go to Europe, even if we had to swim, was another turning point.

I think the important moves I made were those which put me in the way of seeing the world and which led to independence. I don't believe that a man who writes for a living should sacrifice everything in order to get the money. I think it important and highly convenient for him to direct his efforts so that he will get some money which will enable him to take orders from himself instead of all the time being a creature of circumstances . . .

. . . I am, with best wishes,

Sincerely,
George Ade

The Lesson:

Education well used can lead to financial independence and freedom.

Mr. Kakyak Decides to Be a Republican

From *Stories of Benevolent Assimilation*, edited by Perry Gianokos, 1985[191]

"Now Mr. Kakyak, we will begin the course of instruction by telling you something about the great political parties," said Mr. Washington Conner, the missionary from the United States of America. He and Mr. Bulolo Kakyak, the Tagalo agriculturist, were seated in the shade of the nipa hut.

"As I am now an American subject and have a proprietary interest in American politics, I am naturally anxious to find out what is what," said Mr. Kakyak, squatting into a comfortable attitude.

"Have you made up your mind which you wish to be—a republican or a democrat?" asked Mr. Conner.

"What is the difference between a republican and a democrat?" asked the Filipino.

The missionary whittled fine shavings from a piece of split bamboo and half closed his eyes as he meditated upon his reply.

"There are supposed to be certain live issues dividing the two

---

[191]. This was originally published circa 1899 after The Philippines became part of the USA.

parties," said the missionary. "For instance, the republicans are supposed to favor a high protective tariff—although not all republicans are high protectionists and not all high protectionists are republicans. The democrats are in favor of free trade, a tariff for revenue only, a tariff for revenue exclusively, a tariff for revenue with incidental protection and a tariff affording protection to the products of democratic states. The republicans are in favor of a gold standard, all except the bimetallists and the silver republicans. The democrats are in favor of free silver, at a ratio of 16 to 1, or any other ratio that will win, all except the gold democrats, who are not in favor of any ratio at all. Each party is in favor of civil-service reform when the other party tries to make a sweep of the offices. Both parties are opposed to all trusts and combinations of capital, as nearly as you can gather from the late platforms. Although the platforms for 1900 have not been framed, I have every reason to believe that all republicans, except the anti-expansionists, will indorse President McKinley's plan of colonial extension and benevolent assimilation, while all democrats, except a large body of imperialists, will denounce the campaign of conquest in these islands. And there you are!"

"That being the case," said the Tagalo, "I think I will take to the woods."

"Nonsense," said the missionary. "You must make a choice."

"But I can't see that there's very much difference between the two parties. You say that some democrats indorse nearly everything in the republican platform and some republicans are opposed to expansion, high protection and the gold standard. How can they be republicans?"

"They are republicans because they vote the republican ticket. A republican is one who votes the republican ticket. A democrat is one who votes the democratic ticket."

"In your country how does a man make up his mind which ticket to vote?"

"He usually follows the example of his father. That is always a safe and easy plan."

"But my father was neither a republican nor a democrat. He was a rebel."

"An insurgent patriot, you mean."

"You called them 'rebels' yesterday and warned me not to use the term 'insurgent' any more."

"Those of your countrymen who fought Spanish rule were insurgent patriots, as nearly as I could learn from reading the publications in my own country a year ago. Those who are now resisting American authority and trying to thwart our scheme of benevolent assimilation are rebels. There is a wide distinction between an insurgent patriot and a disorderly rebel and you want to get it clearly fixed in your mind."

"Well, insurgent or rebel, he did not give me any instruction in American politics and I fear I am not qualified to make a choice between the two parties you mention. At the same time, as I am now a subject of the United States, I suppose I ought to be something."

"By all means," said the missionary. "I can assure you that I well understand your hesitancy because there are no geographical predilections here in the island of Luzon. If you lived in Reading, Pa., you would have no trouble over coming to a decision. You would be a republican by instinct. Or, if you were a resident of Talladega, Ala., you would be a democrat, so as to get into society. But here in Luzon it is different, I will admit. Still, as you say, it is highly important that you should be something."

"Hold on! I have it!" exclaimed Mr. Kakyak. "You say that the issues have become rather cloudy and indefinite here of late and there are varying beliefs in each party. Why wouldn't it be a good idea for me to hold aloof from both parties for awhile? By declining to ally myself permanently with either of these political organizations I could be free to act upon each issue independently, as it were. That is, I might support the republican ticket this year, and next year, if the republican administration had made serious mistakes or nominated candidates of low intelligence and bad records, I could change around and vote the democratic ticket. By doing that I wouldn't bind myself to the democratic party forever, mind you. I would simply vote to give it a chance to correct temporary abuses of power."

"Great Scott!" gasped the missionary. "How did you ever get that perverted idea into your head? Do you know what you would be if you ever went to changing about like that?"

"Why—no," replied Mr. Kakyak, somewhat frightened at the missionary's manner.

"You'd be a mugwump."

"A what?"

"A mugwump."

"That doesn't sound very nice."

"A mugwump is the most detestable of all creatures. All true partisans recoil from him as from a deadly adder. Little children hoot at him as he passes along the street with an umbrella under his arm. He is represented in the comic papers as wearing side whiskers and gum shoes. He cannot vote at primary elections. No mugwump may ever hope to get on the police force. He is the torment of the political prophet and the day-bogey of the campaign manager. You ought to read what the *New York Tribune* says about him. I implore you, Mr. Kakyak, not to make this supreme mistake at the very outset of your political career. Be a populist, be a prohibitionist, be anything that bears a party name, but don't be a mugwump. Once the brand of mugwump is put on you you are a political Jonah, to be mistrusted for all time. You won't be able to get a political job if you live to be 100 years old. If at any time you venture to address your fellow-citizens on any topic of public interest and claim a respectful consideration of your arguments some editorial writer will pick you up and say, 'This man is a mugwump,' and that will settle it! He won't have to strain himself to refute your arguments. You will be ruled out of the game of politics on your own damning record. No, Mr. Kakyak, be something. Those were the exact words that you used only a few moments ago. Be something! Be either a republican or a democrat, and after you have selected your party stick to it through thick and thin. If you happen to be a democrat and believe in protection and the gold standard you vote for free trade and 16 to 1, understand? It may go a little hard at the time, but after you get to be an old man and want to act as a delegate to something or other it will count largely in your favor if you can swell around political headquarters and say: 'I'm 69 years old, coming this fall, and I never voted anything but the straight ticket.' Then people will respect you. But whatever you do don't become known as a mugwump."

"Perhaps you are right," said Mr. Kakyak. "I am an unsophisticated Tagalo and you are wise with the experience of triumphant democracy. But I don't know which I ought to be. From what you say, I don't believe it makes much difference. I believe I'll toss a coin. Heads, I'm a republican; tails, I'm a democrat."

He pulled a copper coin from the loose pocket of his trousers and tossed it into the air.

"Heads!" ejaculated the missionary. "You are now a republican. Welcome to the grand old party. Remember that hereafter you indorse the administration."

Thus ended the first lesson.

The Lesson:

As it was for Mr. Kakyak, there is as much difference between the Republicans and the Democrats of today as there was 100 years ago. The Republicans used to be the party of fiscal conservatives but that was before Trump's profligate populism. Gone now are the Republican fiscal conservatives: Liz Cheney, Mitt Romney, Ben Sasse, etc, and the last solitary Democrat fiscal conservative, Joe

Manchin, too. Today I believe the most important issue is our nation's debt. Lyn Alden offers an excellent analysis at *Seeking Alpha*.[192] *The Economist* in its recent article[193] seems to agree:

> "The average American has gone through the 21st century with presidents who said we didn't have a problem. So why should anyone bother now with hard reforms?" says Douglas Holtz-Eakin, who led the [Congressional Budget Office] under George W. Bush. "There's going to be a generation of voters that can't get anything they want, because all the money has been spoken for."
>
> Doug Elmendorf, the CBO's boss under Barack Obama, says Republicans have learned that it is toxic to cut entitlements, while Democrats have learned to steer clear of tax rises. "Both those positions are obviously politically popular, but they take off the table the biggest pieces of the federal budget," he says. "So it's increasingly hard for either party to develop a plan that puts fiscal policy on a sustainable path, much less agree on a set of policies."
>
> Keith Hall, boss from late in Mr Obama's time through much of Mr Trump's, thinks it will take a fiscal crisis to force action. "But then we're looking at really draconian cuts that give us a bad recession, simply because they waited too long," he says. "Policymakers, Congress and the president, they just don't take it seriously." . . .
>
> . . . America requires a serious political debate and bipartisan agreement to put its budget on sounder footing. Alas, its leaders are inclined neither to seriousness nor to agreement.

---

192. https://seekingalpha.com/article/4560090-long-term-fiscal-spiral?gt=351f291429160d69, accessed January 11, 2024.
193. https://www.economist.com/finance-and-economics/2023/05/03/america-faces-a-debt-nightmare, accessed January 11, 2024.

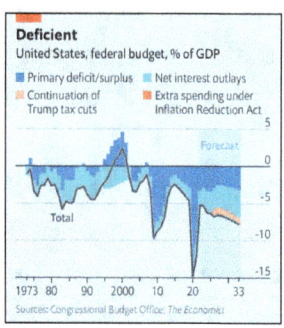

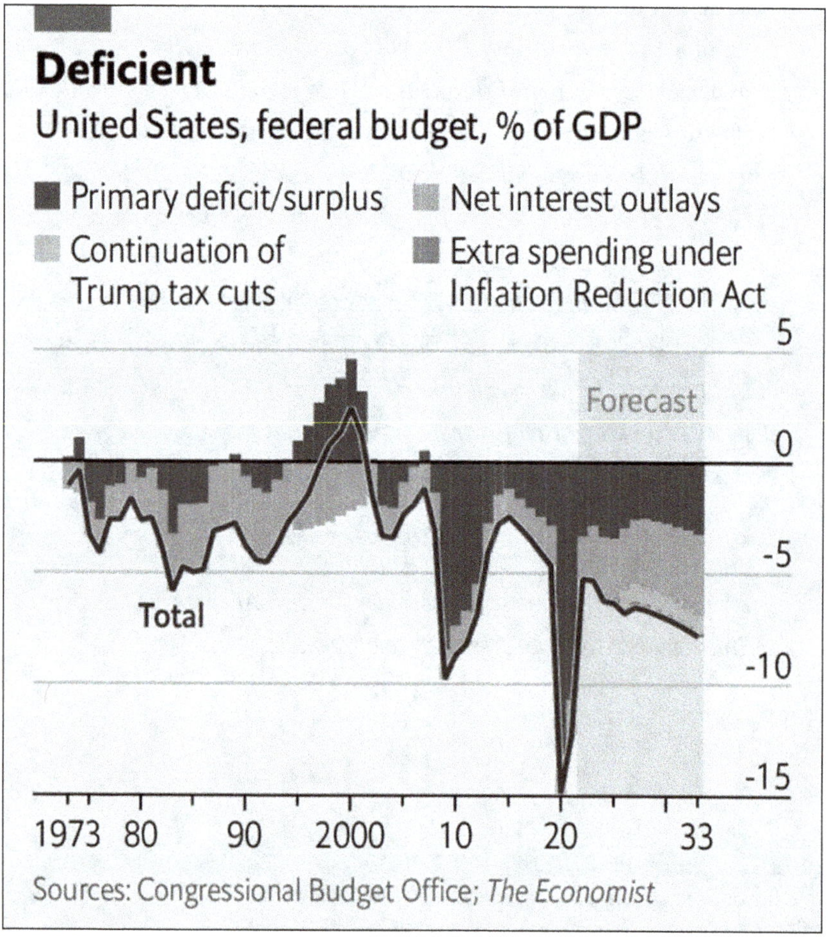

The Economist

Regrets

Lamentations on the Joys of Single Blessedness

From *Single Blessedness*, 1922

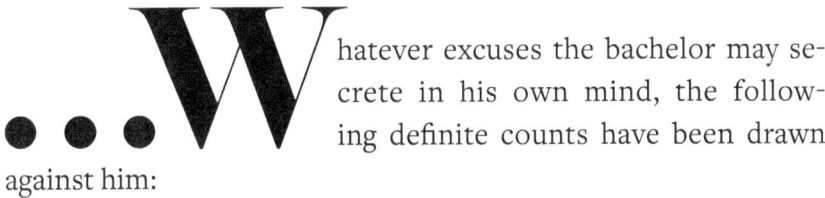

Whatever excuses the bachelor may secrete in his own mind, the following definite counts have been drawn against him:

1st. It is the duty of every good man to become the founder of a home, because the home (and not the stag boarding-house) is the cornerstone of an orderly civilization.

2d. It is the duty of every high-minded citizen to approve publicly the sacrament of marriage, because legalized matrimony is the harbour of safety. When the bachelor ignores the sacrament, his example becomes an endorsement of the advantages offered to travellers by that famous old highway known as "The Primrose Path."

3d. It is the duty of every student of history and economics to help perpetuate the species and protect the birth rate.[194]

These are the damning accusations. Any representative woman's club, anywhere, would bring in a verdict of "guilty" against a notorious bachelor, in two minutes, without listening to witnesses . . .

---

194. Today the USA and most First World countries are in population decline, some bordering on population collapse.

. . . Possibly you expected from me a wordy attempt to prove that a man may acquire happiness by avoiding matrimony. Well, you cannot secure contentment by a mere avoidance of anything. The only worth-while days are those on which you sell a part of yourself to the brotherhood of man and go to the mattress at night knowing that you have rendered service to some of the fellow travellers. The more you camp by yourself the more you shrivel. The curse and the risk of bachelorhood is the tendency to build all plans around the mere comforts and indulgences of the first person singular.

Sometimes a bachelor gets to taking such good care of himself that he forgets that some day or other he will need six friends to act as pallbearers.

Next to solitaire, probably the most interesting single-handed pastime is trying to visualize one's own funeral. The bachelor often wonders if it will be an impressive function.

No use talking, when a transient undertakes the journey alone, he is compelled to be in doubt as to terminal facilities. His friendships are insecure and all the arrangements unstable. He has a lot of liberty, but he doesn't know what to do with it.

No man can cheat the game by merely hiding in a hotel and having his meals served in his room.

He can run in the opposite direction from matrimony until he is all out of breath, but he will never travel far enough to get away from himself. When he flees from the responsibilities of family life he is incidentally leaving behind him many of the experiences which belong to a normal career. He cannot get away from the double-entry system of accounts revealed in Doctor Emerson's essay on Compensation. The books must balance.

No man can take twelve months' vacation each year. A vacation is no fun except when it comes as a release from the regular routine. Each July the married man is supposed to sing:

"*My wife's gone to the country! Hurrah! Hurrah!*"

Thereby he gets an edge on the bachelor. He has a chance to throw his hat in the air at least once a year. When does the bachelor pull his "Hurrahs"? Think it over.

If the locked-up hubbies believe that the boys still at large are raising Cain seven nights a week and fifty-two weeks in the year, let them cease to be envious. It can't be done. The most fatiguing activity in the world is that of roystering.[195] It is terrible to be fed up on roystering. Almost any group of case-hardened bachelors would rather row a boat than sit around a table and sing.

Bachelors do not regard their respective caves and caverns as modified cabarets. Their so-called home life is merely a recognition of the physical fact that no one can entirely dispense with slumber.

The "jolly bachelor" in his own retreat is often just as jolly as a festoon of crape. He is not discontented. He is calmly reconciled. But not celebrating.

He has been saved from the shipwreck by miraculous intervention, but he finds himself on a lonely island and not a sail in sight.

The bachelor doesn't have to watch the clock, and no one is waiting to ask him where he has been; but how about that rapidly approaching day when he will not find—in all the world—ham and eggs that are cooked just right or coffee fit to drink?

As the autumn days grow shorter, and each milestone begins to look more like a tombstone, the bachelor becomes less and less declamatory regarding the joys of single blessedness.

He doesn't weaken, mind you. He can explain why it would have been manifestly impossible for him, at any time, to undertake such a crazy experiment. His training, his temperament, the conditions enforced by his employment, the uncertainty of his financial outlook—these and thirty other good reasons made it utterly impossible for him even to think of playing such a ghastly joke on a nice woman.

---

195. Enjoying yourself in a loud and energetic way.

He is there with a defense; but when you ask him to add up the net blessings and benefits which accrue to the bachelor, his discourse becomes diffuse and unconvincing. If he is past forty, he doesn't brag at all. If he is past fifty, he begins to talk about the weather.

And now, having received all of this secret information from the camp of the enemy, you know as much as we do regarding the joys of single blessedness.

The Lesson:

When culture changes to such a degree that more and more of the population becomes self-centered and selfish, focusing on instantaneous gratification, eating the seed-corn and gobbling the marshmallow as soon as it appears, there are consequences. The first and most obvious is population decline. Without immigration, the United States would quickly fall in population, perhaps all the way to a population collapse.

This is something that George foresaw and believing as he did—that one should know oneself—it is his chief regret in the way he conducted his life. But I think even George would be surprised by how much women have become like men in this selfishness post "the pill." If one looks at literature and movies made prior to George's death, the role of women as mothers is upheld as an ideal. That is no longer the case.

In the past, women received privileges as they were considered the vessel of life and therefore had a higher calling than any man could ever aspire to. Because you could never tell when a woman was with child, all women were honored. Whenever a woman entered a room in which men were sitting, immediately the men were expected to stand up—just the same as if their king or commanding officer had entered the room. They were expected to cease smoking and using "bad language" too. The man always walked on the street side of the sidewalk to protect the woman. When ascending the stairs, the man followed the woman so if she stumbled he would catch her. When descending the stairs, he went first so he would break her fall. He always pulled back the chair for her at the dinner table. He always opened the door for her and let her enter first. He would walk slightly ahead of her for her protection until one came to, say, a restaurant where the maître d' would take on that role. The man would then follow behind the woman as her protector. Once shown to their table, the man would sit facing the door so he could detect any sign of trouble coming in from the outside. In the event of danger, the man was honor bound to protect the woman from man or beast. If the ship was sinking, it was strictly women and children first into the lifeboats. If there were not enough lifeboats, the men were expected to go down with the ship without remark or complaint.

A man was expected by culture, custom and law to absolutely support his wife financially. So great and so important was a wife and mother that any man whose wife worked was seen as a poor provider and a disgrace to his family.

My grandfather Charles Roland Ade would not allow his well-educated wife to work for money even though she wished to because it would be "disgraceful." Instead he encouraged her to take on the numerous charitable (never paid!) executive positions that she did throughout her lifetime with the church, the women's clubs, the March of Dimes, Easter Seals, the American Legion Auxiliary, Girls State, theatre directing and acting, painting and so on. He relented only during World War II.

This was the culture in George's day. In the early 20th century one of the most popular songs was "Mother Machree":

> *There's a spot in my heart,*
> *Which no colleen may own.*
> *There's a depth in my soul,*

Never sounded or known;
There's a place in my mem'ry,
My life, that you fill,
No other can take it,
No one ever will.
Sure, I love the dear silver
That shines in your hair,
And the brow that's all furrowed,
And wrinkled with care.
I kiss the dear fingers,
So toil-worn for me,
Oh, God bless you and keep you,
Mother Machree.
Ev'ry sorrow or care
In the dear days gone by,
Was made bright by the light
Of the smile in your eye,
Like a candle that's set
In the window at night,
Your fond love has cheered me
And guided me right.
Sure, I love the dear silver
That shines in your hair,
And the brow that's all furrowed,
And wrinkled with care.
I kiss the dear fingers,
So toil-worn for me,
Oh, God bless you and keep you, Mother Machree.

I challenge you, Dear Reader, to find any popular song these days that honors the self-sacrifice and greatness of motherhood. Today's culture has declined into self-indulgence and resentment.

Any actuarial scientist will tell you that married people live longer than unmarried people. The recent Nobel prize winning economist Angus Deaton received his honor in large part for his focus on "deaths of despair." Unmarried white males are becoming useless drug addicts and committing suicide in incredible numbers. Men and increasingly women without marriage and family are at greater risk of Deaton's deaths of despair and new evermore powerful drugs, like fentanyl, are accelerating how fast one can travel down this road.

Darwin's laws apply just as much to culture as they do to DNA, so we should all be warned: if our culture does not change to give mothers the honor, respect and compensation they deserve, then our culture will die out. In my opinion it's all about valuing women as mothers, not just as workers. In George Bernard Shaw's *Pygmalion*, Professor Higgins asks, "Why can't a woman be more like a man?" My answer to the Good Professor's question: because that would lead to extinction!

In some countries, they can't even pay people to have more children.[196] It is frightening for me to think that the culture of Islamic State or something similar could actually win the war in the long run—not by lifting women up, but by subjugating them and forcing population growth. Demographics is destiny.

The final demeaning insult is renaming a mother a "birthing person." Being a mother and motherhood is just as valuable a career as anything offered at Harvard University.

---

196. https://www.vox.com/23971366/declining-birth-rate-fertility-babies-children, accessed November 28, 2023.

Benediction

The Yankee's Prayer (1924)

Help me to get things straight. Give me an outlook on the whole world. Open my eyes to the truth regarding the material wealth and the golden opportunity of my native land, but strike me with swift punishment if I roll my 'r's in speaking the word "great" or feed the vanity of my ignorant neighbors who think that the U.S.A. has become a symbol of perfection.

Help me to understand that the comforts and luxuries and pleasant accessories of modern life abound in my bailiwick because my friends and I have moved into a new country in which there is much recent wealth to be divided. Teach me to modify my sense of importance with an humble thankfulness.

Save me from delusions regarding continued and abounding prosperity. Give me the wisdom to preach against wastefulness.

Incline me to avoid boasting, but keep me from being an idle weeper or an idle faultfinder. Let me read history aright and learn that a people seldom can be made happy and prosperous by involved and ponderous legislation. Assist me and my associates to look to ourselves and not to Congress.

Give me patience and tolerance and strength to brace myself against sudden and hysterical and gusty changes of popular feeling. Let me not construe the rule of the majority into a fool axiom that the majority is always right. Cause me to bear in mind that in every age of which we have record, an unpopular minority advanced measures, which, later on, were accepted by the majority.

Protect me against labels and memberships and binding obligations which will submerge me as an individual. Save me from being enslaved or hampered by catch-phrases. May I never take orders which will make me a coward in the sight of my conscience. Let it not be said of me that I "belong" to a political party.

Lead me to an understanding of the new meaning of "service." Help me to believe that the man prospers best and longest who is concerned as to the welfare of the people about him. Compel me to see that our organization is a huge experiment in cooperation and not a scramble for prizes.

Give me large portions of charity with which to regard the performances of my easy-going countrymen. Help me to judge every act by the intent of it.

Increase my usefulness by giving me an X-ray vision, so that I may detect the goodness and deservedness of those who do not wear my kind of clothes, worship in my church or live in my township. Make it open to me that integrity and patriotism cannot be monopolized.

Keep me from trouble, but make me dangerous if I am drawn into a fight. Convince me that every battle should be fought to a finish, so there will not be any argument later on.

Let me remain level-headed when I am envied by the people of other lands, but do not take away the things which arouse their envy. Permit me to retain my heritage as long as I know how to take care of it.

The Lesson:

Written in the midst of the Roaring Twenties, George's prayer is a cornucopia of common sense, each line a haiku of wisdom. He writes, "Save me from delusions regarding continued and abounding prosperity. Give me the wisdom to preach against wastefulness." Within five years of writing those lines came the stock market crash of 1929 and the Great Depression.

The Yankee's Prayer reads as fresh and relevant today as it was 100 years ago. I have recited it to my family every Thanksgiving for decades. These truly are words to live by.

Appendix

Theories X and Y

George Ade was generations ahead when it comes to business and management theory. It was not until Theory X and Theory Y[197] was devised by Douglas McGregor[198] in his 1960 book *The Human Side of Enterprise* that George's view that there is no such thing as lazy people was taken seriously.

Theory X assumes that individuals are base, work-shy and constantly in need of a good prod. It always has a ready-made excuse for failure—the innate limitations of human resources. Theory Y, however, assumes that individuals go to work of their own accord, because work is the only way in which they have a chance of satisfying their (high-level) need for achievement and self-respect. People will work without prodding; this has been their fate since Adam and Eve were banished from the Garden of Eden.

In his classic *Up the Organization*, Robert Townsend wrote powerfully in support of Theory Y:

> *People don't hate work. It's as natural as rest or play. They don't have to be forced or threatened. If they commit themselves to mutual*

---

197. https://www.economist.com/news/2008/10/06/theories-x-and-y, accessed January 23, 2024.
198. https://www.economist.com/news/2008/10/03/douglas-mcgregor, accessed January 23, 2024.

objectives, they'll drive themselves more effectively than you can drive them. But they'll commit themselves only to the extent they can see ways of satisfying their ego and development needs.

This is why young people should work at many different summer and part-time jobs. They should take a variety of college classes that could lead not to just a job, but to a career that they could enjoy for a lifetime. You can't know what work you will like if you never try it or take a class about it.

Thomas Edison was once asked how he could put in so many long days at his laboratory and business. His famous reply: "I never did a day's work in my life. It was all fun." Warren Buffett's partner Charlie Munger was said to have "died in harness" at age 99 because he loved his work at Berkshire Hathaway so much. Many doctors also work long past the so-called retirement age. Few members of TIGER 21 and R360 ever really retire; they love building companies, serving on the boards of both businesses and charities, lecturing and writing.

What is retirement anyway? Golf? Travel? TV? Isn't it just an admission that the retiree failed to choose a career that they loved?

As you have learned in this book, George loved to write, made it his profession and enjoyed it his whole life. He also learned quickly how to make smart decisions about business and investing so that he could choose to do anything he wanted with his life.

Sitting at the city desk of a newspaper cranking out copy as on an assembly line was a job he liked well enough, but being self-employed writing highly successful Broadway plays was a profession. Being independently wealthy enough to write whatever he wanted, whenever he wanted, took business and investment skills equal to his literary skills.

Ade Returns to City Room to Perform Labor of Love

From *Miami Daily News*, December 11, 1939

Humorist Tells of Pal

EDITOR'S NOTE: *George Ade, veteran newspaper man, and famous Hoosier humorist, returned to his first love at the Daily News copy desk today, to write of the passing of an old friend, Orson Collins Wells. His story follows:*

By George Ade

I get word from Clearwater, Fla., that my old side-kick and friendly pal for many years, Orson Collins Wells, better known as "Ort" Wells, has been called to the great beyond. He was in his 80th year. Because he was a rare and lovable character and had a host of friends who are scattered all over the map, I feel called upon to tell something about him.

He was born in Neenah, Wisconsin. His father died while he was very young. His mother and his brothers and sisters were desperately poor.

For a while, he lived with his uncle, Orson Collins, for whom he was named, at Lafayette, Ind. When he was a resident of our Hoosier state, he sold newspapers on the street. He was peddling newspapers on the old Lahr House corner when the body of Abraham Lincoln came to Lafayette on the slow cavalcade back to Springfield, Ill. "Ort" was permitted to gaze upon the mortal remains of our great president.

He returned to Wisconsin and, as a young man, learned to be a telegrapher. Soon he was an expert. He worked in New Orleans and later was assigned to taking press reports over the wire in the Chicago office. While he was handling the telegraphic market reports in the brokerage office of Schwartz-Dupee & Co. in Chicago he became so useful in dealing with the customers that he was made assistant manager of the office and held the job until he became of a member of the firm of Charles G. Gates & Co. Charley Gates was a son of the famous "Bet-a-million" John W. Gates. For many years "Ort" was closely associated with John W. Gates, John B. Drake, "Uncle Ike" Elwood and other members of the colorful and highly pugnacious "Gates crowd," the outfit that successfully stormed Wall Street and became a headache to Morgan and many more of the rather placid and conservative New York speculators. They made many millions. "Ort" went along with them and picked up about a million for himself. He was a careful operator and kept nearly all of his money.

After he retired many years ago, we became close friends. In 1910 we went around the world together. Before that he had been my guide, counselor and friend when my plays were being produced. We travelled together in Europe, toured the West Indies and played golf together on many courses, including some in Florida. He was a fairly good player and a red-hot enthusiast.

Always he had a brusque manner and a fairly harsh and vivid vocabulary and was sometimes rated as a "hard egg" but under the surface he was kind-hearted, sympathetic and generous. Those who came to know him well had a tremendous liking for him.

For a long time he was a regular at the race tracks. He went to Saratoga every year. One of the great sprinters of all time, "Ort Wells" was named for him by John Drake. This horse was bought by the kaiser and taken to Germany shortly before the World war. "Ort" often surmised that he was eventually eaten by the hungry subjects of Wilhelm.

I am speaking in praise of him on behalf of an army of his friends who knew him at the Lambs club in New York, the Chicago Athletic and Chicago Golf club at Wheaton, Ill., the Belleview in Florida and the Flamingo in Miami Beach.

Charles Francis Coe was one of his intimates. The last time I dined with him in Chicago the guests of honor were Grantland Rice and Clarence Budding Kelland. He knew many stage celebrities, Wall Street magnates and professional golfers. Tom Meighan and Gene Sarazen were his buddies.

He was a jovial mixer and a royal host. His memory will be cherished.

About a year ago he took up residence in Florida, because this state promised to be merciful in the matter of taxation. He deposited a tidy sum with Ed Romfh here in Miami and bought a house at 315 Jasmine Way, Clearwater. He has been somewhat of an invalid for a couple of years. He blamed his illness on an unreliable "ticker."

On Sunday morning he was sitting on the porch of his home when he lapsed into unconsciousness and passed away. In accordance with his wishes, there will be no formal funeral ceremonies. His body will be cremated, probably Wednesday morning, and the ashes scattered to the four winds of the Florida which he loved so well.

He was a great guy. Along in the years but never senile. Only a few days ago I had a letter from him, hand-written and full of the old pep. He put up a brave fight to the end of a long and picturesque career.

P.S. I nearly forgot to mention that in recent years his most intimate and sympathetic friend has been Kenesaw Mountain Landis, czar of baseball.

Wells Wills Nurse $50,000; Like Sum to Judge Landis

From *The Tampa Bay Times*, December 29, 1939

CLEARWATER—Bequests of $50,000[199] to Judge Kenesaw Mountain Landis, high commissioner of baseball, and to Mrs. Nina Callahan Skorcz, of Galesburg, the nurse who attended him during his last illness, are contained in the will of Orson Collins Wells, retired Chicago stockbroker, who died at his home on Dec. 10.

Except for $217,000[200] in specific bequests to relatives, friends and employees, the bulk of Wells' estate, estimated at more than $1,500,000,[201] is left to the University of Chicago to establish an endowment to be known as the "Orson C. Wells Fund of the Frank Billings Clinic."

Filed for probate in county court here yesterday, the will designates the First National Bank of Miami and Scott L. Probasco of Chattanooga and Clearwater as executors. Letters of administration were filed by E. C. Romfh as president of the bank.

Judge Landis was long a close friend of the Chicagoan, who also numbered George Ade, humorist, and John T. McCutcheon, cartoonist, among his intimates. Wells was a partner of John W. Gates, steel magnate.

---

199. The equivalent of $1.1 million in today's dollars.
200. The equivalent of $4.7 million in today's dollars.
201. The equivalent of $32.8 million in today's dollars.

Orson Wells was the godfather of Orson Welles, actor and radio impresario, who was not mentioned in the will.

Fifty thousand dollars was willed by the Chicagoan to the Presbyterian hospital in that city to establish the "Orson C. Wells Fund for Urology."

Twenty thousand dollars[202] was left to the Continental Illinois National Bank and Trust company, Chicago, to be paid in quarterly installments to a brother, Benjamin C. Wells, 84, now residing in West Palm Beach. This principal and income will revert to the University of Chicago upon the brother's death.

Mrs. Skorcz, in addition to the cash, was left the Wells home in Harbor Oaks, with its furnishings and automobiles.

Washington A. Reinke, chauffeur, was willed $1,500.[203]

Mrs. L. J. Cassell, Vincennes, Ind., was given an annuity of $10,000.[204] A membership in the South Shore Country club, Chicago, was bequeathed to the club.

Lloyd R. Steere of Chicago was appointed to administer the will. Evans, Mershon and Sawyer are handling the legal details. Judge White named A. J. Quinn, New York city, and Jean Grams, Chicago, to verify the will.

The Lesson:

With an estate worth over $33,600,000 in today's dollars, it's clear that Ort Wells, George's financial mentor, was a master of fiscal acumen, especially when you realize that he was able to hang on to such a fortune through the Great Depression. That's financial savvy in anyone's book!

---

202. The equivalent of $438,000 in today's dollars.
203. The equivalent of $33,000 in today's dollars.
204. The equivalent of $219,000 in today's dollars.

George's Last Will and Testament

I, George Ade, of the Town of Brook, County of Newton, State of Indiana, being of sound and disposing mind and memory, hereby revoking any prior Wills and/or Codicils by me heretofore made, do hereby make, publish and declare this as my last Will and Testament.

ITEM I.

I think it proper to declare, before listing devises and bequests, that one purpose in parceling out the lands of which I may now be possessed is to insure a number of relatively small holdings rather than to keep my landed estate intact. I believe it to be good public policy to divide the land of a farming community among many owners, and I believe that the interests of the community are best served when the various tracts are finally owned by the farmers who cultivate them.

ITEM II.

I direct that my just debts, funeral expenses and expenses pertaining to my last illness be paid as soon as conveniently may be done after my death by my Executor. It is my further will that all Inheritance or Estate taxes, which may be levied against my estate or against the specific devise or bequest given to any devisee or legatee, shall be considered as a debt of my estate and shall be paid by my Executor as such from the sale of real and personal property as hereinafter provided. It is my further hope and wish that none of the personal

GEORGE ADE (SEAL)

PAGE ONE

effects in my home or on my home grounds shall be offered at either public or private sale in order to meet any debts and obligations.

ITEM III.

To GEORGE ADE DAVIS, of Oklahoma City, Oklahoma, I give and bequeath the interests and rights and titles which I may have in published books, plays, photoplays and all manuscripts, and all published and unpublished writings, for his absolute property, EXCEPTING, HOWEVER, it is my will that this bequest shall not include any unpublished or original manuscripts in my home which are not merchantable for publication, dramatization or as photoplays but have only an intrinsic or sentimental value, which said manuscripts are to remain in my home and subject to the further provisions of this Will.

ITEM IV.

To ARDIS ADE KURFESS, wife of William Frederick Kurfess, of Hinsdale, Illinois, I give and devise the following described real estate in Newton County, State of Indiana, to-wit:-

> The North half of the South East quarter of Section Ten (10), Township Twenty-eight (28) North, Range Eight (8) West;
>
> also,
> The North East quarter of the South West quarter of Section Ten (10), Township and Range aforesaid;
>
> also,

_____GEORGE ADE_____(SEAL)

The South East quarter of the South East quarter of Section Ten (10), Township and Range aforesaid;

also,
The North half of the south West quarter of the South East quarter of Section Ten (10), Township and Range aforesaid;

also
The North half of the South East quarter of the South West quarter of Section Ten (10), Township and Range aforesaid;

also,
Ten (10) acres, more or less, of even width off of the North side of the North East quarter of the North East quarter of Section Fifteen (15), Township and Range aforesaid, to include all farm buildings and lots,

and containing in all of said tracts two hundred and ten (210) acres, more or less.

ITEM V.

To CHARLES ROLLAND ADE, of Kentland, Indiana, I give and devise the following described real estate in Newton County, State of Indiana, to-wit:-

All of that tract of land owned by me situated in the North West quarter of Section Fourteen (14), Township Twenty-eight (28) North, Range Eight (8) West, and containing one hundred and thirty-eight (138) acres, more or less.

also,
Thirty (30) acres, more or less, of even width off of the South side of the North East quarter of the North East quarter of Section Fifteen (15), Township and Range aforesaid;

also,
The North West quarter of the North East quarter of Section Fifteen (15), Township and Range aforesaid;

also,
The South half of the South West quarter of the South East quarter of Section Ten (10), Township and Range aforesaid,

and containing in all of said tracts two hundred and twenty-eight (228) acres, more or less.

          ___GEORGE ADE_____(SEAL)

PAGE THREEE

ITEM VI.

To NELLIE ADE RATHBUN, wife of James D. Rathbun, of Kentland, Indiana, I give and devise the following described real estate, in Newton County, State of Indiana, to-wit:-

    All of the real estate which I own in Sections Thirty (30) and Thirty-one (31), Township Twenty-eight (28) North, Range Eight (8) West, containing two hundred and thirty (230) acres, more or less, and known as "Brookside Farm".

ITEM VII.

The devisees named in Item IV, V and VI herein are my nieces and nephew, they being children of my deceased brother, William H. Ade, and the real estate specifically devised to them shall include the improvements situated on the several tracts. It is my will further that if any of said devisees named in said Items IV, V and VI herein be not living at the date of my death, the portion devised to such deceased person in my Will I hereby give and devise to his or her descendents then living, PER STIRPES and not PER CAPITA.

ITEM VIII.

To ADAH RANDALL PLUGGE, of Wahington, D. C., my niece, being the daughter of my deceased sister, ANNA L. RANDALL, I give and devise the following described real estate in Newton County, State of Indiana, to-wit:-

    The South half of the North half of Section Fifteen (15), Township Twenty-eight (28) North, Range Eight (8) West;

also,

_____GEORGE ADE_____(SEAL)

PAGE FOUR

The North East quarter of the South East quarter of Section Fifteen (15), Township and Range aforesaid;

also,

The North East quarter of the North West quarter of Section Fifteen (15), Township and Range aforesaid;

also,

Thirty (30) acres of even width off of the South side of the North West quarter of the North West quarter of Section Fifteen (15), Township and Range aforesaid;

also,

The South half of the South East quarter of the South West quarter of Section Ten (10), Township and Range aforesaid;

and containing in all of said tracts two hundred and ninety (290) acres, more or less.

If my niece, ADAH RANDALL PLUGGE, be not living at the time of my decease, the devise to her shall go and is given and devised to her surviving children, share and share alike.

ITEM IX.

To ELLA M. McCRAY, WIFE OF Warren T. McCray, of Kentland, Indiana, my sister, I give and bequeath a life estate only in and to the following described real estate, together with all of the improvements thereon, in Newton County, State of Indiana, to-wit:

All land owned by me situated in Sections Four (4), Five (5), Eight (8) and Nine (9), in Township Twenty-seven (27) North, Range Eight (8) West, containing about four hundred (400) acres. This tract is known as the "Streight Farm".

And the fee in remainder in and to said real estate I give and devise to LUCILLE McCRAY EVANS, MARIAN McCRAY and GEORGE McCRAY, children of the said ELLA M. McCRAY, share and

_____(SEAL)

PAGE FIVE

share alike, or to their descendents PER STIRPES and not per CAPITA if any of them be not living at the time of my death.

At the time of drawing this my last Will and Testament, the tract of real estate herein devised and bequeathed and described in this ITEM of my Will is one of two tracts of real estate totaling about seven hundred thirteen (713) acres which are encumbered by a mortgage indebtedness of Fifteen thousand ($15,000.00) dollars owing The Mutual Benefit Life Insurance Company, and the bequest and devise herein is made upon the express condition that the above named legatee and devisees assume the payment of a total of Five thousand ($5,000.00) dollars of said mortgage indebtedness, or any renewal or extension thereof, and the bequest and devise herein shall not become binding and/or effective until my estate is released and discharged from Five thousand ($5,000.00) dollars of said total mortgage indebtedness.

ITEM X.

To ALICE M. DAVIS, of Kentland, Indiana, my sister, I give and devise the lands I own in Sections One (1) and Two (2), Township Twenty-seven (27) North, Range Nine (9) West, in Newton County, State of Indiana. This tract of land is known as the "Brecount Farm", and contains about three hundred and thirteen (313) acres.

In the event my sister, ALICE M. DAVIS, shall predecease me, I hereby devise to the children of the said ALICE M. DAVIS, the realty devised to her in this ITEM of my Will, said

_____(SEAL)

Page six

children being GEORGE ADE DAVIS, of Oklahoma City, Oklahoma, and HARRY W. DAVIS, whose present address is unknown. If this devise passes to the children of the said ALICE M. DAVIS, and the said HARRY W. DAVIS be not living at the time of my death, his share shall go to and is given and devised unto the said GEORGE ADE DAVIS, now of Oklahoma City, Oklahoma.

At the time of drawing this my last Will and Testament, the tract of real estate herein devised and bequeathed and described in this ITEM of my Will is one of two tracts of real estate totaling about seven hundred thirteen (713) acres, which are encumbered by a mortgage indebtedness of Fifteen thousand ($15,000.00) dollars, owing The Mutual Benefit Life Insurance Company, and the devise herein is made upon the express condition that the above named devisee assume the payment of a total of Ten thousand ($10,000.00) dollars of said mortgage indebtedness, or any renewal or extension thereof, and the devise herein shall not become binding and/or effective until my estate is released and discharged from Ten thousand ($10,000.00) dollars of said total mortgage indebtedness.

ITEM XI.

To HAZELDEN COUNTRY CLUB, a corporation of Indiana, I give and devise the following described real estate together with the improvements thereon, situated in Newton County, State of Indiana, to-wit:

All that part and portion of Section Twenty-two (22), Township Twenty-eight (28) North, Range Eight (8) West, lying

_____(SEAL)

PAGE SEVEN

North of and adjacent to Indiana State Highway sixteen (16), including the club house and its contents;

also,

Beginning at a point twenty one hundred ninety-eight (2198) feet East and twenty (20) feet South of the North West corner of Section Twenty-two (22), Township Twenty-wight (28) North, Range Eight (8) West and from thence South fifteen hundred eleven (1511) feet, thence East one hundred thirty-four (134) feet, thence South eight hundred sixty-one (861) feet, thence West three hundred thirty-six and five tenths (336.5) feet, thence North six hundred seventy-nine and five tenths (679.5) feet, thence West eleven hundred eighty-one and five tenths (1181.5) feet, more or less, thence North three hundred thirty nine (339) feet, thence East one hundred seventy-four (174) feet, thence North eight hundred eighty-five (885) feet, more or less, to the public highway, thence in a Northeasterly direction along the Southern boundary of said highway to the place of beginning,

and containing in both of said tracts sixty (60) acres, more or less.

The private roadway, as now established, on the West side of the tract last above described shall at all times be kept open for the joint use and benefit of all present and future owners and successors in title of the real estate devised in this ITEM and the owners of the real estate immediately West and South thereof.

This devise and bequest in this ITEM of my Will is on the express condition that said Hazelden Country Club assume and undertake to pay all taxes due or a lien on the real estate and/or personal property devised and bequeathed to said Hazelden Country Club, and all other indebtedness of said Club and that this testator and/or his estate shall be released from all liability or cost on any indebtedness of said Club, and the devise and bequest herein shall not be effective or valid until the conditions herein specified are complied with by said devisee.

                                                                          GEORGE ADE   (SEAL)

PAGE EIGHT

Provided, however, that this bequest and devise to Hazelden Country Club shall not become valid, binding and effective in law until an elapse of five (5) years from the date of my death, and if for any reason the said Hazelden Country Club shall cease to operate as a social organization within five (5) years of the date of my death, then, and in that event, the said Hazelden Country Club shall forfeit all rights in and to the property herein conditionally devised and bequeathed to it and said property shall revert to my estate and shall be merged in and become a part of ITEM XII of this my Will and be bound by all of the terms and conditions of said ITEM XII and added to the property therein bequeathed and devised.

ITEM XII

I give, devise and bequeath to a Board of Trustees composed of the following persons:-

1. The President of the Board of Trustees of Purdue University at the time of the probating of this Will;
2. The President of Purdue University at the time of the probating of this Will;
3. Joseph A. Andrew, Attorney-at-law, LaFayette, Indiana;
4. James D. Rathbun, Kentland, Indiana;
5. Joseph W. Reeve, Rensselaer, Indiana;

the following described real estate in Newton County, State of Indiana, to-wit:-

> All of the tract of land commonly known as Hazelden Farm located in Sections Twenty-one (21) and Twenty-two (22) of Iroquois Township of Newton County, Indiana, including my private home, out-buildings and surrounding grounds, comprising a total of about four hundred thirty (430) acres (except the sixty (60) acres described in ITEM XI, the same being conditionally

_____(SEAL)

PAGE NINE

bequeathed to the Hazelden Country Club), containing 370 acres, more or less,

together with all improvements thereon and the contents of my dwelling house or home on said premises, which includes all furniture and furnishings, rugs, pictures, china and glass ware, table linens, bed linens, bedding, hangings, curios, ivories, antiques, kitchen furniture and utensils, books and both published and unpublished manuscripts which have only an intrinsic or sentimental value. The devise and bequest herein is <u>in trust</u> to said Board of Trustees for the uses and purposes and on the conditions hereinafter set forth.

It is my wish that the Trustees above named shall have full authority to make final disposition of all property held in trust after they have considered all plans submitted to them, including the following, which I take the liberty to submit:

<u>First</u>: The takeing over of the entire tract by Purdue University, on condition that my private home and the out-buildings and the grounds be maintained and kept in a good state of preservation. It is my wish that the Trustees should have large discretionary powers as Purdue University may not have any corporate authority to maintain an estate under the unusual conditions here suggested.

<u>Second</u>: The turning over to the Conservation Department of the State of Indiana all or part of the heretofore designated tract of three hundred seventy (370) acres on condition that my home and the out-buildings and surrounding grounds be maintained ina good state of preservation and that a part of said tract shall be permanently set apart as a recreation park for the use of the general public under such conditions as shall be named by said Department of

                                      <u>GEORGE ADE</u>   (SEAL)

Conservation. Already I have had surveyed and carefully mapped a portion of Hazelden Farm which might be set aside as a memorial or recreation park, the said real estate being described as follows, to-wit:-

> Beginning at a point fourteen hundred and one (1401) feet South of the Northwest corner of Section Twenty-two (22), Township Twenty-eight (28) North, Range Eight (8) West, and running from thence East nine hundred ninety-six and five tenths (996.5) feet; thence North eight hundred eight-five (885) feet, more or less, to Indiana State Highway Sixteen (16), thence along said highway in a Northwesterly direction to the West line of said Section; thence South on said Section line to a point fourteen hundred and one (1401) feet South of the Northwest corner of said Section; thence West to the Iroquois River; thence in a North and Easterly direction along the East bank of said river to said State Highway Sixteen (16); thence Southeast to the Section line, and containing thirty-three (33) acres, more or less.

It is my wish that if said Department of Conservation should take over any part of Hazelden Farm that it shall have large discretionary powers in regard to the details of operation of said Hazelden Farm.

<u>Third</u>: If it shall prove inadvisable or impracticable for Purdue University, or the State of Indiana, to take over the real estate above indicated, I suggest the possibility of the formation of an Association or Foundation which will undertake to control and manage all or part of the thirty-three (33) acre tract described above in this section, under such terms and conditions as shall be prescribed by the Trustees. It is my Will that they would have legal authority to transfer to such Association or Foundation any part or all of the tract known as Hazelden Farm.

<u>Fourth</u>: If no one of the above named three plans shall prove to be feasible in the judgement of the Trustees, it is my wish that they

_____(SEAL)

PAGE ELEVEN

shall adopt any other plan, determined by conditions and which meets the approval of a majority of said Trustees.

It the Trustees find that it is impossible or impracticable to maintain the home and grounds and preserve the personal effects, they shall have authority to adopt some other plan not suggested in this instrument. I would not favor this extreme latitude of power were I not convinced that the Trustees will be governed by unselfish motives and a desire to avoid the calamity of having the contents of the home dispersed by a sale.

ITEM XIII.

It is my further Will and wish that I be buried on the tract known as Hazelden Farm in a spot designated to James D. Rathbun and that the Trustees in charge of said tract accept this reservation to the devise in ITEM XII.

ITEM XIV.

I give and bequeath to James D. Rathbun my watch, jewelry, wearing apparel and personal effects having no sentimental relationship with my home; and it is my wish that the said James D. Rathbun shall dispose of said articles in accord with private instructions given him. If any question shall arise as to what articles shall be left in the home and what articles shall be included in this ITEM to be distributed, by the said James D. Rathbun, to friends and relatives, it is my Will that the decision of the Trustees herein heretofore designated

_____(SEAL)

PAGE TWELVE

shall be final and binding.

ITEM XV.

All the rest and residue of my estate, including all real estate not otherwise disposed of as well as all stocks, bonds, securities of every kind and character, all choses in action and all other personal property not otherweise disposed of, shall be sold by my Executor, hereinafter named, within one year from my decease at the best possible terms and for the best advantage of my estate and the proceeds from such sale or sales shall be applied in the payment of my indebtedness, inheritance and estate taxes, costs of administration and Executor's and Trustees' fees, provided, however, my indebtedness shall not include the Fifteen thousand ($15,000.00) dollars of mortgage indebtedness specifically described in ITEMS IX and X, provision having been made in these ITEMS for the assumption of this mortgage by the several legatees and/or devisees.

It is my Will that the property herein ordered sold may be sold without order of Court, either at public or private sale, and on such terms and conditions as my Executor shall deem wise and expedient.

ITEM XVI.

When the Executor, hereinafter named, shall have disposed of the property, the sale of which is authorized

_____(SEAL)

PAGE THIRTEEN

in ITEM XV, and shall have paid all taxes and other indebtedness authorized by this instrument, the residue and remainder of my estate, as represented by a cash balance, shall be disposed of as follows:

To MARY B. FLETCHER, the sum of One thousand ($1,000.00) dollars. If she is not alive when this bequest is due and payable to her, the sum bequeathed shall revert to the estate.

To KATE KRUE, the sum of One thousand ($1,000.00) dollars. If she is not alive when this bequest is due and payable to her, the sum bequeathed shall revert to the estate.

The sum remaining after the payment of these bequests shall be divided as follows:

To JOSEPH W. REEVE, twenty (20%) per cent of said sum. If the said Joseph W. Reeve is not living at the time of such distribution, such bequest shall be paid to his then heirs at law, such heirs at law to be determined by the Statute of Descent of the State of Indiana, in force at the time of such distribution.

To JAMES D. RATHBUN, twenty (20%) per cent of said sum. If the said James D. Rathbun is not living at the time of such distribution, such bequest shall be paid to his then heirs at law, such heirs at law to be determined by the Statute of Descent of the State of Indiana, in force at the time of such distribution.

To FRED KURFESS, ten (10%) per cent of said sum. If the said Fred Kurfess is not living at the time of such distribution, such bequest shall be paid to his then heirs at law, such heirs at law to be determined by the Statutue of Descent of the State of

_____(SEAL)

Illinois, in force at the time of such distribution.

The balance, consisting of fifty (50%) per cent of the actual cash residue of the entire estate, is devised and bequeathed <u>in</u> <u>trust</u> to the five (5) Trustees designated in ITEM XII of this instrument, they to have power to transfer, assign or expend any or all of the sum thus bequeathed and devised, it being my wish that the sum shall be used for the improvement, repair, maintenance and up-keep of my home and out-buildings and surrounding grounds and such other parts of the tract known as "Hazelden Farm" as the Trustees or their assignees may decide to retain.

In ITEM XIII of my Will where I make reference to Purdue University I have in mind Purdue University situate at West LaFayette, Indiana.

ITEM XVII.

I hereby nominate and appoint JAMES D. RATHBUN, of Kentland, Indiana, as sole Executor of this my LAST WILL AND TESTAMENT, and direct that he be not required to give bond for the faithful performance of his duties as Executor or Trustee, if same can be legally done.

In the event that the said JAMES D. RATHBUN shall fail, refuse or be unable to qualify or act as Executor or Trustee under this my LAST WILL AND TESTAMENT, I then appoint, with all the powers and authority given to the said JAMES D. RATHBUN, either as Executor or Trustee, JOSEPH A. ANDREW,

_____(SEAL)

PAGE FIFTEEN

Attorney, of LaFayette, Indiana, or such person as he shall designate, in writing, to the Court in which this Will may be offered for probate.

IN WITNESS WHEREOF, I have hereunto set my hand and seal at Miami Beach, Florida, this 21st day of March, 1934.

                    ___GEORGE ADE_____(SEAL)

The foregoing instrument consisting of sixteen (16) typewritten pages, written on one side only, and each page of which has been signed by said Testator, was signed, sealed, published and declared by GEROGE ADE, the said Testator, as and for his last Will and Testament, in our presence, who, at his request, and in his presence, and in the presence of each other, have subscribed our names as witnesses thereto.

                    ___JESS C. ANDREW_____
                    ___JOHN G. JENSEN_____

PAGE SIXTEEN

PROOF OF WILL

Comes James D. Rathbun this 29th day of May, 1944, and presents to the court an instrument in writing purporting to be the last will and Testament of George Ade, deceased, and requests that the same be admitted to probate.

Jess C. Andrew having first been duly sworn, testifies to the following:

Question: What is your Name?

Answer: Jess C. Andrew

Question: Did you witness the signature of George Ade to his last will and testament so presented for probate?

Answer: Yes.

Question: Was George Ade on the 21st day of March, 1934, in your opinion, twenty-one (21) years of age, and a person competent to devise his property?

Answer: Yes.

Question: Was George Ade at the said time and place, in your opinion, under any coercion?

Answer: No.

Question: State the residence of said decedent at the time of his death.

Answer: Newton County, Indiana.

JESS C. ANDREW
Subscribing witness to the last will and testament of   Deceased

ATTEST:

Gilbert H. Stucker
Clerk of the Newton Circuit Court

The court having heard the testimony of Jess C. Andrew, which appears above, and which is now attested by the clerk, does now find that said will should be admitted to probate, and it is so considered, adjudged and decreed.

RALPH BOWER
Judge of the Newton Circuit Court

CODICIL NO. I

        I, GEORGE ADE, of the town of Brook, County of Newton, State of Indiana, do make this my dodicil, hereby confirming my last Will made on the 21st day of March, 1934, so far as this Codicil is consistent therewith and do hereby state:

First: ITEM XIII of my last Will I hereby revoke and declare void and in lieu thereof I direct that my Executor, hereinafter named, shall have the power and authority to determine the place of my burial.

SECOND: By the terms of ITEM XVI of my said Will, I gave and bequeathed to KATE KRUE the sum of One thousand (1,000) dollars, now I do hereby revoke said legacy, and do give and bequeath unto the said KATE KRUE in lieu thereof the sum of Five thousand (5,000) dollars, in recognition of her unfailing and faithful attention to me during periods of illness and convalescence.

    AND, I do hereby ratify and confirm my said Will in all other respects.

    IN WITNESS WHEREOF, I have hereunto set my hand and seal to this a Codicil to my last WILL AND TESTAMENT, this Eleventh day of August, 1937.

                                          GEORGE ADE   (SEAL)

Signed, sealed, published and declared by GEORGE ADE, the said Testator, as and for a CODICIL to his last Will and Testament, in our presence, who, at his request, and in his presence and in the presence of each other, have subscribed our names as witnesses thereto.

                      A. L. Engle

                      Walter T. Clark

PROOF OF CODICIL

Comes James D. Rathbun this 29th day of May, 1944, and presents to the court an instrument in writing purporting to be the last will and testament of George Ade, deceased, and requests that the same be admitted to probate.

A. L. Engle having first been duly sworn, testifies to the following:

Question: What is your name?

Answer: A. L. Engle.

Question: Did you witness the signature of George Ade to his last will and testament so presented for probate?

Answer: Yes.

Question: Was George Ade on the 11th day of August, 1937, in your opinion, twenty-one (21) years of age, and a person competent to devise his property?

Answer: Yes.

Question: Was George Ade at the said time and place, in your opinion, under any coercion?

Answer: No.

Question: State the residence of said decedent at the time of his death.

Answer: Newton County, Indiana.

A. L. ENGLE
Subscribing witness to the last will and testament of   Deceased

ATTEST:

Gilbert H. Stucker
Clerk of the Newton Circuit Court

The court having heard the testimony of A. L. Engle, which appears above, and which is now attested by the clerk, does now find that said will should be admitted to probate, and it is so considered, adjudged and decreed.

RALPH BOWER
Judge of the Newton Circuit Court

CODICIL NO. 2

I, GEORGE ADE, of the Town of Brook, County of Newton, State of Indiana, do make this my Second Codicil to my Last Will and Testament, made on the 21st day of March, 1934, and my First Codicil thereto made on the eleventh (11th) day of August, 1937, hereby confirming my said Last Will and Testament and the First Codicil thereto so far as this Second Codicil is consistent therewith and do hereby state:

FIRST: ITEM IX on page 5 of my Last Will I hereby revoke and declare void and in lieu thereof I substitute the following:

To ELLA M. McCRAY, my sister, I give and devise the following described real estate, together with all of the improvements thereon, in Newton County, State of Indiana, to-wit:

All land owned by me situated in Sections Four (4), Five (5) Eight (8) and Nine (9), in Township twenty-seven (27) North, Range Eight (8) West, containing about four hundred (400) acres. This tract is known as the "Streight Farm".

If my sister, Ella M. McCray be not living at the time of my decease, the devise to her shall go and is given and devised to her surviving children, share and share alike.

SECOND: ITEM XVI on page 14 is modified and changed as follows:

The bequest of One thousand (1,000) dollars to MARY B. FLETCHER is hereby revoked and declared void.

THIRD: It is my wish that the Board of Trustees provided for in ITEM XII of my Will make some definite and freindly arrangements with the Hazelden Country Club, a Corporation, named in ITEM XI of my said Will, so that water service for the locker building and Club House of said Club may be secured and provided for.

                                         _____GEORGE ADE_____(SEAL)

And I do hereby ratify and confirm my said Will and the First Codicil thereto in all other respects.

IN WITNESS WHEREOF, I have hereunto set my hand and seal to this the Second Codicil to my Last Will And Testament, on this 26th day of October, 1939.

         GEORGE ADE (SEAL)

Signed, sealed, published and declared by GEORGE ADE, the said Testator, as and for a SECOND CODICIL to his Last Will and Testament and FIRST CODICIL thereto, in our presence, who, at his request, and in his presence, and in the presence of each other, have subscribed our names as witnesses thereto.

         David C. Miller
         Otto Hood

PROOF OF CODICIL

  Comes James D. Rathbun this 29th day of May, 1944, and presents to the court an instrument in writing purporting to be the last will and testament of George Ade, deceased, and requests that the same be admitted to probate.

  David C. Miller having first been duly sworn, testifies to the following:

  Question: What is your name?

  Answer: David C. Miller.

  Question: Did you witness the signature of George Ade, to a codicil to his last will and testament so presented for probate?

  Answer: Yes.

  Question: Was George Ade on the 26th day of October, 1939, in your opinion, twenty-one (21) years of age, and a person competent to devise his property?

  Answer: Yes.

  Question: Was George Ade at the said time and place, in your opinion, under any coercion?

  Answer: No.

  Question: State the residence of said decedent at the time of his death.

  Answer: Newton County, Indiana.

DAVID C. MILLER
Subscribing witness to the last will
and testament of   Deceased.

ATTEST:

Gilbert H. Stucker
Clerk of the Newton Circuit Court

  The court having heard the testimony of David C. Miller, which appears above, and which is now attested by the clerk, does now find that said will should be admitted to probate, and it is so considered, adjudged and decreed.

RALPH BOWER
Judge of the Newton Circuit Court

CODICIL NO. 3

This instrument is an addition or codicil to my Last Will and Testament drawn at Miami Beach, Florida on March 21, 1934. Since that date, my intangible assets have decreased in value and conditions have arisen which indicate that the proceeds resulting from the sale of such assets will not be sufficient to meet Federal and State Inheritance Taxes, to say nothing of providing a residue to take care of certain bequests. To meet a possible emergency, I am now directing that the Board of Trustees, indicated in Section XII on page nine of my Will, shall be given full and unlimited authority to sell all of the tract known as Hazelden Farm, except the portion given to the Hazelden Country Club, as indicated in Section XI on page seven, and the tract surrounding my home and known as the Home Grounds, on such terms and under such conditions as seem advisable. This tract comprises about three hundred and seventy acres. It is my hope that the proceeds from such sale, added to the sum received for securities and other intangible assets, as indicated in Section XV on page thirteen, shall be sufficient to meet all Federal and State Inheritance Taxes and a ll debts except the mortgage indebtedness, for which special provision is made, also all expenses incidental to my funeral and last illness and administration of the estate, and leave a balance sufficient to provide for the bequests indicated in Section XVI on page thirteen, including a special bequest to Kate Krue. Inasmuch as the sale of this farm property will deprive the estate of the income which was to be devoted to the upkeep and maintenance of my home and the grounds surrounding it, I further direct that the Board of Trustees shall be given full authority to dispose of my home and the contents and the surrounding grounds on such terms and under such conditions as seem advisable and necessary. I do not wish to hamper them in any way because I realize that no one may forsee what circumstances may arise.

SIGNED AND SEALED at Hazelden Farm, Brook, Indiana, on the seventh day of June, 1941.

GEORGE ADE

Witnesses:
Janet Roth
Lillie Balensiefer

PROOF OF CODICIL

Comes James D. Rathbun this 29th day of May, 1944, and presents to the court an instrument in writing purporting to be the last will and testament of George Ade, deceased, and requests that the same be admitted to probate.

Lillie Balensiefer Mead having first been duly sworn, testifies to the following:

Question: What is your Name?

Answer: Lillie Balensiefer Mead.

Question: Did you witness the signature of George Ade, to a codicil to his last will and testament so presented for probate?

Answer: Yes.

Question: Was George Ade on the 7th day of June, 1941, in your opinion, twenty-one (21) years of age, and a person competent to devise his property?

Answer: Yes.

Question: Wash George Ade at the said time and place, in your opinion, under any coercion?

Answer: No.

Question: State the residence of said decedent at the time of his death.

Answer: Newton County, Indiana.

Lillie Balenseifer Mead
Subscribing witness to the last will and testament of   Deceased.

ATTEST:

Gilbert H. Stucker
Clerk of the Newton Circuit Court

The court having heard the testimony of Lillie Balensiefer Mead which appears above, and which is now attested by the clerk, does now find that said will should be admitted to probate, and it is so considered, adjudged and decreed.

RALPH BOWER
Judge of the Newton Circuit Court

CERTIFICATE OF PROBATE

I, Gilbert H. Stucker, clerk of the Newton Circuit Court, certify that the last will of George Ade has been admitted to probate in the Newton Circuit Court, and that a complete record thereof and the testimony of Lillie Balensiefer Mead a subscribing witness thereto, had been duly reorded, and that the same can be found in Will Record No. 6, at pages 174 to 184.

GILBERT H. STUCKER
Clerk of the Newton Circuit Court

By: JOSEPH E. HIESTAND
Deputy Clerk

Recommended Reading

Regarding Tariffs

- Dr. Milton Friedman made the case for free trade in consumer goods in the following article, which first appeared in *Newsweek* in 1993. His argument still holds water today:

    Friedman on Free Trade. https://www.minneapolisfed.org/article/1993/friedman-on-free-trade#:~:text=Friedman's%20denunciation%20of%20protective%20and,economies%20is%20a%20timeless%20lesson.&text=We%20have%20heard%20much%20these,government%20to%20protect%20the%20consumer, accessed November 1, 2023.

- The case for selective trade tariffs on essential military goods is made by Oren Cass, executive director of American Compass, in this article from the *Wall Street Journal*:

    https://www.wsj.com/economy/trade/why-trump-is-right-about-tariffs-3cad4097, accessed November 1, 2023.

- No discussion of tariffs would be complete without a word from Donald Trump, who in 2018 tweeted ignorantly, "Trade wars are good, and easy to win."[205] Although he said his mission was to shrink America's trade deficit, his tariffs on everything from washing machines to steel only widened the gap and angered our allies. As I write this, he's threatening to do it again if re-elected in 2024. For an informative article about why that would be a disaster, see *The Economist*:

https://www.economist.com/finance-and-economics/2023/10/31/donald-trumps-second-term-would-be-a-protectionist-nightmare, accessed January 11, 2024.

Regarding Easy Money Interest Rates

- Howard Marks discusses interest rates and how they affect inflation and asset allocation in this memo from *Seeking Alpha*:

    https://seekingalpha.com/article/4662147-latest-memo-from-howard-marks-easy-money, accessed January 11, 2024.

---

205. https://twitter.com/realDonaldTrump/status/969525362580484098, accessed December 8, 2023.

Bibliography: Notable Writings Almost Included

Should you wish to delve even further into George's common-sense wisdom and advice—and I hope you do—I suggest the following pieces that were close runners-up for inclusion in this book but were excluded due to space constraints.

From *Knocking the Neighbors*

- The Undecided Bachelors
- The Long and Lonesome Ride
- Two Unfettered Birds

From *In Babel*

- The Judge's Son
- The Relative's Club

From *Fables in Slang*

- The Fable of the Visitor Who Got a Lot for Three Dollars

- The Fable of the New York Person Who Gave the Stage Fright to Fostoria, Ohio
- The Fable of the Parents Who Tinkered with the Offspring

From *Handmade Fables*

- The Fable of the Civic Improver and the Customary Reward
- The Fable of the Ripe Persimmon and the Plucked Flower
- The Fable of Her Birthday and the Dwindling Generosity

From *Forty Modern Fables*

- The Fable of the Undecided Brunette and the Two Candidates
- The Fable of the People's Choice Who Answered the Call of Duty and Took Seltzer

From *People You Know*

- The Periodical Souse, the Never-Again Feeling and the Ride on the Sprinkling Cart
- The Patient Toiler Who Got It in the Usual Place
- The Effort to Convert the Work Horse Into a High-Stepper
- Self-Made Hezekiah and His Message of Hope to This Year's Crop of Graduates

From *Little Stories of Our Country*

- The Fourth of July

From *Stories of the Streets and of the Town/Stories of Chicago*

- Mr. Benson's Experience with a Maniac

From *Letters of George Ade*

- Letter to Mrs. Carl F. Wertz
- Letter to Alexander Guerry

From *Ade's Fables*

- The New Fable of Susan and the Daughter and the Grand-daughter, and Then Something Really Grand

From *True Bills*

- The Fable of Another Brave Effort to Infuse Gentility into our Raw Civilization
- The Fable of What Our Public Schools and the Primary System Did for a Poor but Ambitious Youth

From *Breaking into Society*

- The Sorrows of the Unemployed and the Danger of Changing from Bill to Harold
- The Unhappy Financier and the Discontented Rube

From *The Girl Proposition*

- The Fable of the Long-Range Lover, the Lollypaloozer and the Line of Talk

Glossary

Abattoir: Slaughterhouse.

Albert J. Beveridge: An orator, historian and United States Senator from Indiana.

Al Smith: Alfred Emmanuel Smith (1873-1944) was a four-term Governor of New York and the Democratic presidential nominee who lost to Herbert Hoover in 1928.

Arnold Bennett: A prolific English author.

Aubrey Beardsley: An English author and illustrator aligned with Aestheticism.

Bass viol: Also called a *church bass* or *Yankee bass viol*, this is a type of bowed string instrument which enjoyed popularity in early 19th century New England. When referring to a woman, it is a way of saying she was shaped like an hourglass.

Blackstone and Cooley: Issued in 1870, Sir William Blackstone's *Commentaries on the Laws of England* was a book of English common law edited by Thomas Cooley.

Blue pencil: Censored out.

Bradstreet: This later became Dunn & Bradstreet, the publishers of the Who's Who of the corporate world and corporations.

Brannigan: A drinking spree, especially Irish style.

Breech-Clout: A type of loincloth made of tanned leather, fabric or fur, tucked between the legs and held up by a strap or strings. Typically American Indian.

Bridewell: A jail for petty offenders.

Brown Study: [As in *"In a brown study"*] Daydreaming or deeply contemplative.

Buck Dance: A type of folk dance, like clogging, where the dancer's footwear is used percussively.

Camouf: To deceive, as in camouflage.

Cap Sheaf (Capsheaf): The top sheaf of a stock or stack of grain; the crowning point, the climax.

Carusos: Young workers, possibly Italian immigrants.

Century: A $100 bill.

Charles Frohman: An American theatre manager and producer.

Chauncey M. Depew: A U.S. senator from 1899 to 1911, best remembered as an orator and storyteller.

Chinner: A talkative, bombastic person.

Choate Family: A prominent New England family, several of whom were graduates of Harvard and were lawyers, judges, ambassadors, politicians and doctors.

Cognomen: Name or nickname.

Contumely: Insulting language or treatment.

Coon Song: A genre of music by Black people, or that presented a stereotype of Black people.

Corn Juice: Whiskey made from corn.

Crape: Old-fashioned spelling of crepe: thin, wrinkled paper for making decorations. Black for funerals.

Cravat: A neckband, the precursor to a modern necktie or bow tie.

Croesus: The king of Lydia (present day Turkey) in the 500s BC known for his wealth.

Cupid and Dove-Tail Pieces: Fancy finishing details.

De Beers: De Beers was (and is) a diamond consortium founded in the late 1800s, so George was referring to a diamond.

Dopester: A person who collects and supplies information, especially on sporting events and elections. As in, "He's got the dope on that."

Dreyfus Case: A criminal justice scandal in France at the turn of the 20th century.

Drummer: Slang for a salesman. As in, "He's out drumming up sales."

Duck: Leave hurriedly.

Durbar: British Indian word for any official meeting of importance. The most famous was the Delhi Durbar, an Indian imperial-style mass assembly organized by the British in Delhi, India to mark the succession of an Emperor or Empress of India.

Duse: Eleonora Giulia Amalia Duse, often known simply as Duse, was an Italian actress, rated by many as the greatest of her time.

Euchre: (pronounced You-Kur) As a noun, Euchre is a card game. Used as a verb, to euchre means to gain advantage over someone.

Flavius Josephus: A Roman-Jewish historian and military leader born in 37 AD.

Four Hundred: A term created by Ward McAllister (the 1880s version of an influencer) who said that there were only 400 people in fashionable New York society.

Fliv: Slang for cars, usually of poorer quality.

Florida Water: An American version of Eau de Cologne.

Foliage on the Sub-Maxillary: Facial hair beneath the lower jaw; chin whiskers.

Frank Gotch: A champion professional wrestler.

Fripperies: Things that are not necessary, not serious, not important.

Gallinipper: A large mosquito.

Gaspard: The man in charge of royal treasure.

Gazelle: An attractive, aloof girl.

George Vaughn: Professor of Law at University of Arkansas.

Gillie: A man or boy who attends his male employer or guest.

Gink: An odd man or boy.

Grips: Slang for suitcases.

Gugg: Dimwitted or silly person.

Henry: The Henry was a car built by the Henry Motor Car Company in Muskegon, Michigan from 1910 to 1912.

Herbert S. Stone & Co.: A Chicago-based publishing house that published some of Ade's works, namely *Artie, Pink Marsh, Doc' Horne, Fables in Slang* and *More Fables*.

Hied: Went quickly.

High-Binder: An unscrupulous person, originally a New York gangster.

Hop: Slang for "full of nonsense." Also slang for opium, heroin, or other narcotic or psychoactive drugs.

Ibsen Club: An organization devoted to the promotion of the works of the Norwegian dramatist and poet Henrik Ibsen.

Jack: American slang for money.

Jan Wheelock: Joseph Wheelock Jr., a turn-of-the-century American stage actor.

John Drew: An Irish-American actor who was considered a matinee idol at the turn of the 20th century.

John W. Gates: John Warne Gates, also known as "Bet-a-Million" Gates, was an American Gilded Age industrialist and gambler. A native of the Chicago area, he was a pioneer promoter of barbed wire. He was also the business partner of George's mentor in business and finance, Ort Wells.

Julia Arthur: A Canadian stage and screen actress.

Kelly: A type of pool game played with sixteen balls.

Kerosene Circuit: Villages and small towns where obscure opera companies played one-night-stands in the late 1800s/early 1900s, thus named because the opera houses were lit with kerosene lamps. A step down from electric lights and limelights.

Kuhn, Loeb Co.: An investment bank in New York City.

Legerdemain: Deceit, trickery.

Lorgnette: A pair of spectacles with a handle to hold them in place rather than fitting over the ears or nose.

Maarten Maartens: A Dutch writer.

Macadam: The small pieces of gravel compacted in layers to surface roads.

Maeterlinck: A Belgian playwright.

Marshall Wilder: An American actor, monologist, humorist and sketch artist.

Mary Mannering: An English actress.

Mater: From the Latin for mother.

May Wright Sewell: An American reformer who was known for her service to the causes of education, women's rights, and world peace.

Mazuma: Slang for money.

McCormack: John McCormack was a famous Irish tenor.

Mouchoir: Handkerchief.

Mrs. Fiske: Minnie Maddern Fiske, billed simply as Mrs. Fiske, was one of the leading American actresses of the late 19th and early 20th centuries.

MSS.: An abbreviation for manuscripts.

Naphtha Launch: A small boat powered by an external combustion engine (Naphtha engine).

Nobby: Fashionable, elegant, stylish, chic; as per Nob Hill, the poshest part of San Francisco.

Pass-book: A booklet provided by a bank to keep track of deposits and withdrawals.

Pauline Hall: A popular turn-of-the-century prima donna in America.

Pepsin Tablets: A digestive aid.

Pig Iron: Crude iron, an intermediate good used by the iron industry in the production of steel.

Plug Hat: A round hat with a narrow brim. Also known as a derby or bowler.

Porte Cochere: A porch where vehicles stop to discharge passengers.

Raglan: An overcoat with sleeves that extend in one piece fully to the collar.

Rhino: British slang for money.

Roman Colours: The bright colors favored by Ancient Romans in clothing and décor.

Roystering: Enjoying yourself in a loud and energetic way.

Rube: A country bumpkin.

Running Amuck of the Bulls and Bears: Wall Street booms and crashes.

Ruskin Club: The Ruskin Art Clubs, founded in 1888, promoted the arts and culture, and furthered women's causes.

Samoleons: Slang for dollar.

Seven-Up: A Dutch card game originally called All Fours. It was first written about in England in the 1600s. In the 1800s it became popular in America and was called Seven-Up.

Shepheard's: The leading hotel in Cairo and one of the most celebrated hotels in the world from the middle of the 19th century.

Shyster: A person, especially a lawyer, who uses fraudulent or deceptive methods in business.

Sinking Fund: A fund established by setting aside revenue over a period of time to fund a future capital expense, or repayment of a long-term debt.

Skin Game: A rigged gambling game or swindle. Or, a dishonest business or scheme.

Soubrette: A flirtatious young woman.

Spats: A type of footwear accessory for outdoor wear, covering the instep and the ankle.

Spondulix: 19th century slang for money or cash.

Subscription books: Popular in the 18th and 19th centuries, these were books "lent" to readers for a fee (by subscription).

Surcingle: A wide strap or belt.

Sussiety: George's take on the phonetic spelling of "society."

Swivel: Strength of mind or character.

Tidies: A tidy is a small cloth draped over furniture to protect it. Today we might call it a doily.

Time-Tables: A printed schedule of train departure and arrival times.

Tontine Policy: An early system for raising capital where individuals pay into a common pool of money. Tontines were popular in the U.S. in the 1700s and 1800s, then faded in the early 1900s. Tontine investors paid lump sums upon joining and received annual dividend-like payments until death.

Tremolo Stop: A piece sometimes added to a guitar to enhance the tone.

Trunk Line: The main line of a railroad.

Twin Six: Packard's roadster with a 12-cylinder engine, the first of its kind.

Two-Spot: An unimportant person or thing.

Victoria: A doorless French carriage with a forward-facing seat for two persons covered with a folding top, or calash, and a removable, elevated coachman's seat above the front axle.

Waldorf Diet: Food served at the Waldorf Astoria hotel in New York, renowned for being very rich and fattening.

Walter Pater: An English essayist, art and literary critic, and fiction writer, regarded as one of the great stylists.

Weskit: An informal word for waistcoat.

Yap: A mouth that talks continuously and/or a hillbilly-type person.

Yeggman: A person who breaks open safes; a burglar.

Acknowledgements

Firstly, my thanks go to my cousin James Ade Kurfess, who knew George from golf outings and family Thanksgivings at Hazelden. He learned George's common-sense wisdom directly, not just from his writings. Jim read the complete manuscript of this book, offering many valuable insights and corrections.

My cousin Donald Kleinkort, thanks for his permission to include some of his writings in this book, and for his valuable criticism of the manuscript. Also, my cousin Karl Kleinkort and my sisters Marguerite and Adair for their comments and suggestions.

My Cordelias: Mary, Sarah and Karen, who read the entire manuscript with great enthusiasm and provided me with valuable feedback. Also to Alan, Anna and Sean.

Charlie Garcia, Managing Partner and South Florida Chapter Chair of R360, for his review and endorsement and for his dedication to mentoring the rising leaders of the next generation.

Gary Zwerling, retired partner at Goldman Sachs, for his detailed review of the manuscript and very helpful comments.

My friend Louis Chiavacci, who is one of the most savvy investors in the TIGER 21 organization, for his reading and valuable comments on the manuscript.

Miguel Poyastro, master of Miami real estate as well as master of his own ship (literally and figuratively) for reading and commenting on the manuscript. A Cuban immigrant, Miguel worked his way up from penniless to the very top of the real estate business in Miami. He knows a lot about real estate, investment and life!

This book would not be possible without the cooperation over many years of the Purdue University Library Archives and Special Collections. Their assistance in going through many of the yet to be digitized papers and letters is much appreciated.

The Newberry Library also provided access to their fine collection of George Ade books and papers.

Krissy Wright for her help with the cover, and Ryan Scheife at Mayfly Design for his photography of the cover and his outstanding work creating the book's layout and design.

Last but not least, to Pamela Suarez for her valuable assistance, researching and correcting enumerable facts, references, fractured grammar and syntax, as well as her enthusiasm in researching many obscure references.

About the Author

William C. Ade is an independent petroleum geologist specializing in international new ventures. He was born and raised on a small family farm in Indiana where he worked his way through Ball State University earning degrees in geology (B.S. honors), physics and geology (M.S.) and an MBA. In 2008 he received the Distinguished Alumnus Award from the BSU Department of Geology. Will also serves on the BSU Geology Alumni Board.

Will began his career in 1975 as a field geologist and geophysicist for Phillips Petroleum in the western U.S. Since 1978 his work has been mostly in Asia. In 1986 he founded his own consulting company in Singapore generating "wildcat" exploration prospects, new ventures, and also mergers and acquisitions for publicly-held companies and private investors. Over the course of his career as a geologist, he has found commercial oil and gas with an estimated recovery of over 1 billion barrels of oil equivalent. He holds royalties on several of the oil and gas fields he discovered.

Will is a past-president of the Southeast Asia Petroleum Exploration Society (SEAPEX), former long-time member of the Singapore Scout Check and also served as a delegate to the American Association of Petroleum Geologists (AAPG). He has authored papers on exploration for oil and gas in Southeast Asia published in SEAPEX, Indonesia Petroleum Association, Geological Society of Malaysia, AAPG and other journals. He has spoken at many industry conferences and his comments have appeared in *Forbes, The New York Times, The Wall Street Journal* and *Barron's*.

In 1997 Will was named Jasper County Farmer of the Year and in 2017 received the River Friendly Farmer Award from the Newton County Soil and Water Conservation Division. In 2013, he was given Ball State University's Founders Alumnus Award. Will funds several scholarships and ongoing research projects at BSU, also contributing to the Boy Scouts of America and the Mayo Clinic (Jacksonville).

Will divides his time between international travel and his homes in Indiana and Florida. He was a member of the TIGER 21 Investment Group (South Florida) for more than ten years and is a founding partner of R360 as well as a member of the Columbia Club of Indianapolis. He is the author of *The Artworks of LuEthel Davis Ade* (2005), *Plays Worth Remembering: A Veritable Feast of George Ade's Greatest Hits* (2020), *A Pioneer in the Fullest Sense: The Wit and Wisdom of George Ade's Father* (2020), *Wildcat Road Vols I* and *II* (2021, 2022), and is the co-author with Kathryn Ade Kleinkort Sprinkle of *Food Fit for Heaven: Favorite Ade Family Recipes* (2024).

www.ingramcontent.com/pod-product-compliance
Lightning Source LLC
Chambersburg PA
CBHW070743060526
44119CB00092B/430/J